After
RAISING
SUGAR CANE

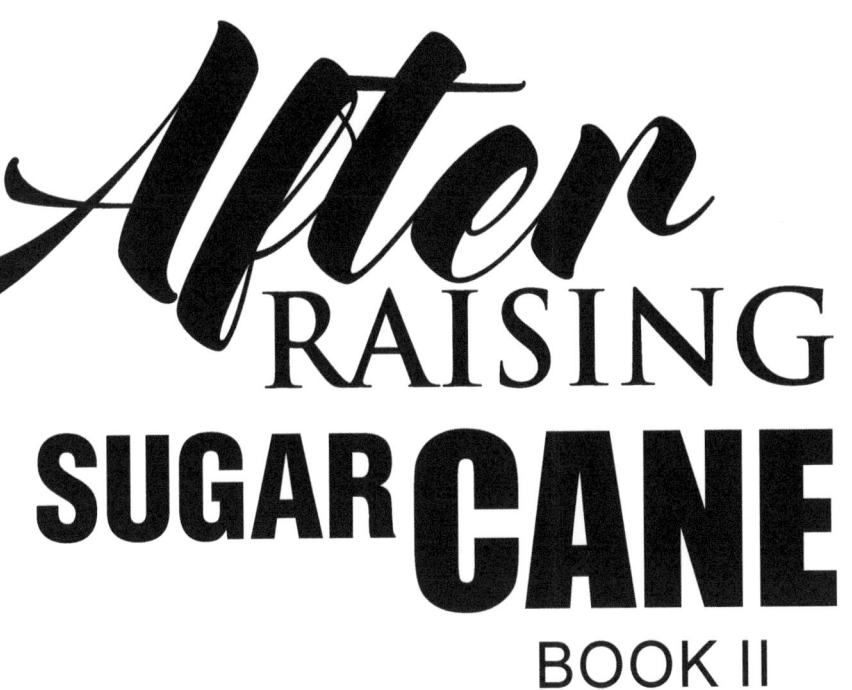

After Raising Sugar Cane
BOOK II

*A MEMOIR
CONTINUE*

BY *BARRY RAFFRAY*

After Raising Sugar Cane Book II
Copyright © 2022 by Barry Raffray. All rights reserved.

No part of this publication may be reproduced, stored in a retrieval system or transmitted in any way by any means, electronic, mechanical, photocopy, recording or otherwise without the prior permission of the author except as provided by USA copyright law.

The opinions expressed by the author are not necessarily those of URLink Print and Media.

1603 Capitol Ave., Suite 310 Cheyenne, Wyoming USA 82001
1-888-980-6523 | admin@urlinkpublishing.com

URLink Print and Media is committed to excellence in the publishing industry.

Book design copyright © 2022 by URLink Print and Media. All rights reserved.

Published in the United States of America

Library of Congress Control Number: 2022904354
ISBN 978-1-68486-131-6 (Paperback)
ISBN 978-1-68486-132-3 (Digital)

14.12.21

DEDICATION TO MY SONS

I dedicate this book to my sons, Kent Steven, Lane Anthony, and Todd Nolan Raffray. This is a continuation of my life before they knew me. I am hopeful that they will enjoy reading it and also learn from the struggles of life and trying to make a living and supporting a family through the effort of trying to get a better education to do a better job and have more opportunity for advancement. Sometimes good old fashion hard work makes up for not having the brain of a Albert Eistein.

With that being said, this book is dedicated to Kent, Lane and Todd.

Love Dad

TABLE OF CONTENTS

Dedication To My Sons 5

Chapter 1 - The Army Physical In New Orleans 15
My Second Airplane Ride 17
Joe Bougeois And Us 19
The Army-Arrival At Fort Jackson 21
Start Basic Training 22
Meeting The Non-Coms 24
Mess Hall During Basic Training 26
Tear Gas Shack 27

Chapter 2 - Something Wrong 30
I Met The Base Doctors-A Lot Of Them 31
In Base Hospital Ward 31
Made New Friends In Hospital 32
Johnny Rivers (Roverstelli) 34
Tony Kubeck 35
While In The Ward 35
The Dye Test 36
Walking The Hall With Piss Again 38

Chapter 3 - Coming Home 40
Arrived Home- Saw Doctors 41
After Final Discharge 43
1962 Sugar Mill Job 44
Mr. Luban Chewing Tobacco Story 46
Making Raw Brown Sugar 47
Working For Atwell And Blankenship 51

Chapter 4 - 1963 Sugar Mill Job 60
Relief In My Darkest Hour 61
Donald (Duck) Aucoin 64
Working For Dominick Sciortino 66
Side Story 69
Back At The Story 70
A Gift From Louisiana 71

Chapter 5 - My River Road Wreck 74
Looking For A Job 77
Getting A Job And J&L Engineering - In 1965 77
Cars That I Had Part 1 80
Trip To Houston To See The Astros 81

Chapter 6 - My First Wedding 87
The House In Baton Rouge 88
The Baton Rouge Job Hunt 90
Working For Foster Grant Chemical 92
Trip To Orange Park Florida 95

Chapter 7 - Changing Oil On My Sport Fury 100
First Son Born, Two More To Come 104
Lane's Early Arrival 108
Still Working For Foster Grant Chemical Company 112

Chapter 8 - The 1973 High Water On The Mississippi River 117
Times Of Low Water On The Mississippi River 120
Loading The Ocean Going Chesapeake, Virigina Barge 123
Benzene Unloading During Low Water 126
Selling Of Foster Grant Company 129

Chapter 9 - Todd Came A Calling 131
I Donated Blood 132
Kent's Magic That Did Not Work 134
Kent's First Waist Watch 135
Cars That I Owned By Purchase Or Gift 136

Jumping Way Ahead Of My Story Because Of Cars 143
Cars From The Stoltzs..145

Chapter 10 - Changing Shocks On The Dart 148
In-Laws Move To Oklahoma..151
Oklahoma- A Hot/Cold Place 153
Oklahoma's Crossroads Mall..154
Kent And Lane In Private School 157
Lane Is Above Average- We Have The Papers To Prove It..........157
In-Laws Move Back Into Baton Rouge Area 159

Chapter 11 - Plant Union Help Us Regular Office Workers........162
Women Doing "A Mans" Job ???..164
Tank Truck Driver-Eighteen Wheelers......................................165
Women Working In The Plant..167
First Woman Deck Hand 168
More First- Marine, Railroad And Rail Car Leasing
Sales Women...169
My Move To Texas...170
Good Times With My Team 173

Chapter 12 - The Boondaggles Were Just Great 176
Big Changes Over Time 183
Moms Passing 184
Daddy Remarried...186
July 1984- Tubing On The Guadalupe River 190
Daddy's Passing...196

Chapter 13 - In 1985 A Change Was Gonna Come..................198
Tubing The Guadalupe In 1985..199
1986 A Big Bad Year 205
The Sale Of Our Business To Huntsman 207
1987 208
Big Change Happened 210

Chapter 14 - Thank God For Ron And Reggie 212
December Divorce 1989 215
Sold Big House In 1990 216
Todd Misbehaving 218
Las Vegas Trip In 1990 219
Welcome To Vegas World 222

Chapter 15 - Big Mamou Mardi Gras 230
Mardi Gras Morning 232
Very Large Crowds... 240
Time Just Moving Along 242

Chapter 16 - Lajitas On The Rio Grande In 1992 250
1993 Summer Trip To Belpre, Ohio Plant 259
White Water Rafting 262

Chapter 17 - 1994 Houston Flood 267
1994 Las Vegas Trip 273

INTRODUCTION

This book is about the life of a young man after graduating high school. As with many rural young men, the first thing he does, is join the armed services after graduating from high school. This get them away from home and a chance to see different places in the world. And in many cases, a skill that one could work at after the hitch is over.

It is a continuation of the life of Barry. The good, the bad, and the ugly is all included as it is in everyone's life.

Re-live the pain, enjoy the good times, and rejoice in his triumph as Barry, at times, struggle his way through life trying to have a positive meaning of it all - such as it was.

ACKNOWEDGEMENTS

I want to take this opportunity to apologize for several errors that I made in my first book printing of "Raising Sugar Cane". I especially want to apologize to my good friend, Bobby Pearce, for referring to him through-out my book as Bobby Pierce. I am truly sorry that after all the proof reading I did that I did not catch this mistake. You just have to wonder how can I make a mistake like this for some one that is my good friend since we've been in the seventh grade. Weeeeeeeeeeeell, all I can say is "SHIT HAPPENS" - apparently my head is full of it - shit that is.

ALSO

My story in the book about the glove that Leon Miller gave to Me. The first baseman's mit was given to Dicky Barbier and NOT Sonny Barbier, as I stated that section of the first printing of my book. I do not know how or why I did not catch it when proof reading so many times. But I missed it for the same reason as mentioned above.

ALSO, ALSO

I apologize for all the misspelled other names in the book. If you read the book, you know who you are unless your brain is like mine and now full of you know what.

Another correction I would like to make is in the section where I wrote about our high school janitor whom I referred to as Easy Ed Brown. His name was Bill Brown. So it was Easy Bill Brown. I recently found out that Mr. and Mrs. Brown lived on Cedar

Grove Plantation for a couple of years while Mr. Brown worked as a mechanic there. This would have been when I was very young as I do not remember it. He worked for Mr. George Cunningham, who was the Shop Manager before Mr. Ashley (Lou Lou) Henry took over. I do remember Mr. George and Mrs. Lizzy. Mr. George built a very nice brick home in White Castle. It was, and still is, on the corner of Moss St. and Adams Drive. It used to have a big C on the front of the fireplace chimney.

Back to Mr. Bill Brown. He was wounded during World War II and did not have the full use of his left arm. At school he always work at a sturdy pace and did not get overwhelmed or in a such and always stayed calm whatever the situation. As I mentioned before, he picked up the moniker of Easy Bill Brown or just Easy Brown.

THE ARMY PHYSICAL IN NEW ORLEANS

EARLY JUNE 1962

Seven days after graduating from high school, Davis Callegan, Donald "Duck" Aucoin and I went to the Army Induction Center in New Orleans for physicals.

During the physical part of our testing, I had to pee in a bottle and have it tested. I failed the first test. I was told by a doctor to hang around and drink plenty of water. After an hour, they had me pee in a bottle to have it tested again. I failed this test also. I did not know what was going on. This time it was a black haired doctor that gave me the test and he knew that it was my second test. His hair was mess up and he sort of had that far away look in his eyes. As I think back now, he would remind me of the TV detective character, Columbo, but with darker hair. This doctor told me that I had one more chance to pass and that I should drink more water, which I did and sat around waiting to have to pee. I drank plenty of water and waited. I passed the third test by another doctor this time. At the time I had no idea what the problem was with me and pee. Since this was my last test of the day, after finally passing the pee test, all of us recruits were released for the week-end. As I mentioned at the end of my first book, "Raising Sugar Cane", Davis decided not to go into the army for a three year hitch - which is what we all was going to sign up for.

Early the next Monday morning, Daddy and Momma drove Duck and I to the New Orleans Army Induction Center for a swearing in ceremony.

While Daddy and Momma were telling me and Duck goodbye outside the Customs House, the weird doctor was passing by. He stopped and said "hi son, I see that you made it". I was shocked that he would remember me from a couple days ago with all the other guys that were being tested. Maybe it was that Dr. Tomney thing since we all had to walk around without any clothes on while doing the physical. Well, maybe not. I don't know. Anyway, Daddy asked what is he talking about. I answered that I did not know, but everyone here thinks that he is cuckoo, another word for crazy, strange. I found out later what this doctor was talking about. He was the only one giving me a hint of what was going on with my body.

Duck and I went inside and checked in. We got sworn in, in a very small room backed from wall to wall with recruits. They (the Army brass) made some speeches before the swearing in. I started to sweat profusely. I felt like I was being squeezed in. I started having trouble breathing. I thought if they don't get on with it, I going to have to make a break for the door to get some air. They got through just in time. I realized now that I did not like to be in tight and crowded places. I had this problem before while attending LSU basketball games in the old Coliseum . Most of the time the place was almost empty but if they won a couple of games, the place would fill up. I could not go there with the place packed full of people. I felt all closed in on. This affected me some years later at LSU football games until I finally got over it.

After getting our orders and being grouped together with five other guys that was flying to Columbia, South Carolina (Fort Jackson), we headed to the airport on transportation that the Army paid for.

Duck was the youngest of everyone and the only one with a last name starting with the letter A, as in Aucoin. The officer in charge gave Duck all our tickets and our orders and said "you are in charge and responsible to get these men to Fort Jackson". There were some guys that were going by train with a different group. We would have preferred to be in that group. We did not know why some went by air and some went by land.

MY SECOND AIRPLANE RIDE

This would be my second airplane ride and I was not that happy about it. My first ride was when I was about twelve or so. One Sunday, Daddy's boss from Lake Charles flew to Cedar Grove Plantation, which had our own airstrip for small planes. He was meeting with someone else. We drove to the airstrip to see if someone had picked him up. When we got there, the boss was already gone but the pilot was there. He also worked for W. T. Burton Industries and asked if we wanted to go for a ride while he was waiting for the boss to come back. Right away daddy said no. I begged to go and momma wanted to go also. Momma and I climbed into the seats behind the front two seats. This was a Sunday afternoon and I was suppose to serve as alter boy for the Catholic afternoon services at church. I sort of forgot about my altar boy duties for the time being. I was serving with Pat Tomney and he never showed up anyway. Today I decided to quit being an altar boy. This was not a smart thing to do at this time. I would miss church and it is a MORTAL SIN to miss church service on Sundays. If we would have crashed and I died, I would have gone straight to HELL. Even Purgatory would have been out of the question. When a Catholic die with a big sin on their sole, they were a sure shot for hell. And all the praying by the family afterwards was not going to get them to that halfway house called Purgatory. I would have to hurry up and go to confession for missing Sunday service the first chance I got.

This four to six passenger plane had pontoons on it. It could land on water or land. We took off. We flew over our house then over the Mississippi River. Mr. Bob, the pilot asks daddy if he could see any ducks. Daddy said that he was not looking for any damn ducks. Mr. Bob said how about landing in the river. I said sure. Daddy said no. Momma did not say anything. So he asked Daddy to look out his window an see if the wheel were locked in the up position. Daddy could not give an intelligent answer. I look out and after being told again what to look for, I confirmed that the wheel were up into the pontoons where they must be to land into the water. Down we came. We had to land against the current, which we did. It was very bumpy because the River was choppy. We did not stay floating very long. Mr. Bob gave it the gas and we took off again. At the time I think I was having fun. We then came back to the Cedar Grove landing strip and landed. I thanked Mr. Bob as Daddy also did and we were off. I then told Daddy and Momma that I had miss my altar boy assignment for the day and that I wanted to quit. They did not like it very much but honored my wishes.

As stated before, this was my second air plane ride. It was very big four-engine jet. We had to fly standby, which is what all service personnel must do. When boarding was announced, we were told to stay out of the way until they called for us. After all the other people boarded, they counted the seats to see if there were enough for all us service guys. We had four white guys and three black guys. They called for us and we lined up. I was second to last in line. The three black guys were in the front of the line. Duck was in front of them with our tickets. We walked outside on the tarmac and lined up to board the plane. Duck gave the lady all of our boarding passes and looked at the plane from his close up position. Duck stepped to the side and the black guys started our line moving forward. Duck made an about face and was walking back pass us. When he got near me, I grabbed his arm and asked him where was he going. He did not really know but did not care to get on the plane. I pulled him toward me and said, "WE got to go". I wasn't going if he was not going to go. We inched ourselves forward until we got to the steps to board the plane. Duck was in front of me, I made sure of that. He stopped. I nudged him and we went up the steps and boarded the plane. It was a huge airplane. When we got into the first class after saying hello to the stewardess and the pilot or someone dressed like a pilot, then we saw the three black guys and one white guy sitting in first class seats. Duck said what's this? They said that they were told to sit there because there would not be any room in the back for everybody. I was pissed. The seats looked to be pleated and rolled leather and tan color as I recall. But they were cut out like in a mold. These seats did not lean back. You sat straight up. These seats were larger than ours were, and at the time I thought those guys had it made. I almost asked Duck to order two of them out of those seats so we could have them and let those two go to the back of the plane where the second classers were. But I kept my mouth shut. We were the last to get on and the Stewardess was trying to make us hurry so we could sit down and they could take off. I kind of liked it like it was - just sitting on the ground and keeping still.

Duck and I got the last two seats side by side and the plane took off after the stewardess did their little thing about the breathing oxygen thing and the cushion flotation device and such. I did not care to hear any of this stuff. I am nervous enough without all that. We took off. We were finally heading for Atlanta, Georgia. There were four good-looking stewardesses on this plane. These days they were all young, single, and good looking. Like any of them was going to notice me, huh. They had closed the curtains between the two classes. After we were in the air for a while, the stewardess came around offering cold drinks and hard drinks and peanuts an such. They opened the curtains and we could see our guys up front sitting straight up and moving around in their seats trying to get comfortable. We were in our Grey Hound Bus type seats, leaning back and relaxing, which was very hard to do when I am in the air. I could not relax at all on take off and landings. I still do not like that part. I would fly more, if I did not have to sit through taking off and landing.

JOE BOUGEOIS AND US

Joe Bourgeois, who was from Reserve, Louisiana, was in our group. Joe was twenty-seven and married. The Army had drafted him. He did not care to go in. He had to serve two years because that is how the draft works. Joe was also deathly afraid of flying. Duck and I had to coax him unto the airplane in New Orleans. Joe was a big guy and I was happy he did not pitch a fit getting him on the plane with us. I did some talking with him that it would be all right. I was scared shitless too, but if I had to get on the plane, I wanted everybody there to get on it too. Joe was more scared than me an Duck. Joe sat a number of rows behind us, so we could not keep and eye on him. He had started to sweat profusely while on the tarmac waiting to board the plane. Every now and then, Duck or I would look back at Joe to see if he was all right. After being in the air for about fifteen minutes or so and after the stewardess had made their first round, I looked back and there was Joe, soaking wet from sweat, sitting in the very back of the plane. There was a stewardess sitting on both sides of him. One had a cold towel patting his forward and wiping his face and the other was patting his hand while holding it. He was sitting very quite and grinning from ear to ear. I was pissed again.

We arrived in Atlanta and had to change plane. Ole Duck took over again He led us off the plane, found out where the other plane was and we arrived there way ahead of take off time.

This was a much smaller airplane than the one we came in on. It had one propeller on each wing. One thing that I can say about that big jet is that is sure was smooth while in the air. I sure wished that the big plane were going to Columbia, South Carolina. But it was not.

The little plane had only two stewardesses. I only remember one. This girl was not pretty. At the appointed time, we took off. This plane was not loaded down like the big plane was. There were a number of empty seats. They told us where to sit. We could not sit together. I sat on the right hand side and the propeller was just outside my window. I could not tell you if Duck sat close to me or not. In fact I cannot remember where anybody but me sat. The weather was not good when we started out. I had white knuckles on take off. After that the pilot said not to move about the plane that there was a storm and we could not go around it. Well, we was bouncing around, dropping one thousand feet at a time, and shacking all over the place. It was dark when we left Atlanta, so we could not see anything. After some time in the air, I saw Joe in the back of the plane with the stewardess. We were bouncing all over the place. I was the only one in my row. I looked out the window and saw what looked like smoke. I hollowed that the plane is on fire. That got a lot of attention. I had taken off my set belt and was trying to get out of this seat while hollowing that I see smoke. The stewardess arrived and informed me that it was just water vapor from the rain hitting the propellers. This settled me down a little. But, I kept a close eye on that engine the rest of the way just in case she was wrong. I never was so happy as when this plane landed and I got off it. I said never again do I want to fly. And I didn't for many years.

THE ARMY-ARRIVAL AT FORT JACKSON

We got to the base at Fort Jackson, South Carolina about one in the morning. They had the whole group of us sit in what looked to be high school desk to fill out paperwork. The whole group consisted of us fellows who arrived by airplane and the guys who arrived via train from New Orleans and other guys who came from other places. There were about thirty recruits. We listened to the sergeant talk and filled out more paperwork. We were all tired. The guys who were more tired than the rest, dozed off. The sergeant said that he had all night and we would not get to bed until everyone was awake and all paperwork was completed and turned in. He left it to us recruits to wake anyone who dozed off. We did just that. After an hour or two, a corporal came to get us and head us to where we were going to sleep. We went into one barracks and walked all about downstairs and then went upstairs looking for bunks. The guys in there trying to sleep were pissed off and made remarks at us. No room there. We then went into another barracks and the same thing happened. I got the message. I believe Duck got it too. This was the Army. Since our arrival, they were messing with us. This is their way of showing us who the boss was. We found empty bunks in the third barracks we entered. It was only part filled with recruits, which I believed that the corporal knew all along. It was about three in the morning now. We all flopped out on bunks and went to sleep. There was no talking or mumbling whatsoever.

They got us up about six in the morning and we hung around until about seven thirty. I sat on the steps of the barracks the first morning and wondered what the hell did I do. I made a mistake and I actually ask God to get me out of there.

They assembled us at about seven thirty-five and took us to breakfast at the mess hall. After eating they march us back to the barracks. We really did not know how to march yet. During the day they had us police (clean) the area grounds. We were made to even pick up cigarette butts and any other debris no matter how small. We did this for about seven days until more recruits arrived to complete our unit. We ended up with about three and a third barracks of recruits. Usually a full unit is four barracks full of guys.

START BASIC TRAINING

As a full unit, we were issued our clothes (uniforms) and supplies. They issued each of us an M-16 weapon (rifle). Then we started basic training. We were moved to Tank Hill. We were in Company C, the third set of barracks on Tank Hill. Each set of four barracks help a Company. This was our unit. Company B was just below us and Company D (the paratrooper unit) were just above us as you go up the hill.

Some recruits were picked as barracks leaders and squad leaders and Company leader. They had a little more authority than the rest of us. They also asked for volunteers to work on the barracks. They were repainting and fixing up all the barracks in Company C. These were huge two story buildings. I got put in the fourth barrack building that only had half of the bottom floor occupied. We were over one hundred guys short of a full barrack. Duck got put in another barrack. We could have asked to be together, but we were not smart enough to ask or just did not want to risk asking. After all, this was the real Army. We did not want to be teased or made examples of.

We had to set up our clothes in footlockers and wall lockers. They had suggested that each recruit buys padlocks for our lockers. I had a padlock on each locker and kept one set of keys on me at all times. After being there a few days, I gave the other set of keys to my bunkmate that slept next to me. We had become friends. You put all your things in the lockers in a neat and folded position. We were instructed on how to store our stuff and on how to make our beds/bunks. Our lockers and bunks would get inspected almost every day.

I happened to be in the last barracks that was to be repainted outside and inside. It looked pretty bad on the inside and there was not much the few guys that lived in there could do about it. Because we could not pass barracks inspection through no fault of our own, we failed every barracks inspection, which meant that we got to serve most of the meals each day in the mess hall. The times that someone in our squad did not serve a meal, someone else had messed up. This was sort of a punishment detail.

Back to the classroom I go. I thought when I joined the Army that the classroom time would be over. Just kidding, I knew it was not over, especially since I had nine more months of radar school waiting for me in Fort Mammoth, New Jersey after I got out of basic training. We had classes on hygiene, VD, taking orders, breaking down your weapon and cleaning it and putting it back together, and explosives, and communications, and I don't remember what all.

We had to learn self-defense. We had to learn how to march as a unit. They marched us everywhere. We marched up the mountain, down the mountain, on the parade grounds, to training classes, to areas where they made us police the area. Etc, etc, etc.

They also ran us in the mornings. We had to run out in the countryside and run up Drag Ass Hill. This was the hill/mountain that all the barracks were located on. After you made it this far, which some guys did not, it was easier the rest of the way because we came out at about Company L, and was running down hill on black top to get back to our barracks.

MEETING THE NON-COMS

The first several weeks that I ran, I made the run fine. I was not in as good of shape as I thought I was for a nineteen-year-old from the farm. The C Company sergeants and corporals training us would take turns running us each morning.

Sergeant Wells was a lifer. You could see on his uniform where he was once a Master Sergeant with over seven strips. When he worked with us, he was a Buck Sergeant with only three strips. This is the lowest sergeant rank. He must have really screwed up. He was in his upper forties, about five feet nine inches tall and weighed over two hundred and fifty pounds. He was really fat. He ran the complete route with us. When you see sergeant Wells running in the shape he looked to be in, you had to run. If he could do it, you had to believe that you could do it too. No one wanted to let this man show them up.

Sergeant Gonzales was about six feet tall and in very good shape. He ran with a sawed off cue-stick handle that he used to poke you with. We hated to see Sergeant Gonzales. He said "when Gonzales runs, everyone run", and he meant it. I saw him hit several recruits with his club. I managed to stay just ahead of him, even though I would seam to get really tired and sluggish. He was coming for me one time to poke me but just in time for me, a guy just behind me stopped and Gonzales got pre-occupied with him. I really felt sorry for that guy. He was being hassled. I sort of walked up Drag Ass Hill this time. Something was happening because I do not usually get this tired on a run.

Corporal Church was another soldier that had made it past First Sergeant but lost his strips for some reason. When Church ran, he did not care much if you ran or not. He reminded me of Roger Maris the baseball player with the New York Yankees. He looked very much like Maris. I would sit near Church at chow and all he would talk about was getting out of this damn Army when his current hitch was up. Losing his strips/rank, really got him against the Army.

Sergeant Harris was our Platoon leader. He was in charge of our barracks. We did not meet him until about the third week of basic training. He was on vacation or as Army personnel say it, on leave. He was a well-spoken black man. After and extended conversation with him, he told me that I would make a good soldier. He did not force us to run when he did, but he expected you to try and it least go through the motions.

One of our officers was Lieutenant Davis. He gave me twenty push-ups because I did not solute him. I was hoping that he did not see me because I was running late as it was from mess hall after serving another lunch.

I cannot remember our Captain's name or all our other Commissioned and Non-Commissioned officers that ran our Company. I do remember Corporal Church, Sergeant Wells and Sergeant Gonzales. Lieutenant Davis was really young and would run with us almost every day. But the non-coms were in charge of the running.

Every morning we had to fall-in for roll call. The non-com would call out each recruits name and he would have to answer here or present or otherwise acknowledge that he is in attendance. They do this, of course, to account for every recruit. There were cases of recruits running off and going AWOL. Well the pronouncing of some of the names that the non-com called out was really funny and amusing- but DO NOT LAUGH out loud. Being from South Louisiana, it was my guess that the most unusual names came from my state. In my case, that was not a problem. Raffray is a very simple name to pronounce. You just say Raff – ray. How hard could that be? Nobody had any trouble with my name. But Donald (Duck) Aucoin (O-koyn or O-kwin), that was a little different.

Since Duck's last name started with an A, it was one of the first names to be called out at roll call. After the first full formation, Duck caught on fairly quickly. The non-com call out "A coin". There was no response. He called out again a little louder, "A Coin". Still there was no response. The non com moved closer to the formation and shouted, "A COIN". Duck realized it was him and said, "here". The non com stepped even closer than shouted at Duck, "what's wrong with you A Coin, don't you know your own name"?

Duck became A-coin after that for the rest of his stay at Fort Jackson, and perhaps the rest of his three year hitch.

MESS HALL DURING BASIC TRAINING

After the morning run, we went straight to the mess hall for breakfast. I was among the last to eat because I could not finish with the top runners in our Company. I was always hurrying to try and catch up with the others after eating far fall-out to go to our next activity.

Before the noon and supper meals, we had to go through the monkey bars. If you made it straight through, you went to eat and had more time to relax then the others. If you fell at any point, you got back in line and tried it again. I just could not do it. After four or five tries, the Lieutenant would let us who could not do it, do ten push-ups. I would be really tired and had a hard time even doing the push ups after the damn monkey bars. My arms were always too weak for the rest of my body. They still are.

A lot of the time, I was a server of the meals. Our barracks was undergoing renovations and we were inspected each morning. We failed inspection, we got the shit detail to serve the meals for that day. The good news was that I did not have to go through the damn monkey bar when I had to serve a meal. Those that served had to get to the mess hall and get ready for the several hundred guys that were coming. The bad news was that we ate after everyone else so we had to hurry to clean things up a bit and really hurry to find your group for the next activity. I did not have any time to relax. But that was alright because I did not have time to think about how things were going. The real screw ups got do the hardest work in mess hall like wash dishes, peel potatoes, and the worse job of all, clean the grease pit. You actually got in this pit to clean the cooking oil out of it. It was some really nasty stuff. I never did this- thanks be to God.

It seamed like most of the non commissioned officers were screw offs that lost their rank and was demoted to training the recruits. This seam to be their "shit detail" until they got their rank back or just got out of the service.

TEAR GAS SHACK

We had to learn how to put on and ware a gas mask. We had classes on this subject. Then we went out in the woods where smoke booms were thrown at us and most of us died because about ninety eight percent could not get our gas mask on in time to stay alive according to your trainers. This pissed off our trainers. They acted pissed-off most of the time anyway. I guess I would have been also if I lost all my rank. Anyway, this meant more school on emergency usage of gas mask. They marched us to the Tear Gas Hut. I saw the ambulance standing by just in case. I was the first in a row as they marched us into the gas hut. It was a frame building with one large open room. I was the first in my squad to go in. Our gas mask was buttoned up in its container on our belts. This is where it goes when not in use. You carried everything. What was not in your backpack was hooked on to your belt like your water canteen, combat knife, and other stuff like your tear gas mask. They briefed us again on how to use the gas mask then departed for the building. They added the gas. It was real this time. They counted to ten or some other higher number while we held our breath and then the alarm went off and then we but on our gas mask. This was the real thing. My mask did not seal all the way. I did take in some gas. They gave the order to left face to march us out single file. And suggested that we stay in single file and not panic or else. Since I was the first to go in, yes, you guessed it, I was the last one to come out. I was chocking and trying to tell the Sergeant that my mask was not fitting properly. He said to stay in line. I could not see anything. We had placed our hands on the next recruit's shoulders and just followed him out. When I got to the door, I was really happy. I saw this flash as I got to the steps. I tore the mask off, I was couching and my eyes were crying and burning a little. After four or five minutes, I was all right. I looked over the mask really good and could not find a problem with it. I just did not have it sealed properly. I did not ask for nor was I given any medical attention. I was very happy this training was over.

The flash I saw was a picture being taken. Duck had a basic training photo album that the Army took pictures of different activities during our basic training. He purchased it at the end of his full eight weeks of basic training was over. I never got the chance to purchase one since I was not there at the end of this training period. I believe that there is a picture of me coming out of the Tear Gas Hut in that book.

Barry (Butch) Raffray - June 1962

SOMETHING WRONG

During the third week of basic training, I starting feeling like something was wrong with me. I seam to get tired to easy. I was not in the greatest shape when I joined the Army, but I was raised on a farm and worked hard and was in better shape than I was showing. I the five weeks or so that I was there, I saw fat guys losing weight and really starting to look good. I also saw really skinny guys putting on some weight and filling out. This regular routine that the Army had was good for all of us.

Starting the fourth or fifth week of basic training, I was really swollen up. I had looked forward to this week because it was the week we go to rifle range. I wanted to shoot my weapon and see how I match up against the other guys. But today, I could not lace up my boots. My feet were to swollen. I could not make a fist. My fingers and hands were to swollen. My face was puffy and my eyes looked like Japanese eyes. The swollenness around my eyes made them look slanted and squinty. I had trouble to see good. At fall- in, I checked out for sick bay and my Company marched off to rifle range without me. I was upset for two reasons now. I felt bad seeing them go, and I could not talk to Duck. He was in another part of the formation and marching out.

At this point, I started to worry about me. What happened to me? What did I have to make be swell up like this? How did I get this? All kinds of thoughts go through your head in a time like this. I waited for the van that passed by in the mornings to pick up guys that had to see the base doctors for one thing or another.

I MET THE BASE DOCTORS-A LOT OF THEM

I waited for a doctor to see me for three or four hours. I had to sit on the floor of a very large waiting room because so many guys were there. Sometime after twelve noon, I was put in a room where a doctor would see me. He came in and asked me what was the problem. I said that I did not know and showed him my hands and feet. He then looked at my face and realized that I was not that fat. He had me take my fatigues and my boots and socks all the way off. He was really puzzled. I lay on this table. He would press his thumb on my right leg above my knee. It left an indent about a quarter of an inch or more deep. After a minute or two, the indent would fill in like a slow sponge coming back to it original shape after squeezing the water out. He did this several times in different places. The impressions would disappear after a minute or so. He than went down the hall. He came back with a lady doctor and several other men doctors. They all started poking me with their fingers. Before I knew it, there was about six doctors and nurses in the room with me. It was getting crowded. They were poking and asking each other questions. They took blood to test. They did not have a clue as to what it was that I had.

I never went back to my barracks after this. The only visitor I had for the next five weeks was Duck a couple of time when he could leave our Company C area after about the sixth or seventh week of basic training.

IN BASE HOSPITAL WARD

The doctors place me in a hospital ward which was it this complex. This was very odd. The ward that I was placed in had only about ten guys in it the whole time that I was in the hospital. It had about fifty or sixty beds but very few guys. We all seam to have something different to contend with. But the oddness was, I was in a three quarters empty barracks in Company C and now I am in a four fifths empty hospital ward.

They weight me in at one hundred seventy eight pounds. They had me stay in bed for the first four days and nights. I was monitored by a male nurse that had an office at the entrance into the ward. I even had to use the bathroom in a bedpan. I did not care for that to much. On the fifth day they reweighed me. I weighed one hundred and fifty five pounds. This was my going into the Army weight. My natural weight at the time. I had lost twenty-three pounds of fluid in four days. The swelling was all gone. I felt lighter and my face, which I had not seen in over four days, was back to normal. Now to find out what I have.

When I could move around, I had to go to the hospital orderly's office. They had to break into my wall locker and get into my foot locker at Company C to get all my Army issue clothes and the rest of my stuff. I had left a key to both lockers with a guy that bunked next to me. They thought both keys were for one locker. They ruined one of my good locks. I got it back too, broken. When my unit found out that I was not coming back from the hospital quickly, I was transferred to the Hospital Unit. All my belonging was sent there except my rifle. The Orderly at the hospital unit knew that I was not going to another company later I guess, because he told be to pick a set of dress clothes for me to keep and shoes, socks, belt and hat and underwear. They kept all the rest of my new Army clothes including my boots. Before I even left the area, they were dividing up my new stuff. If my jackets would fit, they would trade their old one for it and did this with all my stuff. While in the hospital, I was issued several sets of patience clothing. They were light blue. A short sleeve top and long bottoms with this lace up tie around the waist. I was issued slippers to ware. While in the hospital, everywhere you wanted or needed to go was inside. You could walk on the grounds, which was well kept up in the type slippers that were issued. But you could not go to town in them.

MADE NEW FRIENDS IN HOSPITAL

While in the hospital ward, I got acquainted with several recruits who also had medical problems. Most was in there for just several days than back to their units. Some of the guys in my ward were not going to stay in the Army for one reason or another. If you were in basic training and lost a week or more by being in the hospital, you had to be re-cycled. This meant that you missed important training at your unit and would be placed into another unit that was just getting to the week of training that you left for the hospital. You were not allowed to miss one week of training and go back to the guys/unit you knew. You went to a bunch of strangers and started training where you left off from.

One guy in the hospital was from Troy, New York. He was a tall ole boy. Well over six feet. He was a checker and chess champion. So he said. I did not know how to play chess but I would beat him eight out of ten times playing checkers. He had a problem with this.

Another guy named White had diabetes. He refused to sign a release that the Army wanted stating he had it before he joined even though his mother had a history of diabetes. I believe White beat the system. He wanted a pension and free medical treatment (insulin) for the rest of his life. I do not know how long he was in the Army before he went into the hospital.

Another guy, Riveria, could not eat meat. He told me and everybody else that he was allergic to meat. The hospital used to grind it up and sneak it in his meals. They thought that he was a faker. I saw him throwing up on many occasions. He would get the red ass because he knew that they were putting meat into his food secretly. I do not know what happened to him.

A guy was there with chronic back problems. He would cry during the day and night when they held back his medication. He said that they would fake his medication but he could tell when his back started hurting that they did not give him the correct pain medicine. He was not allowed to leave the ward area ever. He did put his uniform on one Saturday and told me that he had been locked up to long and he was going to town. He skipped out that week end and came in late Sunday night. He missed Sunday roll call. Yes, we had roll call every day just like being in the regular Army. This meant that the guy went AWOL- absent without leave. A serious offense. He slept in the bed next to me. Early Monday morning the M Ps and his nurse came in and got him. She chastised him for skipping out. He augured back. I had seen them two go at it almost each day. They just did not like each other. They took him away. I never saw him again but I slept better after he was gone. I did not have to put up with all that crying and moaning all night.

Another guy was a Section Eight fellow. He was really COCKOO. He stole my radio ear plug one time which I left on my bed, but I could not prove that it was him who took it. It was a small devise attached to a plug in cord. You could plug it into a special socket that was by every bed in the hospital ward throughout the hospital. We would listen to the music and other entertainment that our Base hospital radio station would put on. I was going to have to buy it if it did not turn up. One day he came by my bed and threw it on my bed and said "it don't work no more". I knew he a taken it. I took it apart and re-attached a lose wire inside and put it back together again. To my surprise, it worked. I would not leave it or anything else unlocked from that day forward.

JOHNNY RIVERS (ROVERSTELLI)

I mentioned our Base radio station. It was located in the hospital. The listening devises was issued from the radio office. I had to sign for it which meant that I was responsible for it. I used to go with some of the guys and sit in the sitting room of the radio station and read magazines or talk or listen to pop music or just to kill time. We could also watch the disc jockey work through the large plate glass and talk with them when the records were being played.

All the time that I was in Fort Jackson, Johnny Rivers was the afternoon disc jockey. He played pop music and even played some of his songs. I had something in common with him. He was from Baton Rouge and I was from just down the highway from Baton Rouge. Johnny was doing a six month hitch and this was his job for the six months. He was a big star back then so he did not want to serve two or three years. He could not be out of circulation that long or his fans may forget about him and not buy any of this records, then he is a has been. He changed his name from Roverstelli to Rivers and made the big time. He had to go to California to do it, but it paid off for him. All the years that he was Roverstelli, he could not get a break. It just goes to show how show business is. The same thing had to be done for Richie Vallens- Valenzulla, because the white people would not accept any name that did not sound white, no matter how good they sounded.

TONY KUBECK

Tony Kubeck, who played short stop for the world champion New York Yankees was at Fort Jackson also. He was serving his six months tour of duty there. This was during the baseball season so he could not play for the Yankees while in the Army. This must have cost Tony big bucks. He would come by the hospital to cheer everybody up and also be on the radio station in interviews as such. While at Fort Jackson, he played on the Base baseball team. I never made it to one of the games. I did not leave the hospital grounds after getting there until I came home.

WHILE IN THE WARD

I learned to play several card games while in the hospital. One game was crazy Eight which I showed to family and friends after getting back home. We got many hours of pleasure from this game and several others that I've since forgotten how to play. I even played crazy eights with my sons when they were small, and still play occasionally.

While in the hospital, I met this one guy that I communicated with for several years than just lost contact with him. His name was Barney Carroll. He was from Raleigh, North Carolina. He was over six feet and a good looking kid. He was only in the hospital for about three or four days. We became friends and would talk for hours well into the night. He had ancestors (great Grandfather for one) that was in the Civil War. He promised to send me a Louisiana Confederate bill when he got home. He said that his family had trunks full of confederate money. His family was what we call "well to do" folks. I guess money has been in there family for over one hundred years. He as very well educated and stood tall. He just looked like he came from money.

After arriving home, I received a letter from Barney telling me what he was up to. We wrote back and forth during the summer. In my letters, he realized that I had joined the Army for three years. He was a six month guy. He just did not understand how I, being from the South, could join the Yankee Army for three years. He could never serve that long in the Yankee Army. During the winter months, his letters arrived from Spray, North Carolina. This was his family's winter home. They lived in Raleigh during the summer months and Spray during the winter months. I still have his letters picked up somewhere. I always wanted to go to North Carolina and try and look him up. Maybe some day I will.

He could not find a Louisiana confederate bill to send to me so he sent a five dollar North Carolina confederate bill that I have in my safety deposit box in a bank nearby.

THE DYE TEST

One morning, my breakfast was held without warning before hand. I was stopped by our ward orderly and told to wait. A male nurse came by and said "I have to put dye in your system". He shot the dye into the vain of my left arm and told me that I had to drink eight glasses of water. He was standing by me to see that I drank the eight glasses. I got sick and needed to use the toilet. I got diarrhea. I was in the stall quite a while. He came to check on me, I felt like I would pass out. The nurse saw that I was in distress as I was sitting on the toilet and he told me to try and lift my head as he was holding down on it. I did and my head cleared up quickly. This procedure rushed blood back into the brain and stop the light headedness right now. This is a procedure I used on many occasions afterward when I was getting dizzy and felt that I would pass out.

I recovered satisfactorily from this episode and before the nurse left, he gave me a gallon jug and told me to pee into it for the next twenty-four hours then deliver the whole amount to the hospital lab. I knew where the lab was because of all the blood tests I had being doing. He left and I went on to a late breakfast in the mess hall.

The next morning, on my way to breakfast, I carried this gallon jug to the lab. All along the way folks snickered at me for caring my piss. Some of them even laughed. Now I knew why my buddies in the ward did not want to walk with me to the lab before going to breakfast. They left early so that I would not tag along with them.

Two days later, I was leaving our ward with some of the other guys, heading to mess hall for breakfast, when our orderly shouted Raffray. I said "sir". He told me that breakfast was held on me again. I said "shit- why?" He did not know or just would not tell me. The other guys left. I went back to my bed and waited.

In about a hour, here come the nurse again. He said we got to do the dye again. Why?, I asked, "Because the lab messed up the test with your piss", he said. "A whole three quarters of a gallon, I asked. "Oh no, he said, "they took a syringe full and poured out the rest". "Those bastards", I said. Then I said "AAAUUUUUUGGGGGGGGGG". We did it again. The dye into my vain, the eight glasses of water, the almost throwing up and the pissing in a gallon jug for the next twenty-four hours.

I had not given blood before I went into the Army. Daddy used to do it on a regular basis at the White Castle Hospital or whenever someone called and needed blood. As a teenager, he tried to get me to give blood. He said it made you feel good to give and your heart replaces it with new fresh blood. I just could not do it. I was afraid of needles and I thought it was very painful.

When I made the decision to go into the Army, they took blood on several occasions. While in the hospital there, I got used to giving blood. It did not hurt much. But this dye thing was something else. I much rather give blood fifty times than get the dye once. It just was not natural. They were pushing/forcing the dye into my vain. I could feel the burning and the pressure in my arm that you do not feel when they are taking blood. It is not the natural flow. It was like the dye was trying to push my blood back into my heart. It was forcing its way into my blood stream.

WALKING THE HALL WITH PISS AGAIN

The next day, here I am again walking the halls with almost a gallon of my yellow piss, holding the jug really tight. I did not want to drop it and go through that all over again. When I delivered it to the lab, I told the guy there to hold on to the damn piss until after he knew all test was completed. He did not like what I said. I got worried that this bastard might screw my test up on purpose just to have me go through this shit again. I wished that I had not said one damn thing. I worried for a couple of days over this. As it turned out, I never did another dye test.

Several days later, the doctor that I had been seeing called me into his office. He told me that I had a Kidney disease. It was Nephritis or Nephrosis meaning an inflammation of the kidney. It is a malfunction of the kidney. The doctors did not know much about it. It was a relatively new disease. They did not know of any treatment for this disease.

The Army started the process for getting me out of the service after a week or so for the paperwork to get to the right folks. They told me I would get an Honorable Discharge and not a Medical Discharge. The reason for this is that I had the disease before I went in to service. This meant that I could not go to any Base hospital or Veterans hospital or get help from the Red Cross because the Army/Government would not pay. I got pissed off at President Johnson. I wrote a letter to him but did not mail it. This is one of my biggest regrets that I did not mail the letter. I have long since lost it.

Daddy got help from the local Veterans Administration in Plaquemine, Louisiana. a Mr. Dupont was in charge and knew Daddy well. We asked for and got permission to come home and go to my local doctor before signing any releases at this time.

COMING HOME

I became friends with and older black orderly that worked at the base hospital. I treated him with curtsey and respect. He treated me with the same. He had empathy for the situation that I was in. When I got my orders to go home, he offered to drive me to the Grey Hound Bus Station in Columbia on his way home after he worked his shift. I took him up on it.

Columbia was about fifteen miles from the base. We talked the whole way. He was a good man. He drove me direct to the station, we shook hands. I told him how much I appreciated his help and assistance during my hospital stay and again thanked him for the ride and we said our good bys. He took off while I was going into the station. I got my ticket for Baton Rouge, Louisiana. I had notified Momma and Daddy of the scheduled time of arrival and the bus trip number that I would arrive on.

I left Columbia, South Carolina on August 3, 1962. I arrived back home on August 5th. The ticket I held called for the bus to stop at every stop along the way, which they did. They even stopped to pick up folks on the side of the road. There were not any interstate highway back then. At lease not any in the South.

It took twenty six hours to get to Baton Rouge from Columbia. At one point, when I was on the road for eighteen hours or so, an old man boarded the bus, sat beside me and asked how long I've been riding the bus. I told him a very long time, eighteen hours. He laughed and said that he had been riding for five days. He got on the bus in San Francisco and was heading to Florida. He had a couple more days to go.

Along the way, we stopped on the side of the road to pick up a fair and the engine died. The driver could not restart it. He announced that he could call for another bus which may take several hours or we could try and push it to see if he can get it started. All the men piled outside and went behind the bus. When the driver gave the signal we pushed and moved the bus about fifteen feet and it started. We all hollowed and piled back on it and was on our way again.

When I got to Baton Rouge, Momma and Daddy was waiting for me. We rejoiced, hugged and kissed each other, got in our 1955 Pontiac two door and headed for Cedar Grove Plantation. I drove. It felt good to drive again. It had been over two months since I last drove a car.

The next morning, I sat up in bed and cried like a baby. I do not know if I was crying because I was happy to be home again or because I did not know what I would do next or what would become of me or if I only had a short time to live. All I know is that I cried out loud. Momma heard the noise, came by and looked in my bedroom, saw what was happening and closed back the door. She never said anything to me about it. I was a confused and unhappy young man.

ARRIVED HOME- SAW DOCTORS

I arrived home one week before Duck came home on leave after basic training. He had two weeks before he reported to his next base in Alabama for airplane mechanic school. Duck and I spent most of this time together just running the road and visiting folks.

Dr. Daigle, my doctor in White Castle, did not know much about this kidney disease, so he sent me to see Dr. Kern, a re-known kidney specialist in Baton Rouge. In due time, I made the appointment to see Dr. Kern. He did all the usual test. Test like, blood taken to test later, pee in a bottle to test later, finger in the butt to test at that moment. Until now, I had not mentioned about how often I had a finger poked into my butt hole. Dr. Kern was a large German doctor with the largest hands I ever saw or felt. I saw his hands two or three time over the next month, which was more often than I wanted too. Since I (we) did not have insurance, Daddy paid for the doctor visits and tests that they ran on me.

When the results came in, I made the trip to Baton Rouge to see Dr. Kern again. It was explained that I had this kidney disease a long time before I went into the Army. It takes several years to get to this stage. I had felt good all through high school. I had perfect attendance my sophomore, junior and senior years of school. I miss one half day in the ninth grade to go to Uncle Andrea Ponsano wife's funeral. I like the old lady very much. She was Mattie and Margie's Momma. They are the twins that I cannot tell apart.

I was healthy and it was hard to believe that I had this for that long a time before I joined the Army. But I remembered the doctor at the induction center in New Orleans and the three times that I had to pee in the bottle to be tested. Something WAS wrong then.

Doctor Kern advised me, a nineteen year old, to go into business for myself because no plant or business will ever hire me with a kidney disorder. I was down, way down, but not out.

Daddy and I visited with the Veterans Administration representative in Plaquemine, a Mr. Dupont, but could not get any help from him or them. I signed the release from the Army stating that they were not responsible for my condition. I volunteered for three years. I was in the Army for four months and nineteen days of active duty. I received an Honorable Discharge. A medical Discharge would have given me benefits and they did not want to do that. I cannot go to a VA hospital or receive any medical benefits whosoever, or any other kind of benefits for that matter.

I kept on seeing Dr. Daigle in White Castle, who had prescribed penicillin pills for me to take one a day. He did not know if they would help me, but did not think that they could/would hurt me. They did not help. I stopped taking them after two months or so. I did not want to chance getting allergic to them and one day need them to save my life and could not take them.

AFTER FINAL DISCHARGE

Over the next several years, I worked at the sugar mill (house) on Cedar Grove Plantation during the grinding/harvesting season. In late 1962, I worked about sixty five days straight. In late 1963, I worked almost one hundred straight days during grinding. All jobs in the mill were twelve hours on and twelve hours off. There were no holidays and no overtime pay. I worked a minimum of eighty-four hours a week. I averaged more than this because of working during WASH-OUT. This was something we had to do in the mill several time during grinding season. We had to clean all the grit and muck out of the system. This meant the several tanks, feeders, Oliver filters, etc. I worked a couple of thirty-sixes to get my part completed during WASH-OUT. I would work my twelve hours. Then my relief came in. He was old and could not climb into the tanks, so I worked his shift cleaning our tanks. He would give me instructions/direction from above and point out the dirty spots that he could see. I would clean them with a high pressure water hose. Then I would work my shift again during the start up.

In between the 1962 and 1963 sugar mill jobs, I worked for an oil well repair company named Atwell and Blankenship. Mr. Atwell lived in White Castle and was Dianna and Ricky Atwell's father. Dianna married my cousin Pee Wee (Steve) Doiron Jr. If I did any other work for pay, I do not recall it.

In early 1964, I went to work in a grocery store in White Castle. I worked six days a week. Eleven hours a day during the week and twelve hours on Saturday. I went in on Sundays to restock shelves and price items that were being placed on shelves for the first time.

Every item had a price on them during these times. Nobody would buy something that did not have a price stamped on it. Folks did not like getting to the counter with the item then asking how much it costs. I made thirty-five dollars per week. This was for about seventy hours work a week.

When I got home from the Army in August of 1962, I just knock around trying to do odd jobs until I got the grocery store job in early 1964.

1962 SUGAR MILL JOB

Mr. Luban Caillet, the sugar mill Superintendent, hired me to run the Heaters. This was the first place that the cane juice came after being squeezed/crushed from the cane stalks.

The heaters would heat the juice to about two hundred thirty degrees to boil off the water, then pump the juice to another storage area to be processed later. When the mill had a jam and stopped crushing the stalks of cane for any reason, the flow of juice stopped. I needed to watch it very close. When the flow stopped coming to the heaters, the temperature would rise sharply. The danger was that it could blow up the heaters, me and about one fourth of the mill. We had water control valves about twenty feet over my head. The valve had a chain hanging down to my level. If the temperature got over two hundred thirty-five degrees, we could have major problems of making/cooking sugar in the heaters. This would surely plug the tubes inside and the whole thing would blow up. To keep this from happening, when the feeder where the cane was crushed got jammed and the juice stopping flowing to me, I had to open the water valve and let in water so the heaters would not get over heated and blow up because of steam pressure. Now, I had to be careful because I did not want to put to much water into the heater to soon because this could cause it to blow up also. A lot of cold water mixed with very hot steam and metal is not good. I had those two old heaters just a whining and humming on several occasions. I got scared, but I had to hang in there, that was my job. I was taught by Mr. Luban to feel the side of the header for heat in addition to reading the temperature gauge on both tanks in case the gauges were wrong. I got pretty good at feeling the heat and guessing what temperature it was. We were damn lucky that I did not blow the whole place up.

In 1962, Mr. Luban lived in the mill during grinding. He had this room on the ground floor. The heaters and I was on the second or third floor. Anyway, when we got a jam at the feeder, one of the places he came to check was the heaters. He would stay with me a while and give me pointers on what to look for. Mr. Luban was a good man and I respected him very much. He was a big, strong and powerful man that my Daddy, another big man, had respect for. His sons, Gerald and Calvin (Pochie), who I went all through high school with, both work in this mill after they grew up to support their families. Both worked in the sugar mill for years until it was shut down several years after Southdown purchased it from the W. T. Burton family sometime in the 1980s, I think.

When I was about eight or nine years old, I can remember a car wreck that Mr. Luban got into. He used to drive kind of fast. During the grinding season when the mill was running around the clock, he did not like to be gone from it for very long. So he went everywhere in a hurry so he could get back to work quicker. He had this light blue big 1950 or 1951 Buick. He was driving from the mill on the shell road coming toward the Texas and Pacific Railroad track and La. #1. He hit the tracks going to fast and his car flipped over. Daddy and I heard it from our house and we knew that somebody had a wreck. I jumped into Daddy's truck with him. In fifteen seconds we were at the scene. It was less than one half mile. Mr. Luban had crawled out of a window. I don't know how he did it. I thought he was way too big to get out of a window. He was alright. He said he was not hurt. He started walking around his car looking for damage. Someone shouted that the wrecker would be on its way shortly to right his car.

Mr. Luban looked toward White Castle. From here we could see all the way to town. He said, "I don't see them, I got to go, I don't have time to wait". Before anyone could get around to his car where he was, he crouched down and got a hold on something and started grunting. Daddy said, "wait a minute, Luban." But by that time he was moving the car and it flipped back over on it tires. He jumped in, started it up and drove off. What a man. All the adults there and us kids also, just scratched our heads and said, "Jesus Christ". I knew from that time on that Mr. Luban Caillet was not a man that you wanted to make mad at you.

MR. LUBAN CHEWING TOBACCO STORY
(As I saw it)

When working around the clock during grinding, Mr. Luban used to ware coveralls. The one with the bib, trap door in the back and built in suspenders, with nothing under them. He did not even ware a shirt during the whole winter time. I don't think that he wore any drawers either. He had the whole mill to run and was a man on the go. We were all men in the mill, so he did not have/take the time or need to put more clothes on. The one vice or joy that I knew he had was chewing tobacco. He would buy it from the company store. He was always chewing tobacco. He like the kind that came in a bar shape..

Mr. Grainier and Mr. Barby Miller both worked in the mill year round for Mr. Luban for many years. They had worked for Mr. Luban's dad for years also when he was the Chief Engineer or mill Manager. Mr. Luban took over for his dad when he retired or died. I believe Pochie became Chief or if not, was high up in the mill before it shut down. Anyway, every day Mr. Grainier and Mr. Miller would ask Mr. Luban for a chaw (piece) of his tobacco. This one time during grinding in 1962, I was near by when Mr. Barby Miller ask for a chaw. Mr. Luban was upset at something and had the red ass, I guess. I saw him take the whole pack out of his pocket. He reached down inside his coveralls and I could see him moving his arm up and down around his genital area. Then he pulled it out and offered it to Mr. Miller. Mr. Miller put his hand up and said, "I don't believe I care for any now". Mr. Luban spit out the tobacco he was chewing and took a bite from the plug he offered to Mr. Miller. To my knowledge, Mr. Luban was never bothered by folks wanting a chew from his tobacco again. I only told this story several times. I don't know why, but it is a great story. Well, maybe I do know why. It is a sure fired way to break folks from asking you for a bite of anything you might have.

MAKING RAW BROWN SUGAR

The overseers and field hands who were responsible to grow the crop and would harvest it and deliver the cane to the sugar mill. The cane stalks would be stacked up forty feet high or so on the ground just outside the crusher feeder area. We had two derricks that would unload the cane from tractor carts or truck trailers and stack it up while a smaller dragline with a crab on it would feed the mill. The feeding of the mill went on twenty-four hours a day. The unloading of the cane was about ten to twelve hours a day. A large supply was kept on the yard around the mill to be sure not to run out. To get this inventory, the mill accepted cane for two or three days before starting the mill up. You did not want to ever run out of cane during the grinding season. All farmers needed to get their crops to the mill. When the mill processed everything that was on hand in the yard, grinding was over.

So the field got the cane to the mill. The mill had several conveyors. One set, the cane was placed on by the dragline during the day and the derricks during the night. High pressure water would spray on the stalks of cane as the conveyor operator move the product to another conveyor. The sets of conveyors were placed in the shape of the letter T. A conveyor on the right and a conveyor on the left were about eight feet off the ground. Between these two conveyor systems was a conveyor that went straight into the mill. This conveyor was built at ground level. The conveyors on the left and right would feed into the conveyor on the ground. The right and left conveyors were on the outside of the mill. The straight conveyor was also outside but continued into the inside of the mill. This conveyor had the large crushers on them.

As the cane fell into the shoot (the straight conveyor) large knife blades started chopping it into smaller lengths. Water was still being sprayed on the cane to wash off any dirt and grit. This drained away into a collection basin. As the cane came further into the building, different set of water spray systems were used. The stalks would be conveyed through the large crushers. One crusher on top and two on bottom, squeezing the juice out of the cane stalks and spraying some water on the crushed stalks as they continue through another set of crushers and another set. There were four or five sets of crushers in all. The juice and water collected in large long troughs under the carrier or conveyor system. This product was pumped automatically to my area. I had two funnel shaped tanks over a very large opened top square tank. I would stand over these tank most of my working time. Every story in the mill had steel see through floors. From the forth floor a person could see down to the bottom floor if there were not any tanks or equipment in the way. I think the funnel shaped tanks held about two thousand gallons each. As one tank would fill with cold juice mixed with some water, it would trip and the second tank started filling while the first tank emptied into the large open square storage tank beneath it. I also was in charge of an electronic devise that would count the number of time the funnel shaped tanks would fill. I had to change a paper chart every twenty-four hours on my shift. I gave this to the Superintendent when he made his rounds. It went to the office. I guess we changed the very first one on my shift when we started grinding, so it stayed that way for all of 1962 grinding. About two times a week, I had to add red ink to the system. The chart was done in red ink. I do not know why red ink was used.

The large open top square tank below me is where the juice came from that feed my heaters. The heaters were located about twenty-five feet behind where is sat to watch the flow of the juice into my funnel tanks. This is how I could tell fairly quickly if the carrier/conveyor was having problems. The flow of the juice would slow down to nothing. When this happen, I would run between the Oliver filters and the hot juice three story tank to look at what was happening at the crushers on the floor of the mill. I would hollow and try and get someone's attention to find out how long we may be jammed. My buddy that ran the Oliver Filter would be there with me because he needed to know because it affected what he needed to do also. It was during times such as these, that I had to manipulate the chains to add water to the heaters.

After heating the juice as I mentioned earlier, my hot juice went to the hot juice tank that was very large and in front of all my tanks. It was the reason that I could not see the carrier/crusher because it was three or four stories tall. From this hot juice tank, the juice flowed to the Oliver Filter where they sucked the juice and all the dirt, grit and other foreign objects that may be in it out. The clean hot juice then went to the Double Effects tanks. The mud from the Oliver Filters went to the bottom floor. As the filters rotated, the juice went through its screen like surface. The mud stuck about a quarter inch thick onto the screen. As it rotated, it scraped the mud off and re-sucked more juice, etc., etc.

The Double Effects would heat the juice several hundred degrees. You could make molasses here and syrup if we had more equipment. Cora Texas Mill made and marketed Cora Syrup. It was good. If you are not careful, you could make sugar here also and that would be very bad. From the Double Effects, the product was sent to the Sugar Maker on the top floor. He cooked the product some more and made raw brown sugar. You could not tell it was sugar yet, but the Sugar Maker knew it was. When he got through that cooking process, the product was very viscous. The Sugar Maker emptied his product into large vats that had huge mixer blades in them and move very slowly stirring the mixture. This was a very thick mixture. You could put a plank across the product and almost walk across it. It almost looked like toffee but was thicker and reddish brown in color. There were troughs about five feet wide and three feet deep that was used to transfer the product from the vats to the Sugar Dryer who was down on the bottom floor. This thick product was sugar, but it was not in granular form yet. To get the grains that we all know sugar to be, it had to be processed some more. The troughs wind its way to the bottom floor. The product was so thick that it just sort of oozed it way downward. We counted on gravity doing its work to get the product to where the centrifuges were. The equipment look like top loading washing machines or dryers actually. We had nine of these on each side of a conveyor belt system, with small troughs coming off the large trough to feed each centrifuge.

The Sugar Dryer opened the traps on each trough to let enough product ooze in. Then he cut the flow off, than started the centrifuge spinning at a high speed. The then added a small cup of water into each container and let it open for a few minutes. Then he would go over to the nine centrifuges on the other side and complete the same process. When done there, he came back to the first set of centrifuges and stopped the spinning and started scraping the raw brown sugar out. It was granulated now. As he tilted each centrifuge to empty it, the brown sugar fell onto a conveyor that moved it to another conveyor that went up about three stores to another conveyor that transported it out of this area into a sugar warehouse next door where is was bagged into three hundred pound sacks or blown into box cars for sale to other manufacturers that would process the raw brown sugar into fine brown sugar or white sugar. This process of turning brown sugar into white sugar is a very clean and purified process because that sugar from here is sold to consumers/users.

Note: I often told folks that I help to make sugar from sugar cane, rabbits, snakes, rats, mice, birds, etc. I believe all these animals got caught in the stacks of sugar cane that went through the crushing system at one time or another. At our shop, we hauled raw brown sugar in regular dump trucks from one warehouse to another. These were the same dump trucks that we hauled the Oliver Filter mud with. The trucks were not washed between loads. Our brown sugar was nasty but made great tasting ginger bread cookies and other good stuff.

Our sugar was sold to refine sugar producers. It was reprocessed into white sugar. It was purified and not touched by human hands at their sites. At lease this is what I was told. I have never been into a refine sugar processing facility. Always wanted to go, but never did.

WORKING FOR ATWELL AND BLANKENSHIP

OIL FIELD WORK 1963

In the middle part of 1963, I worked for Atwell and Blankenship for several months. They were a local based company. We worked on gas and oil wells. We had a portable derrick on a big truck and would go into the oil fields, where wells had stopped producing because of bad pumps. We pulled the rods from the well casings to get to the pump at the bottom so it could be repaired. Sometime, we pulled casings that were bad and replace with new ones. Casing is a three or four inch diameter pipe/tube that is thirty to forty feet long that have threads on each end. The rods were about one inch solid steel the same length as the casing that went inside the casing that had the pump attached to it. The pump supplied pressure that forced the product to come up the casing to ground level where it was collected and transferred to storage holding tanks. The casing is what the oil/gas flowed up and out of the ground through.

We went into action after the oil or gas had stopped pumping from the well. Usually it was a problem with the pump on the end of the rod that was four hundred to eight hundred feet down in the well. Our rig was designed to pull the rods or casing one at a time until the lowest one was removed from the ground. After the pump was repaired and reinstalled on the last rod section, we would start replacing each rod back into the well.

To explain further, the pump was attached to the rod. The rod went inside the casing which was inside the tubing. We never pulled tubing. They were maybe six to eight inch in diameter. We did pull casings to get to the bad ones and replace with good ones. You needed to replace a casing when it developed a hole in it and the product would leak into the tubing. The tubing was there to shield and protect the casings and keep dirt, rock and such out of the product. The casing was where the oil was sucked up through to the ground level. As mentioned earlier, the rods were inside the casing and had a pump attached on the deepest one.

NOTE: It has been so long since I worked in this industry that I may have the Casings and Tubes reversed. The rods were inside and had the pump attached to it somehow.

Since each rod/casing was thirty or more feet long, the derrick rig we used had to be much taller to get them to above ground level. When we drove on the highway, the rig on the big truck bed was in a lying tied down position. Our truck/trailer rig must have been almost fifty feet long when on the highway. At each site, we had to set the derrick up-right and stabilize it to handle the load of the rods or casings to be pulled.

This work was manual and I just could not keep up physically. I would swell up. The more activity I did, the more I would swell, which was not a good thing. This meant that my damaged kidneys was working harder than normal and not processing the fluids properly. I would get really sluggish and tired and could hardly move. The excess fluids would stay in my body as long as I was active. It took complete rest and bed time for days to come back to my normal weight. I worked in a four member crew. Willie Saunders was our pusher or foreman. He ran the lift machine at the base of the derrick. He operated a power cable unit that lifted each section of rod/casing above where it connected with the one under it. Upon the derrick base section with Willie, was Lil Buck Suarez. Buck was the head hand. His workmate was Lester "Beaver" Hebert. Buck and Beaver's job was to attach the large C clamp type thing around the rod or casing so it would not fall back down into the well shaft, and manually unscrew the sections with large pipe wrenches. Willie would lift the rod out of the ground above where they screwed together. The C clamp was attached to the next rod just under where they were screwed together. This allowed Buck and Beaver to unscrew the top rod and remove it without the rods still under the ground falling back into the hole. This left the first rod pulled dangling on a cable above all our heads inside the derrick's frame.

I was the step and fetch it guy. After the rod was unscrewed, Willie would operate the power unit to lower the rod toward the ground. I had to grab it and walk it out to a lay down area a short distance from the rig. Before the actual laying down of any rods or casings started, I had to lay timbers down on the ground to lay them on. We had to keep them off the ground and try to keep them as clean as possible. All the sections were coated with oil and a petroleum product that looked like chunks of grease. I cannot remember the name of this product but it was place in the hole when drilling the well to keep the steel lubricated and free from rust. This product was really nasty and gooey. This stuff ruined a good pair of gloves in a hurry.

I laid the timbers length ways on the ground. I had to grab a hold and walk out pulling the rod/casings and cable to the lay down area. Then disconnect the connection holding the end of it and walk the cable back to the derrick while Willie was wrenching the cable back on its spool mechanically. The next one went just on the inside of the first one and so on. All of these had to be placed in the order of how they came out of the ground. When we replaced them, we went in reverse order. The last one out was the first one back in and so on.

The first job I did was the hardest. This was manual labor but I made it harder because I did not know better and none of the other guys told me better at the time. I placed the first rod nearest the derrick. The next rod went to the other side of the first and so on. I kept getting further away from the derrick. I was making out all right until about the twentieth rod. I could no longer pull the cable out enough to walk around the rods. I had to walk on them to get to the place where I needed to lay the next one down. I started slipping and sliding all over the place. The pump repair guy had showed up just before I had to start walking on the rods. Willie had called him to give an estimate of when we would get the last rod and pump out. He got there about twenty minutes before we got to it. Each time I would walk a rod out to the lay down area, I would slip and slide. My free arm was flinging all over the place to help to balance me. The guys on the derrick were laughing their asses off. So was the guy waiting to repair the pump. I was not a happy camper. The guy watching was laughing so much he had to stick his handkerchief in his mouth. Now my buddies were laughing at the guy that was laughing at me. I did not think it funny one damn bit.

During this time, I notice that the cable above my buds heads holding the rod was not in the correct position. It was only half way up and it was suppose to be all the way up. I yelled to Willie and got his attention and pointed to the problem. He hurried and stop Buck and Beaver, then work the levers and got it unstuck and hoisted it to the top. Willie thanked me for noticing the jam. He later thanked me again. That was a really dangerous situation for the three of them up on the platform. He again told me "good work". If Buck and Beaver had finished unscrewing it, it would have crashed down on them because the cable was not holding it from the top of the derrick. A jolt like that could have toppled the whole derrick. This made me feel good that I had pointed it out to them.

On the next job I knew to lay the first rod/casing further away from the derrick and all the others inside it. All went well. I did not have to work nearly as hard.

Our crew had several job near Eaton, Louisiana which is near Mamou, Louisiana. One time we were there for four days in a row. Willie found a motel at what was called the Y at Eaton. I never saw a town there. Maybe the Y was name Eaton- I don't know. This "motel" was really cheap. It was a row of one room huts with a bathroom in each one. The way Atwell and Blankenship worked the expenses was that their lead man, Willie, would make all the arrangements for sleepovers and pay for food and each of our share would be taken out of our pay at payday. I cannot tell you if I made money on this job or not. I just do not remember.

At the Y, the main building housed the office, a bar and a restaurant-sort of. Our first night there, we ate supper at the main building in the sort of restaurant. The owner, who was a large fat man, had cooked our meal. It was chicken something or other. This was our last meal there.

In the morning we got some coffee and a roll at the office. We then drove to Mamou which was closer than Ville Platte but much smaller, to buy sandwiches stuff for lunches.

We ate our lunch at the job site because we were several miles away from everywhere out in the boonies. So each morning we drove to Mamou to get our lunch supplies. We drove to Ville Platte each evening for supper. Our first supper in Ville Platte was very lively. Buck was trying to lead us young guys (Beaver and me) in the right direction. He did not think to highly of the younger generation. At one point during the meal, a good looking girl walked by. Beaver said, " man, she have some great tits on her ass". Buck got all undone. He went off. Now that is what I've been taking about he said. You young guys saying things like that. That does not make any since. That woman did not have tits on her ass. That is impossible. Something is wrong with the younger generation. We laughed at Buck's remarks and he got pissed off. Willie jumped up and said, "lets go into the dance hall". This defused things and got Buck's mind off the young folks.

We walked into the next section where a stage show was going on and folks were dancing. We watch the largest black woman I have ever seen sing a rhythm and blues song. She had a very good voice. What was odd about it was that she was singing an upbeat fast foot tapping leg moving song and she did not even twitch an eye. I have never seen anything like it before or since. She could have at least moved a hip. But nothing moved, just her lips. No snapping her fingers or moving her head or moving anything. I was a bashful guy and I could not help but feel the music. She was there to sing and that is all she did. As big as she was, maybe if she started swaying with the music she may have caught a heart attack or something. We left to head back to our huts when the song was over.

At the Y, Beaver and I bunked in one hut and Willie and Buck bunked in the one just before ours. There were about six to eight of these huts in a row on the side of the entrance driveway that we were on. There was just enough room to park a car between each hut. They were close together. We bedded down for the night. About midnight we heard all sort of co-motion going on at one of the huts near ours. There was a lot of coming and going all night long. The next morning Willie decided that we were staying at a damn whore house.

That day was another hard working day. We stayed at it until about six p.m. to finish the job. We cleaned up at the whore house and went back to Ville Platte for supper. Since we got a later start, we came straight back after supper.

For years during high school and since, I would get leg cramps at night. It is commonly called a Charlie horse. I also got them in my back when I tried to put a button down shirt on. I hurt something awful. When the leg cramps hit me, I am awoken even if in a deep sleep. About 1 a.m. a Charlie horse hit my left calf leg muscle. I could not rub it out so I went outside and tried to walk it off. I walked up and down the pathway that ran in front of all the huts. Here I am walking back and forth in the moonlight. An old dog that live in the area came up to me and walked back and forth with me. He was like my best friend. I did this for almost an hour. My calf felt much better so I went back into my hut. It was a hot night. We had a large fan on a stand in our hut. The fan did not have a guard on it. Beaver got up during the night and moved the fan near the one window in the hut to get better circulation of air. During the night I heard a noise but did not get up to check it out. I was really too damn tired too. I had not gotten much sleep. When Willie woke us at six a.m. we found out what the noise was all about. The fan had sucked up the window shade and tore it to shreds. There were pieces of shade all over the room.

It was overcast when we went to work in the morning. We had an accident at the site the day before. The C clamp tool had so much pressure on it that it flew to pieces. We were all lucky that no one got hit by the flying metal pieces. We had to search for the pieces and Willie welded what we found back together to make a makeshift tool. We could use it but not put much pressure on it. Willie called in and Bootsy Parker was on his way with a new clamp thing. We had been working at the site for several hours in the rain. It got muddy there. Bootsy showed up and after replacing our equipment, it was decided that we would knock off early today. The rain was letting up some. Bootsy, Buck and Willie got in the cab of the truck. Beaver and I had no choice but to get in the bed. The damn truck got stuck in the mud. Bootsy was spinning the tires and getting us in deeper. Willie yelled orders for Beaver and me to get out and push the truck. We were already wet from head to toe. We got behind the tailgate and started pushing. Bootsy was gunning the engine and the rear tires were spinning. The truck finally started moving forward. Beaver hurried and jumped upon the back bumper. I did not move fast enough. The tire spit mud on me from toe to head. The truck made it to gravel and stopped for me to get in. I was pissed. I felt twenty pounds heavier. As I made my way to the back of the pickup, Beaver and the rest were laughing there asses off. They laughed all the way back to Eaton and continued to laugh off and on for the rest of the day and into the night. I was so happy that I could make them laugh - NOT.

At the hut, I had to get a hose with a spray nozzle to knock some of the mud off me. My buddies were really having a good ole time.

Our last day at Eaton was not a good day for me. We were putting back the rods after the repair to the pump was completed. We had only about five hours of work to do for today then we were going to take the derrick down and head for home. I had been working steady and carrying my weight- thus far. It was very hot. I started sweating profusely and got really weak. I could not stand up anymore. We only had about an hour to go to complete this job. Willie and the guys helped me toward the front of the big truck. Willie told me to lie down under the truck out of the sun and rest. I was on my back under the truck resting. After some minutes a drop of oil from the motor fell in my right eye. It burned. Rubbing it did not help. I rolled on my left side to be sure not to get hit by any more oil in the face. Here I was, worn out, lying under a derrick platform rig with oil in my eye and still happy to be out of the sun and breathing stuffy air.

The four or five days in a row of manual labor had just taken everything out of me. I was getting some swelling in my limbs also. I knew then that I would not be able to work full time at this kind of job. My kidneys would not allow it.

The guys finished up the job. Pack up everything and we took off for home. I got my last paycheck from Atwell and Blankenship two week later. I was sitting on the front porch on the plantation when Willie drove up. He asked how I was doing and looked at my eye. It was almost back to normal. I did not go to the doctor so it took longer to straighten out than it otherwise would have. I told Willie that I was feeling O K. I thanked him for giving me a chance to work with them and asked him to pass that on to Mr. Atwell for me. Willie invited me to come see him when I felt like it, gave me my check and left.

I visited with Willie often for the next several months. I rode with him when he went to the fields to check out wells for Shell Chemical in the White Castle area. He was building a sugar cane hauling trailer in his spare time behind his house in White Castle. He later purchased a large truck and hauled sugar cane with his rig during the harvesting season.

1963 SUGAR MILL JOB

Mr. Luban died before the 1963 grinding season. In 1963, Mr. Pollet hired me to work the heaters again for this grinding season. During this grinding season, I worked the heaters, Double Effects, Oliver Filters, Lime tanks, and other jobs. I even worked for the Sugar Maker a day or two. If somebody did not show up for work, Mr. Pollet did my job and I did these others. I liked him except for one trait. He was deathly afraid of his boss, Mr. Roper, from the Lake Charles office. Mr. Roper was my Dad's boss also. In fact during this time, he was everybody's boss on the plantation. I watched several times from my high vantage point how Mr. Pollet would look out of the window on my level and if Mr. Roper started for the mill, Mr. Pollet would go running and look for a place to hide. One particular time he circled around me three times with Mr. Roper not far behind trying to catch up to him. The first time around, Mr. Roper asked me if I saw Pollet. "Yes sir", I answered. "Which way did he go" Mr. Roper asked? "That way", I said as I pointed in the direction that I had last seen Mr. Pollet. The second and third time, I just pointed his direction to Mr. Roper and we both just shook our heads.

I had never seen anything like this. My Daddy always said to be a man and stand up for yourself. He also said that a man may be boss but he can not eat you. He is just a man. Neither daddy nor I had ever heard of Jeffery Dormer at that time. Like my Daddy, I have never been afraid or in awe of any boss. They are just people. Most of them are richer than me, that is all. Besides Moses, (who lived in our attic on the plantation), the only thing I was afraid of was the crushers in the mill. I was afraid that if I fell into the carrier and started through the crushers feet first, while it was making a waffle out of me one inch at a time, I would be alive to see and feel it. Now that really scared me. I never even walked close to the crushers. I only imagined what could happen.

This was a longer season than the 1962 season by over thirty days. It lasted close to one hundred days. The sugar cane framers had what is referred to as a "bumper crop". The tonnage per acre was great from all of the farmers. Thus they all had more sugar cane to deliver to the mill. I still worked twelve hours a day seven days a week. I did not have much time to spend any money. In fact, I never had any time to spend money. Every two weeks daddy took my paycheck and deposited it into my saving account at the White Castle Bank of Commerce. I was making a whopping one percent interest.

In 1962, I made one dollar per hour. No overtime was ever paid. Grinding lasted for sixty-two days that year. I 1963, I made one dollar and fifteen cents per hour with no overtime ever paid. They did not have to pay overtime for agriculture type work in those days. Grinding lasted ninety-three days in 1963.

The one thing that they did do when working in the sugar mill during grinding season was - if the mill shut down (broke down) for a few days, and you still showed up for work, they would PAY you. If you did not show up because the mill was down, you did NOT get paid. I showed up every day and Pollet made sure that I had something to do that was NOT my joy each time. One time I did hide from him for a while. He kept coming around looking for me-I was watching him. I finally came down from my hiding place and had to run several errands for him - in my car, using my gas. Sometimes having a conscience is a costly thing. I just could NOT hide for long.

RELIEF IN MY DARKEST HOUR

After coming home in August of 1962, and spending some weeks going to local doctors, then got the job during grinding at the sugar mill, my time was taken up and I did not dwell on how things were and would be to much. I did not have the time to dwell. During grinding I worked twelve hours a day and was in bed sleeping/resting for eleven of the twelve hours that I was off. I really needed this rest time because of my condition. After grinding and going into 1963 without a job and a future, I really hit hard times, mentally. I worked that job on work over rigs for Atwell and Blankenship but could not keep up with the pace and physical labor. My last day there, I ended up lying down under the big truck just to get out of the sun all worn out. Oil dripped into my eye and gave me trouble for several weeks. I did not go to the doctor. It finally cleared up.

I did not have any prospect of a job. I mopped about the house aimlessly with no purpose. I had so much despair, I was angry. I did not care to go to church. I was seeing Dr. Daigle, our family doctor, but there was not a medical cure for Nephrosis. Take aspirin and or penicillin pills. I quit taking the penicillin after a couple months or so. It was during this time that Gail Mabile, Mr. Jules and Mrs. Iola oldest son, started coming by the house. Gail was about four years older than me. He had served his time in the Army and had a family and was working for LeBlanc Gas Company out of Baton Rouge. He drove a delivery truck and delivered butane to households in the countryside that needed gas.

He would show up at the house and blow the horn. I go out and he would say, "come on boy, lets go sell some gas". We rode all over the countryside in Iberville and West Baton Rouge Parish. He would stop in small settlements in the country that only had butane tanks. Only the cities had natural gas in these days. If you lived a half mile out of town, if you had gas at all, it was butane. Gail was a born salesman. He could really talk and he sure could shoot you a line.

In the black settlements, he would search out the Preacher's house, get permission to give him some gas- free, and ask the Preacher to announce at his Sunday Service to by their gas from LeBlanc's Gail Mabile. This worked very well for him. There were several times that

I thought I might get blown up because of too much pressure on some of the old tanks that we were putting gas into. But I am still here I am happy to say.

I had a good time riding with him and I forgot about the troubles I had. I rode with him for about three or four months off and on, until grinding season started sometime in October of 1963. Then I went to work in the sugar mill for the grinding season.

I thank Gail for taking the time to get me living again. Without him I just do not know what would have become of me. At this time in my life, he was in the right place at the right time for me. I even met some girls through him and had a few dates. This boy was a laugh a minute. He did take his work serious but had fun doing it. This is something that I took with me throughout the rest of my working career. Time was getting better for me. Thanks to Tony Gail. He goes by the name of Tony Gail Mabile now.

There are a hundred stories that I can tell you about my pal, Tony Gail but I will just relate this one below.

You must keep in mind that during these years there were not many window air conditioners in our area. We were to damn poor to have even one if there were any. Anyway, Gail ask me to help him install a big window fan in their kitchen window. Or maybe he did not ask me to help but just drove to his house after picking me up on Cedar Grove. We pulled up into his yard, got out of the big gas truck and loaded the window fan onto the back part of the truck. Those old type of window fans had a wooden box built around them. The completed unit was about four feet by four feet or a little bit bigger. You had to nail the unit onto the window sill outside of the house. The height of the butane tank gas truck was just about even with the windows of the house. Almost all of the houses was built on pillows and were off the ground. There were not many houses that were built on cement slabs in those days. I would have to hold the fan in place over the window while Gail hammered the nails in. It was very hot and in the middle of the summer. We were both sweating like mud hogs. Just as we were getting ready to lift the fan to the window, Maxine, Gail's wife, came to the window and said, "Gail, why are you sweating so much." Then Gail replied, "I am sweating for some Pussy, Maxine." To which she jumped back from the window and yelled, "WELL!" And left the window hurriedly and never bothered us again. She did not even bring him or me a class of water. My guess is that Gail did NOT get any of that stuff that he was sweating for-for the next week or two. Maxine was really embarrassed and pissed off at him.

DONALD (DUCK) AUCOIN

In late 1962, Duck and completed has airplane mechanic school in Alabama. He was stationed in Seoul, South Korea. We worked on small reconnaissance airplanes which patrolled the thirty-eight parallel between South and North Korea. He actually got to fly when he ran across a nice pilot. According to Duck, most of them were assholes.

Davis, who decided not to go in the Army for three years when Duck and I joined, signed for the draft and was drafted in the late summer of 1962. When Duck was in South Korea, Davis was in Germany doing I don't know what. We just could not understand how Davis got a tour in Germany for a two year enlistment. Germany was an eighteen month tour and usually three year enlistees got to go their. This is where Duck and I wanted to go after our training was over.

Duck hated it so much in South Korea, he served his eighteen months in about thirteen months. He pulled extra duty which counted as time served on his tour. He ended up in Seattle, Washington having about a year and a half to go and was still just nineteen years old. His age was a problem on the West Coast. He was not old enough to buy a drink in a club there (you had to be twenty-one) and he felt he was too old to hang out with the seventeen year old service guys. He spends a year going to an Olympic swimming pool and just swimming. He really built up his body. He went into the service as a six foot, scrawny fellow of about one hundred fifty pounds at eighteen years old and came out much a man at twenty-one years old and two hundred plus pounds. He had wide shoulders and a big chest and about a thirty-two inch waist. He was one hell of a man.

Davis Callegan filled out a lot too. He went in at about one hundred thirty pounds and come out a hundred eighty pound man. His five foot eleven frame and very broad shoulders took the weight well. He looked very good and was a hell of a man also. He no longer had that chicken breast of a chest. He now had a manly chest.

During late 1964, Davis was discharged from the Army. Several years later he married Kathy Esneault. Donald was discharged in mid 1965 and later married Betty Wunstell who we graduated with from White Castle High School in 1962. I served in both of their weddings. They both had good long successful marriages. Davis and Kathy raised one daughter to adulthood. Donald and Betty raised a son and daughter to adulthood.

Donald (Duck) Aucoin - June 1962   Davis (Day) Callegan - August 1962

WORKING FOR DOMINICK SCIORTINO

After the 1963 grinding season during the first few months of 1964, I got a job with Dominick Sciortino's Grocery Feed and Seed Store in White Castle as the delivery boy and all around go to fellow to get stuff done. I got the job because Clement Hebert was leaving to go to a better paying job.

For the Sciortinos, I delivered groceries in town and in the country along with one hundred pound sacks of feed and seed. I stocked the shelves, I help unload the delivery trucks, I worked in the meat market section, the customer counter, weighed pecans to purchase from town folks, and other jobs that someone had to do.

I work six days a week and went in on Sundays for three or four hours to restock the grocery shelves. I worked eleven hours a day Monday through Friday and twelve hours on Saturday. All in all I worked about seventy hours per week.

I would make a run on Thursdays into the countryside to deliver groceries but mostly feed (cattle, hog, horse, and chicken) and some seeds. This was in one hundred pound sacks. For the older customers, I had to carry these sacks on my shoulder for thirty or forty yards to place into their storage containers in their sheds. I would cut the sacks open and pour out the feed/grain into 55 gallon drums there and recover the drums to keep varmints and other animals out. During this time I would get really tired. I could handle the one hundred pounds alright but I would start to swell up a little from the physical activity. After a night of sleep and rest, I was O K the next morning.

Clement had taught me a way to take a longer time doing this delivery into the countryside. He told me how many hours he took to do it. It could have been done in an hour and a half less time but I did not want to make Clement look bad and besides I needed some time to recoup my energy from carrying the one hundred pound sacks. What the trick was for taking a longer time each week on this run was – after I got out of town, I pulled the chock knob out when going about twenty miles per hour. The truck would run at that speed and not miss a lick. There was NO cruse control in those days. When I got to the first stop, I pushed the chock knob back in and cut off the engine. On the way to the second stop, after reaching twenty miles per hour, I pulled out the chock knob again. I followed this same routine for each stop on my route. This made a two or so hour delivery about four or so hours. Word did get back to the store of how good and safe a driver I was. Ain't life wonderful? The things a person can learn along the way is just peachy.

I really had a good time working there. We always had several high school girls working as clerks and I used to tease and play with them. They all enjoyed my antics and craziness. I have always tried to make people laugh. Life is to damn short to go around with a sour pus look on your face. I tried my best to make all the folks that I had contact with laugh at some point every day. Many of them did, and looked forward to seeing me coming.

During the Lenten season was a big time for us at the store. The Lenten season is the forty days and nights before Easter Sunday. Lent is a time to do penance or to do without something that you like. All good Catholics would do a penance during lent. Other religions would do penance also- I think. Anyway, during these times, it was a Mortal sin for Catholics to eat meat on Fridays- every Friday. Many years later, the Pope of the Catholics made it O K to eat meat on Friday without it being a Mortal sin. But the time that I am talking about now if you ate meat on a Friday you made a mortal sin and if you died before going to the priest for confession and absolution, you were a gone pecan. You go straight to HELL. You do not pass go or collect two hundred dollars or anything like that. Into the fires of hell for your sole and whatever is left of you. I never did understand why my sole on my shoe would go to hell. Suppose I was not wearing any shoes when I died? What then? I am just kidding. I often think about all those pour soles that ate meat on a Friday when they was suppose to NOT do it and went to HELL – what happened to their soles after the Pope of the Catholics made it alright to eat meat on Fridays if they died before having a chance to go to confession and get absolution from the priest, huh? Where are they now, huh? Did the Pope or priest send them up to heaven? It just made me wonder what happened to them, that's all.

So every Friday and especially during the Lenten season we sold a great amount of seafood. Things like fish, shrimp, crabs, crawfish,(if we had any), oysters and even turtle. As long as it was considered seafood it was not a Mortal sin. But is you ate meat during lent on a Friday, even by mistake, you had better haul ass to the priest for confession and do your penance (our Fathers and Hail Mary's' and act on contrition), etc., in a hurry. You had better not die before you get this done. And don't even THINK about eating meat on Good Friday. Holy Mary-Mother of God, you would burn double in HELL for that one.

Around this time of year, The Chauvin Brothers Seafood Company out of Chauvin, Louisiana, would deliver oysters and other seafood along with very large ALIVE logger head snapper turtles. Mr. Dominick, who lived above his store, had a small fenced in area in their back yard where we put these turtles until I had the time to run then out to Mr. Jackie Bourgeois dad's house in the countryside. Mr. Bourgeois would skin the turtles of all the meat and he kept the shell for part payment. He may have painted or put designs on them, then sold them to the public. Mr. Bourgeois did not want me driving on his yard where his skinning shed was, so I had to park some thirty yards or so away. Just like the store delivery of sack of stuff, I had to carry these suckers to the pen. Some of the folks that I delivered to had cross fences and I could not drive up close to them. When I loaded the turtles in the bed of the pickup back at the store, Mr. Dominick helped me. I had to catch a hold of the tail of the turtle to carry it anywhere. To save time and trips, I would try and carry two of them this way. The heads of some of these suckers were as big as softballs. I would start out walking holding on to the tail with my arms a far from my body as possible. About halfway to where I was going my arms started moving closer to my body. This is NOT good. The damn turtles have its neck way out and looking around for something to bite. They get pissed off because of all this tail grabbing and being carried upside down. My legs are the closest things that they could latch on to. I did not enjoy this part of my job. Mr. Bourgeois would help me carry a turtle or two. We usually had ten to twelve turtles to deliver. Mr. Bourgeois would deliver some meat or I would go and pick some up so we could start selling it as soon as it was available. Even in the mid 1960s, turtle meat was over four dollars a pound. To my knowledge, I have never knowing eaten turtle. If I did, I do not remember it.

SIDE STORY

I was outside the Chat and Chew Bar in down town White Castle one night. Well, really I was there many, many nights but this particular night, Joe Callegan, my buddy, Davis's brother, who was also his Godfather, was there. He had backed his car into a parking spot and had the trunk opened. He was showing a number of us a very large snapping turtle. The turtle was in a sack with just his head out of the sack. A rope or heavy string was tied around its neck and the sack. The turtle could not withdraw its head back into his shell because of the rope being really tight. Joe was talking about how he came across this large turtle. He was standing near his back bumper and would point his finger at the turtle every now and again. This one time, he was a little closer to it than he thought when BAM. The turtle snapped at Joe's finger and got some meat from it between the hand and the first knuckle. It was a good thing that Joe had his finger sort of curled in a bit, because he would had lost all of that finger. There was some yelling and cussing and bleeding and a little laughing. I do not remember how many stitches the doctor put in that finger.

BACK AT THE STORY

Shucking oysters was another big job during the Lenten season. The Chauvin Brothers would deliver at least twenty sacks of oysters a week. They delivered during the early part of the week so we would have enough time to open them and place in the cooler for display to sell. Each week during Lent, I was shucking oysters when not delivering groceries or loading feed and water softener salt for customer. When Mr. Dominick was not cutting meat for a customer or for the display, he would help me open the oysters. Every time he did this, I would hear him sucking an oyster down. He would open one to put in the display and the next one, he would eat. After a while, I would say, "Mr. Dominick, how may are you going to eat today?" He would yell, "SHIT" and leave the counter where we would shuck the oysters. He would forget himself and start eating his profit every time he opened oysters. He just could not help it. I usually would know that he was eating them for some time before I would remind him that these were suppose to be for sale. If I told him to quickly, I would have to open more of them. So I would let him eat some before reminding him of what was doing. I guess I opened about seventy percent of all the oysters we got in. I was not good at it for a long time. I would butcher up an oyster pretty bad by the time I got it out of its, shell. But one thing for sure, not one of those damn oysters was going into my mouth. I would NOT eat any oyster on a bet or dare, or for money, and still don't.

Each Friday during oyster season, I would help Mr. Dominick shuck oysters for the High Sheriff of Iberville Parish- Mr. Jessel Ourso. Mr. Jessel would come in about ten thirty each Friday. The three of us would go to the back of the store in the oyster shucking area. Mr. Jessel would sit up high on a section of the counter that we did not use for oysters. Mr. Dominick and I would shuck and Jessel would suck them down as fast as we could get em ready. He'll eat and we talked and he'd eat and eat. He usually stayed with us for about an hour every time he came. When he got read to leave, Mr. Dominick would tell Miss Ethyl, his wife and head clerk, how many to charge Jessel for.

It was always several dozen. Jessel would pay Miss Ethyl in cash and say, "I'll see y'all next week". And he usually did.

It was during this time that I worked for the Sciortinos, that I met Mr. Pierce Sommers with the State Department of Louisiana that had something to do with disability.

I had plenty of good time playing around with and teasing Martha Bolotte, Dianne Brown, Kaye and Susan Sciortino and others. Kaye and Susan were about fourteen and thirteen years old but they also worked in the store. Dominick and Ethyl put everybody to work. J.B. Sciortino, the youngest was only four or five years old, but he would be in the store a lot also. None of us made much money, but we all past a good time. I saw to that.

A GIFT FROM LOUISIANA
(Attending Spencer Business College)

During 1964 I worked at Cedar Grove Plantation Company Store for a couple of weeks replacing Mr. Braus Sciortino who had an operation. I made four dollars a day working from seven in the morning to five in the afternoon. Monday through Saturday was the deal. We had Sundays off. I worked with Milton Ponsano. He had a hearing problem and used a hearing aid. Milton had a slight speech impediment. It occurred probably because of his hearing problem. Milton had been working in the store for almost twenty years at this time. I believe they paid me the same amount that he was making. It just does not make any sense, does it? To get this hearing aid, he received assistance from a Louisiana State Department. Mr. Pierce Sommers was in charge of the department that paid for Milton's hearing aid. It was some sort of disability or reimbursement program that the State had for poor folks. Mr. Sommers would come by the store every now and then to see how it was working and if Milton was satisfied with it. On one of his visits, my Daddy met him and talked about my kidney thing and me and that I could not find a steady job because of it. Mr. Sommers gave his calling card to Daddy and told him to have me go see him. Which, I did as soon as I could get an appointment with him. We met on several occasions. He was expanding the State's aid to poor folks program because the State Legislature had allowed him more money. But they were watching for progress very closely. I decided to go to Business College. The State program would pay for it. Mr. Summers really pushed for me to do this and he impressed upon me to not let him down. I could have gone to LSU, but did not know if I wanted to go to that college long enough to complete it. It also would cost the state a lot of money. And I would have to keep a C average to stay in the program. After thirteen years to get out of public school I was NOT going back to school for four or more years. I decided to attend Spencer Business College in Baton Rouge.

In June of 1964 I started classes at Spencer. They had a one year program that gave you their business degree. It was an excellent program that consisted of accounting, business law, typing (manual and electric), business English, posting machine, adding and calculation machine, short hand, and other courses.

I was the first to get my tuition paid for by the state-sponsored program. Spencer was reluctant at first to begin such a program. I was the pilot program. There was a cripple girl that attended Spencer about one month after me on the same state program. As time went on, we had a number of other kids that the state paid for to attend. The state did get a discount off the regular price. Mr. May, the Administrator at Spencer, kept an eye on all of us. I believe he was reluctant to take state sponsored people into his school at first but he came around after he saw our ability to do the work. I think that he did not know who or what to expect from us. I met this kid there that would have blackouts. We would be talking and he would just disappear for thirty seconds or so. Sometime he would fall down if he was standing up or walking. He was about seventeen as was the cripple girl. We all were very good students and did not embarrass the school, ourselves or Mr. Summers and the State.

My buddy, Nicky Guercio was going to Spencer College at the time also. He quit Nicholls State University in Thibodeaux, Louisiana and went to Spencer. After I started driving to Baton Rouge, he rode with me each day. I picked up several folks in Plaquemine who paid me fifty cents a day for the ride to and from Baton Rouge. This helped to pay for the gas that I was using. One of the riders was King Hebert, whom I liked very much and two others that I cannot remember their names. King is now one of the owners of Hebert Brothers Contractors in Plaquemine. I still have a silver dollar that he swapped with me for a paper dollar because he wanted to buy a soda and only had the silver dollar and did not want to spend it. I offered to lend him the change, but he wanted a dollar bill and insisted on the swap. Maybe he just wanted change in his pocket. This surprised me since his Dad was one half of the Hebert Brothers Contractors Company and had plenty of money. They were rich folks. Several times later in the year, I offered King his silver dollar back for a dollar bill, but he rejected it each time. I still have that silver dollar.

I drove to school in Daddy's 1962 Plymouth Valiant. It was cream colored and had four doors. We had a car load on the days that everybody went to class.

I went to Spencer College for one year. I completed two and a half practice sets of accounting work, which was equal to about three years of a four year university accounting degree. Toward the end of my year there, we started learning some brand new procedures concerning computers. We learned to operate a punch card machine. This was the forerunner of the computers that we have today.

While at Spencer, I met this girl named Valerie Stoltz. She was girl of German descent. We went out together for three and a half years then got married September 1967 in Austin, Texas where she moved with her parents the year before.

MY RIVER ROAD WRECK

One of the few times that I drove to school alone, I had an accident on the way back home. We used to cross the Mississippi River in Plaquemine each day going and coming from Baton Rouge. This was the shortest way to go. And the ferry was state run and free to ride in these days. One day, on my way back to the Plaquemine Ferry I went off the road. Coming from Baton Rouge on the River Road, the levee is on the right the whole way. The River Road was a winding road that was at the base or foot of the levee on the East Side of the River. It had been raining and I was not going over forty miles an hour when I look over to my left at an old tank storage facility. When I look back at the road, I had cross the center line and was in a curve that went to the right and jerked the steering wheel to the right and the car went into a spend. I did a full three hundred and sixty degree spend and then some. Thank God that no traffic was coming from the ferry toward Baton Rouge at the time. Now I was going backwards and heading toward the ditch that was between the road and the levee. This section of levee had been fenced in for cattle and had wooden fence post and five or six strands of barbwire on it. The car is in the ditch going backwards and I see fence post zipping on by. The back end of the car is hitting the post and because of the angle I am going that is all that is being damaged at this time. I finally came to a stop. I could not get out on the drivers side because my door was up against the barb wire fence to tight to open it more than an inch. I slid across the front seat and got out on the front passenger's side. I look at the curve in the road where I had come from. I saw where I hit the grass going backward toward the ditch and barb wire fence. I noticed that I had just missed a railroad crosstie that was used as an anchor post by a foot or so. Thank God. Then I broke six four inch in diameter round post in a row and stopped about three foot from another railroad crosstie anchor post. I thanked God again for me stopping before hitting the second cross tire post. I walked behind the car expecting to see mega damaged. I my surprise there was not much damage at all, just some scratches from the barbwire. This is when I noticed that all the fence post that I hit were rotten at the bottom. The barbwire was still taut because of the crossties and the car leaning on it. The ditch did not have any water in it. The earlier rain only had wet the surface. This was a sloping ditch and I thought that I could drive out of it. I could have but the pulling wheel just kept spinning and would not get a grip of the ground. I finally noticed, after keeling down in the tall grass and looking under the car, that I had back in over a stump or cut off post and this was holding the car from going forward.

On this model Valiant, under the front and rear bumpers were more car. There was sheet metal design and about nine inches more of car. I tried lifting up the rear end of the car but could not lift it up high enough to get over the stump. At this time a young black man who was walking on top on the levee saw me and came to help. I got the jack out of the trunk and place it under the rear bumper. Surely this would work. And it would have too, if the jack stand would not have sunk in the ground. The ground was just too soft for a jack stand and we could not find any wood or trash around the area that would keep the stand from sinking into the ground. So here I am.

Over an hour had passed since I first went off the road. I noticed a number of folks from White Castle had passed by either coming from or to the ferry. Not one damn fool stopped to see if I needed help. These White Castle people really piss me off. Most of them were women that I had delivered groceries to. After a while I ran out of ideas. The black guy left, I locked up the car and put my thumb out for a ride. A guy picked me up and took me to a little store that was a mile or so past the ferry landing than took off. I used a dime to call home. Daddy happened to be there. I told him that I got in a wreck and were the car was. He told me that he was on his way. While talking with the clerk there, a wrecker driver drove up to get a soda. I told him my problem. He asked how much money I had. I show him my wallet. I had ten dollars. He told me to wait a minute. He went to the phone and called someone and said that he was running a little late in traffic or something like that. I think that he was throwing his bosses off guard so he could make ten dollars for himself. He had seen the car on the side of the road when he passed by and knew that it would be an easy ten dollars. I rode with him the three or so miles back to the car. He backed up to the side on the road that I was on after making sure it was not too soft there. I showed him what was keeping the car in the ditch and I wanted to try and jack up the car again so he would not damage the underneath of it. He did not have the time for that. He hooked up to the car front bumper and turned the wrench one. I was standing behind the car and off to the side. I could see what was holding it. I hollowed for him to stop the wrench but was too late. The car sort of jump over the stump and came our very easy. He got the ten dollars. I checked for traffic, made a U turn in the middle of the River Road and headed for the ferry landing.

After I was in line at the ferry landing, I checked the car again. It had barbwire scratches on the trunk and drivers' door. The part of the car under the rear bumper and been crimped up a bit. The scratches would be easy to touch up and buff out. Under the car would take pliers and vice grips and other tools to straighten out, which I did later.

The ferry arrived on my side of the River. Daddy was getting off of it. When he saw me in line, he made a U turn and got in line to board the ferry also. While on the ferry, Daddy came over to the car. He had a surprise look on his face. He asked me where the wreck place on the car is. I showed him the scratches and the crumpled part under the rear bumper and he said, "that's all". I said, "yes". He was really happy that I was alright and the car was alright. I told him that it cost me ten dollar to get out of the ditch. He said to let that be a lesson to me to don't go in a ditch no more. We went home happy. Daddy was more happy than me. That damn River Road cost me ten hard earned dollars.

LOOKING FOR A JOB

When I was attending Spencer, I was still working at the grocery store in White Castle. I worked from three in the afternoon to seven at night from Monday through Friday. On Saturdays, I work twelve hours. Sometimes on Sunday, I stocked the shelves. I was working thirty-two to thirty-five hours a week and Dominick was paying me the same amount as working my full time hours of about seventy hours per week. He really helped me out during this time in my life. I owe a lot to Dominick Sciortino.

I received my diploma from Spencer in June of 1965, and started looking for a real full time job. I had to quit working at the grocery store to look for work in Baton Rouge. I tried working for a computer supply company for a week delivering fax papers and supplies to offices throughout Baton Rouge. The job did not pay much and I had to make the deliveries in Daddy's car. It cost me more to operate the car then I got paid.. I got paid by the mile and not a flat salary, and the way they figured the miles left me in the hole, so I had to quit this job. I now wished that I never left the grocery store job. Dominick had encouraged me to get a better job where I could make more money then he could ever pay me.

GETTING A JOB AND J&L ENGINEERING - IN 1965

I took the State of Louisiana Civil Service test to try and get a job with the state. While waiting for the results to come in, a farm implement company was building a branch sales office and repair shop just south of White Castle. The company, J and L Engineering Co., was headquartered in Jeaneratte, Louisiana. They manufactured the J and L Sugar Cane Harvester and Loader and sold Allis Charmers tractors and farming equipment. My Daddy had dealings with them ever sine he was promoted to Plantation Manager in 1960 and was responsible for purchasing the farm machinery. The Plantation had many old Allis Charmers tractors that needed parts and several J and

L harvesters and loaders. So we knew that they were good folks to do business with.

I placed an application with Mr. Harris Trusclier, the to be Branch Manager, as did several other folks in an around White Castle. My buddy, Nicky Gurecio, was already working for Thompson Harvester Company in Plaquemine, who was a main competitor and seamed to be doing alright financially.

I did show on my application that I have this Kidney disease, Nephrosis. I guess Mr. Harris did not notice it on my application because he chose me to hire. Maybe knowing my Daddy had something to do with choosing me. Before being hired, I had to go to Jeanerette for a physical at their company doctor. My medical tests showed that I had his problem. They started talking about not hiring me. I begged them, saying that I really needed a job and I would not take their medical package if they gave me this opportunity. I asked them to give me a tryout. By this time, I had met the owners who were Joe Lampo and Larry Pugh. Their name is how the Company got its name. It seamed unusual to me that the company was named after Joe and Larry, their first names. This was not the only unusual thing about these guys.

The debate about hiring me was settled by Mr. Buzzy Wormser, who was second in command behind Joe and Larry. Mr. Trusclier and all the other Branch Managers reported to Mr. Wormser. Mr. Buzzy said " hire the boy, I have this same kidney problem and you see me working every day without any problems". They did hire me and that is the other unusual thing about Joe and Larry. What they did was not done by Exxon, Dow Chemical, Borden Chemical and other companies that I place applications for jobs and even past their before hire test and went back for interviews about job placement based on physical outcome, only to find out that the Personnel Manager had not notice the medical area of my application and then told me that they could NOT hire me because of medical reasons. If they were doing their jobs correctly, they should not have invited me to take all the damn mechanical and written pre-employment test only to lay the hammer down on me after I pointed out the kidney thing that I listed on my application.

Joe and Larry hired me with full medical benefits. I thanked Mr. Buzzy every time I saw him for the next year or so. I also thanked Mr. Trosclier, who was a hell of a farm equipment salesman.

I was hired to be the parts man working for Earl Hymel, the head counterman. Mr. Trosclier was the boss and salesman for our branch. Tuppy Pearce, from White Castle, (Bobby's -from my first book- oldest brother) and Clyde Glavinia, from St. James, Louisiana, were the mechanics/repair men. Mr. Ed Major was the handyman and truck driver. Ed was the person that replaced me when I quit working for Dominick Sciortino in the grocery store. This was our whole crew. The building had just got framed and we all started putting the parts bins together and working on shelves, etc. When we were ready for part and supplies, several of us would drive to Jeanertte, load up a big flat bed truck and deliver back to our branch. We made a number of trips such as this to supply the parts department and display area of our shop.

It took about a month or so to set up a system to place, locate, and get a complete record of your merchandise. When Earl and I were getting close to finishing the part department, Ed, Tuppy and Clyde were making trips to Jeanertte and other branch locations to pick up Allis Charmers tractors and farming equipment as well as J&L harvesters and loaders to place on the yard. We actually started operation before everything was set up. We had an open house for the farmers and the rest is history.

I started out making one dollar and forty cents an hour. This was the most money that I ever made until this time. We worked fifty hours a week. We put in nine hours a day during the week and five hours on Saturday. We did get paid for ten hours a week overtime. For that ten hours, I made two dollars and ten cent per hour. Now that was money. During sugar cane planting and harvesting season, we all worked six and an half days a week. It was our busy time of the year. The farmers were also working hard in the fields and needed replacement parts for their harvesters, loaders and tractors. I really made good money then. I was working about sixty hours a week and twenty of those hours were at time and a half. I started saving more money. I was living at home and still doing chores around the yard and paying Momma ten dollars a week rent, just as my uncle Nolan was doing. I did not have a lot of expenses, so I was putting money in the White Castle Bank of Commerce. This was Mr. Cleve Joseph's bank. I was making about one percent interest on my savings account. I still have my saving passbook from that time in my life.

I was still milking a cow or two. I did the shucking, shelling and grinding of corn for the chicken. As long and we milked the cows, we were delivering milk to friends in White Castle. We made butter from the cream that came off the milk. After work, during the week, I cut the grass around the house which usually took two days to complete. I also burned the trash about once a week, but did not play with the fire as I did when I was little.

Just before I got the job at J and L, I received three calls from three different departments with the State wanting me to come in for interviews because of the results of my civil service tests. The pay for each job was less than the amount that I ended up getting from J and L. I took a chance on J and L hiring me. I figured if they did not, I should get another chance for a job with the State later. My best shot at getting a job was with a private company is what my thoughts were.

CARS THAT I HAD PART 1

I started working at J and L in mid 1965. I drove a 1954, black four door Plymouth. It was the second car that I had ever owned outright. My first car was a 1953, two door Chevy Sedan, that I purchased from cousin Mattie and Margie. It was their daddy's (Uncle Andre Ponsano) car. He had gotten to old and sickly to drive it. It had been laid up for a long time and when they finally decided to sell it, the value had gone down because of the condition it was in. I paid one hundred fifty dollars for it. It took me to work at Dominick's grocery store for several years and out on the few dates I had and anywhere around town that I wanted to go.

I mentioned earlier that I used my Daddy's car, a 1962 Plymouth Valient, to go to Spencer Business College in Baton Rouge. I also used the Valient for dates out of town.

After working at J and L for about six months, I purchased a 1965 Plymouth Sports Fury. It was a demonstrator that had several thousand miles on it. As with the 1954 Plymouth, I purchased this car from our cousins, the Dirons. Their company, Dixie Sales and Service is where my uncle Nolan worked as mechanic for about forty-five years until he retired at age sixty-five in the late 1970s. I have more on cars that I owned later.

TRIP TO HOUSTON TO SEE THE ASTROS

When I was working in White Castle for J & L Engineering Company, a local organization in Plaquemine made arrangements for several school busses to make a trip to Houston on a Saturday. It was set for sometime in August of 1965. We were going to watch the Houston Astros play a double header with the Atlanta Braves. My brother told me about this package deal. I do not remember what organization sponsored the trip but I do remember that a number of folks from White Castle joined the Plaquemine folks for this trip.

I rode with my brother to the area in Plaquemine where the buses were loading on the departure date. We had to send in our money ahead of time to pay for the trip and a seat on one of the buses. I cannot remember the cost either. We paid for two games and the bus ride there and back. Everyone on the buses was very excited because the teams were playing in the new building called The Astrodome. It was dubbed the eight wonder of the world. It had a whole baseball field inside the building. None of us had ever thought something like this was possible before the Astrodome was built. The old pro baseball team in Houston was named the Colt 45's when they came into existence in 1960. They played their games in old Colt Stadium near the site of the Astrodome. After the dome was built, the new name of the baseball team became the Astros. Nobody knew what an Astro is. I still don't for that matter. It may have something to do this the Astronauts and the NASA Space Center getting started nearby. I believe it opened during the 1965 season. I do remember hearing that the very first ever home run was hit by Mickey Mantle of the New York Yankees in the first exhibition game before the real season started. The oddity of this is that the Yankees was and still are an American League team and the Astros were a National League team. The Astrodome was not a home run hitters park. The playing field was huge and the baseball just did not carry well inside a building. The hitter really had to poke it to get it out of this park.

We all met where the buses loaded, got boarded and the caravan left on time early Saturday morning. This was a one day trip. We all knew that we would spend a lot of time in the bus over the next twenty hours or so. We sat next to Gary Templet and his dad, Mr. Templet. Mr. Templet was very knowledgeable about baseball and many other things. We passed a good time listening to him tell stories on the drive to Houston. It was about a six hour drive by school bus. What we did not know at the time was that it would be a day/night double header and not a back to back double header as we thought.

We were all very excited when the buses pulled up in front of the Astrodome to drop us off. None of us had ever seen a building this large before and still found it hard to believe that people could play a baseball game inside of it.

After a short time, everyone from the several buses gathered together at one specific entrance and we started going in. After you gave your ticket, someone directed us to the level and section we were going to sit in. I do not remember what section we were in but it was somewhere on the west side in the mezzanine level. Our seats were well back from the playing field. We were sitting under the seats that were above us. If it would have rained in the dome, we would not get wet where our seats were.

I was in awe of the place. I missed a lot of the action during the first game because I was always looking at other things in there. The colors were just pretty. All the ushers were girls and they were all pretty also. There was a million dollar scoreboard that they would show message and cartoons on. It was fantastic. We even had a television set that showed the game and replays above our head in our section. Looking around I noticed the each section had a television set. There were even television sets when you walked in the isles to go buy a soda or go to the bathroom. This was really something.

I had carried my old ball glove that Leon Miller gave to me in the mid 1950s just in case a fly ball would come my way. Well, where we were sitting there was no way a ball could get to us. We were never in danger of being hit by a bat or ball while not paying attention to the game. No way Jose.

It was great watching some of the guys that we heard about on the radio and television and in the newspapers. The first game started about twelve noon- I believe. During the first game Henry Aaron, the slugger playing for Atlanta, hit his 500th homerun. He finished with a career total of 755 homers breaking Babe Ruth's record and then some. I saw his number 500 - live. His teammate, Eddie Mathews hit number 475, I think, in the first game also. I believe that Mathews hit his 500th homer while playing for the Astros the next season. He finished with a career total of 512 homers. You have to have great ability to hit 500 home runs in a career. These were two great baseball players. Atlanta won the first game.

We thought that they would wait thirty minutes and start the second game - but nooooooooooo - they made every fan exit the Astrodome. We had no place to go. The buses were all parked some distance away and there was not any air conditioning on them anyway. It was a very hot and sunny day in Houston, Texas that day - I'm going to told you dat for sho. We exited on the same side we went in on, the west side. It was nothing but hot sunlight. There were no trees or shaded areas for us to get under. We sat or lied down on the ground close to the dome building and just sweated. It never occurred to us to walk around to the other side. We may have gotten a little shade from the building on the east side. Anyway, that would have been a long walk and it was hot and suppose we got lost. What we were going to do then, huh? We just sat there in the sun and sweated and bitched. After about two hours or so, they reopened the dome gate for the night game. We all hurried back inside and sat in the same section as before. It was great just getting out of the sun. It would be another hour or two before the second game started. But that was alright with us. At least we were inside.

The second game finally started. It was a very low scoring game. In fact, the Atlanta Braves did not score at all. The Astros scored a couple runs and won this game. But this was a special game. The Astros pitcher was a fellow from Louisiana by the name of Earl Wilson. He was a fair major league pitcher during his career. After this game he became known as Earl "no-hit" Wilson. That's right. He no-hit the powerful Atlanta Braves. For not having a lot of hits and runs, it was a very exciting game. Wilson had to handle Mathews and Aaron three or four time each during the game. And handle he did. In the top of the ninth with one out, Earl Wilson struck out Eddie Mathews. There were now two outs in the top of the ninth and Hammering Hank Aaron coming to the plate to take his cuts. Wilson struck out the Hammer to not only win the game but to win it with a NO HITTER.

There was jubilation in the Astrodome. This was a wonderful time during the early years of the Houston Astros and the Astrodome and I was there and so was my brother, Put.

The Astros had split their double hitter. The Astros had a losing record at that time and we knew that they were not going into the playoffs but it was great for us to catch a game such as this. I had no idea at this time that I would be moving to the Houston area some fifteen years later and spend many days and nights in this building watching baseball, football (pro and college), tractor pulls, special events and the Houston Livestock and Rodeo.

On our ride home we had fond memories of our first visit to the eight wonder of the world. We also found out that Houston, in August, was just as hot as White Castle and Plaquemine, Louisiana was. The only difference was that we did not have a pro baseball team in South Louisiana. But we do have those L S and U Tigers in Baton Rouge.

A year of so after I moved to the Houston area in 1979, we heard some terrible news over the television. In a special report, they said that Earl Wilson died of affixation in his car in the garage of his home in Houston. His wife and kids who were asleep upstairs survived a near death situation. It seams that Wilson drove his car into his garage and close the automatic door while still in his car and either passed out or went to sleep in the car with the motor still running. His death was reported as an accident. It was such a sad day. We were very happy to hear several days later that his wife and kids would recover and were getting out of the hospital soon.

Inside Astrodome - August 1965

MY FIRST WEDDING

During the time that I was working at J and L, I was dating Valerie. She moved to Austin, Texas with her parents in late 1966. I used to drive to Austin and Visit them on vacation and long week ends. We got married on September 1, 1967 in Austin at a Lutheran Church. We had spent several days with the Pastor going over and learning the things that a soon to be married couple are required to know if they are to get married in a proper church setting. It was not a large wedding. You could even say that it was a very small wedding. In fact it was the Pastor, Valerie, me and her parents. My parents could not make the wedding. Some years later, my Daddy told me that not making my wedding was something that he and Momma regretted for many years. They just did not travel that far from home in those days. I guess we just did not want a big TO DO for a wedding. We wanted ours to be small and simple. And it certainly was. We went out with her parents for dinner at a fancy restaurant in Austin that her parents paid for. Valerie ordered a lobster dinner. It looked like a crawfish on steroids. I had never tasted lobster before so I tasted her lobster. I did not care for it. It certainly is not as good as crawfish. After dinner we parted ways with her parents. She and I stayed our honeymoon night in a hotel somewhere in Austin. We got back with her parents late the next day. After several more days in Austin, I took her to live with me on the Plantation with Momma and Daddy and Uncle Nolan until we got our own place. I was still working for J and L in White Castle.

Valerie Jean and Barry Raffray

THE HOUSE IN BATON ROUGE

When Valerie's parents were transferred to Austin in 1966, they could not sell their house in Baton Rouge for a reasonable amount. They even went down to fifteen thousand six hundred dollars, which was the price that they paid for in 1957 and could not sell it. They ended up leasing the house for one year. After Valerie and I were married, we lived with Momma and Daddy for a short time until the lease was up on the Stoltz's house in Baton Rouge. After the renters moved out, we painted and did some repairs to the house and Valerie and I moved into it.

Valerie had taken a job in Baton Rouge and was driving from Cedar Grove Plantation to Baton Rouge every weekday. This was about forty miles one way. After we moved, Valerie became much closer to her job and I became much further from mine. I was driving from East Baton Rouge to White Castle every day which was forty-three miles one way. I was still working five and a half days a week. During cane planting and harvesting season, I worked six and an half day per week. I had to leave the house before six in the morning to be a work for seven. I would get home after work well after six in the evening. This did not give me much time to try and find a job in Baton Rouge. But we just could not pass up the chance to get our own house no matter where it was.

I drove from Baton Rouge to White Castle for the next seven months. I would wave as I recognized folks from White Castle who was driving to Baton Rouge to go to work. It was very costly doing all this driving. I still had my 1965 Plymouth Sports Fury. I would get twelve miles per gallon on high test gas and nine miles per gallon when I used regular gasoline. I had to fill up the tank each third day of driving to work.

When I married, I also got another car. The car came with Valerie. It was a 1964 Dodge Dart. It was in very good condition. It was my wife's car. It got much better gas mileage than my Plymouth- but Valerie drove it to work and did not care to drive the Plymouth. I had sold my older 1954 Plymouth just before we got married. I was making about three hundred eighty dollars per month. Our house note was one hundred five dollars a month. My in-laws gave the house to us as a gift. We just had to take up the payments on the note at four and a half percent interest. As I stated earlier, this was a deal that we could not pass up. I still had a car note of ninety five dollars a month. Thank God or thanks to the Stoltzs that Valerie's car was paid off. My wife working helped us to pay the electric, water, telephone, grocery and all other bills that folks usually have.

THE BATON ROUGE JOB HUNT

My brother knew that I was looking for a job in Baton Rouge. One of his bowling pals who worked in Baton Rouge told him that his company was looking for a shipping clerk for the office staff. In the meantime I had found out that Mac Trucks in Baton Rouge was looking for a stock clerk and office person. These were two possibilities for a job. I made an appointment with Mac Truck for an interview. A cousin of mine, Sharon Trabeau married Mickey Gautier of White Castle, and Mickey worked at Mac Truck. Sharon is one of my double third cousins from my Momma side of the family. I had a good time visiting with Mickey after my interview. He was trying to help me to get the job there. Two days before the interview with Mac Truck, I stopped by the bowling alley in Plaquemine and met with Tony Boranno who my brother knew. Tony gave the directions to get to Harvey Bourgoyne's house in Brusly. Harvey was the guy that the new hire would be working for at Foster Grant Chemical Company. Yes, this is the Company that produced the product that the Foster Grant sunglasses were made from. I stopped and met Harvey at his house late the next afternoon on my way home from work. I passed through Brusly every day going to work in White Castle. Brusly was about seven miles north of Plaquemine on highway LA.#1. Harvey furnished me with an application for the shipping clerk's job and told me where to mail it upon completion. This was in early April of 1968.

After arriving home that same day, I filled out the application and also noted my medical condition in the proper location on the application.

A week or so later, while I was waiting to hear back from Mac Truck of Baton Rouge, the Human Resources person for Foster Grant called me in for testing and interviews. The week after that, they sent me to the Baton Rouge Clinic for all the pre-employment medical testing. I thought that this would be the end of this job possibility. The third week of April, the big boss, Mr. Charles Sleeth, scheduled an appointment with me to be at his house in Broadmore Subdivision, which was only about four miles from where I lived in Windsor Place Subdivision. Both subdivisions were located off Florida Blvd. in East Baton Rouge. We met at the appointed time and sat in Mr. Sleeth's back yard. He was hand feeding the squirrels when I arrived. We talked. He had my application and medical results. He shocked me by offering me the job. I ask about my blood and urine test results. He ignored me and kept talking. I asked again. He was not concern. I asked a third time and he seamed irritated and annoyed with me. He grabbed the medical test results from a stool near by and flipped through the pages and said that every test came out good, all good, no problems. I was shocked and could not say anything for a moment or two. This was the first time in six years that I did not show any trace of Nephrosis. During years past from 1962, off and on, I had applied at Dow Chemical two times in Plaquemine, and several Exxon plants in Baton Rouge. I was even called in for written test at three different locations and recalled three different times to talk with the personnel Directors as they were known then. I always had the truthful information on the medical portion of the application. When I asked if they checked my application thoroughly, they all asked why. I then would mention the medical portion. At this meeting they all looked at that section and would apologize for having me do all the testing and would not send me on for the medical test. Maybe after the first time this happened, I should have just kept my big mouth shut. But I wanted to be honest and above board as I was brought up by my parents to be. I ended up losing the opportunity for the medical exam. Dow did give me a medical test in 1965 and one of the Exxon plants did also that year. But I was rejected these two times because of the medical results. The other times stated above, I was not even given the medical test. This same thing happened at several of the off shore drilling companies in Morgan City and Houma, Louisiana as well. I also tried to get jobs as truck driver, handy man, Parish (County) Clerk, laborer, oil field worker, welder's helper, and office clerical work, all to no avail.

Getting the job at Foster Grant and finding out that my kidney disease was gone was a God send. Better yet- it was a miracle that I did not realize at the time. This worked out just great for be because our work at J and L Engineering was really slowing down. So much so that we transferred Claude Glaviana to the Thibodeaux, Louisiana shop because we did not have the work in our shop. Mr. Bill Satterwhite, who was now our Branch Manager, was cutting back on my hours and talking about me driving a parts truck in the fields to try and sell to the farmers. I knew that I was the next to go. We were trying to figure how my services could generate income. I was not a mechanic. So everyone was happy for me when I gave them my two weeks notice.

I was very happy also. I would give up driving forty-three miles one way to drive for fifteen miles one way to work. This was a good raise in itself. My starting salary was about three hundred fifty dollars a month. This was less than I was making, but it was for forty hours a week, not fifty and I get to save money on gas and ware and tare on my car and I would be on the road an hour less a day and I would be spending more time at home. This would allow me more time to do chores around the house, and make a garden, which I did. This was just a great break for me. I thanked my brother for giving me the contact for this job. I thanked Tony Boronno and Harvey Bourgoyne many times.

By the way, after hearing from the Foster Grant folks the first time, I called Mac Truck and told them I was trying for another job. They did not try and get me to change my mind.

WORKING FOR FOSTER GRANT CHEMICAL

I started working for Foster Grant Chemical on May 6, 1968. I was really lost for about three months. It was so different. There were a few times that I wished I had stayed where I was or tried for another job in another business. I was slow in grasping a procedure but after I got it, I never forgot it. During the fourth month things started coming around and I got the handle on everything. I was taking orders from customers for tank truck or tank car loads of product and calling truck dispatchers and setting up the proper type equipment to load, typing the orders with specifications for our loaders, and doing the bills of lading when the produce was ready to depart our facility. After calculating the weight or receiving them from the public scales, I entered them into a ledger. I reported the necessary information to the customer by telephone or TWX or TELEX, and made a recap for the accounting department to do the billing. I assembled all the paperwork concerning this order/shipment into one set of paperwork and placed into the customer's file in date order. The latest shipment was in the front of the file of shipments. My numbers needed to be correct as this was the amount we invoiced to the customer. I had a handle on it now. I took orders for and shipped nine different liquid products. Our main commodity was styrene monomer. This is what our sister plants made the polystyrene out of. Polystyrene was the raw material for our Sunglass Division, which molded the polystyrene with heat and made the famous Foster Grant sunglass parts. They were assembled by hand labor at the Leominster, Massachusetts plant which was the headquarters for our company. About three thousand folks worked in Leominster, most of them in the assembly plants.

I am very happy that Stanley Lanson of J&L, who was located at Jeaneratte, Louisiana headquarters for J&L, waited about four months before he called me and offered me a job back with them. He needed someone to work in the parts and distribution department. He knew that I was a good worker. I told him no, thank you. But if he would have called one month before, I believe that I would have taken him up on his offer. I may have lost my wife if we had to move to the Jeaneratte area, but I felt so out of place at Foster Grant at that time that I would have left them. Thirty-four years later, I am still happy that Stanley waited as long as he did to try and rehire me.

After I got my feet firmly on the ground and knew what the business was about and knew that I could handle all aspects of it, I got back to my happy go lucky self. I took my work serious but had a lot of fun doing it. I used to make the ladies and guys in the office and the plant laugh with some of my antics. I got tired of seeing the frowns on everyone faces every day. I got them into a good mood and turned their frowns upside down. Most of them looked forward to seeing me each day. I did Flip Wilson routines each day to keep them smiling. It was a better place to work. I would even make the boss laugh. I made the truck drivers feel at home when they were waiting for me to finish with the paperwork to get them on their way.

Harvey Bourgoyne - June 1992

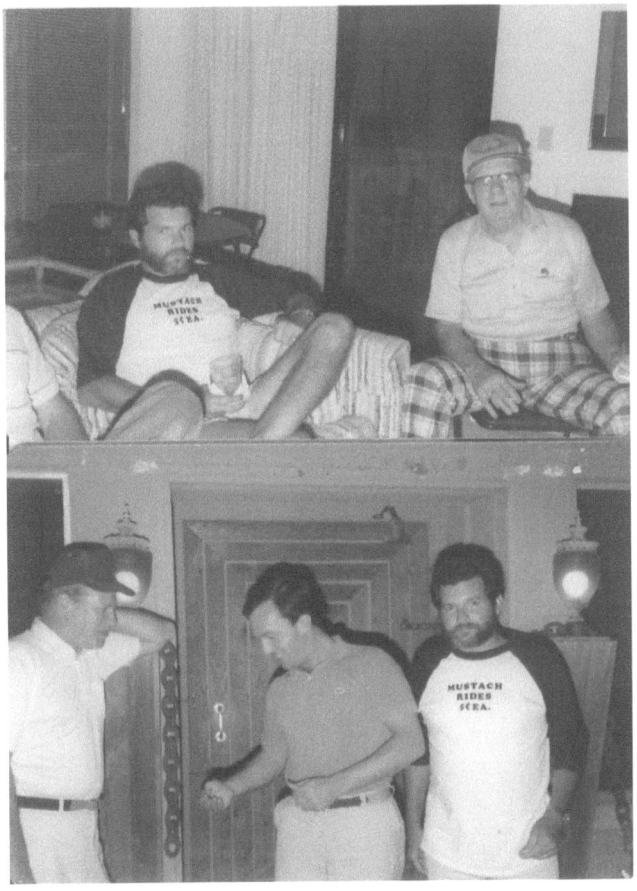

Top: Barry Raffray and Mr. C.V. Sleeth
Bottom: Lars Steib, Bryan Stickney, and Barry Raffray

TRIP TO ORANGE PARK FLORIDA

In 1969 before we had any kids, Valerie and I went to Orange Park, Florida to visit her Momma's sister- Aunt Pauline and her third or fourth husband, Uncle Bill. Orange Park is about ten miles south of Jacksonville.

Uncle Bill had worked for one of the major railroad companies and had an accident about one month before our visit. This was our second visit there. Our first visit was in 1966 before we got married. We had spent a week there and did the sights then. This trip was to see Uncle Bill and Pauline an see how they were doing after Bill's accident. Both of his legs were cut off in the accident. One just above the knee and the other just below the knee. He was a switchman working in the local yard when the Engineer misread the signal and started the string of rail cars moving backward before Bill got out of the way. The first car in the string knocked him down and ran over his legs. Then sixteen other cars ran over them also. The damage was done after the first car but this was a terrible thing to go through.

Bill was recovering really well when we visited with them. He later went into cardiac arrest and have been living with serious heart troubles ever since.

In 1969, both Valerie and I were working full time before we made the trip to Florida. I did not get a chance to change my oil and filter, so the day before we left, I took the Sports Fury to Michelle Gas Station which was at the entrance to our subdivision. I usually purchased gas from him. I had them change my oil and oil filter while Valerie and I were running other late minute errands in the Dart.

We departed for Florida a little after five in the morning the next day. This was about a six hundred mile trip one way. A good twelve hour drive. It was in the summer time so it was hot. I did not like to run the air conditioner on this car because it burn more gas than it already did. It was a real gas guzzler. I had to listen to her bitch most of the way to Florida because it was hot.

On the way back, the "I am hot" bitching started as soon as the sun came up. We were on Interstate-10 maybe fifty miles from Jacksonville. This car was a two door hardtop. I rolled my window all the way down and she rolled her window down also. Then she crawled between the bucket seats into the back seat and rolled both smaller rear windows down. We were looking cool from the outside but were hot in the car.

When on the highway, I usually drive about seventy miles an hour. This was the case this time. I like to make time on the highway. I made sure that she went to the bathroom before we left her Aunt Pauline's house. The next bathroom stop would be when we stop to fill the gas tank up. Since I had already made this trip in 1966, I knew that we would have to stop for gas three or four times before we got back to Baton Rouge.

After an hour or so, she could not stand the hot in the front seat so she crawled into the back seat to get more air. She could bitch from the back seat just as well as from the front one. She did not bitch right away. She had an easy time getting into the back seat because this car had bucket seats with a wide opening between the driver and passenger's seat. It had a floor consol with the shift between the seats but it was toward the front. The layout helped to make this one cool looking car. It had a black vinyl top and maroon body, and automatic on the floor and a reverberation unit on the radio that made it sound like stereo which was not out yet. The interior was black with black vinyl seats that helped to make it very hot in the summer time. After I purchased this car, I ordered see-through plastic seat covers from Fingerhut and installed them to keep the seats in good condition. This cover worked very well keeping the ware and tare from happening, but loved to suck up heat in the summer time and cold in the winter time.

Driving this car a seventy miles per hour I could almost see the gas needle move from full toward empty. I knew that after about three or so hours of driving at this speed that I would have to find a gas station. But for now we were just sailing along. My wife was in the back seat. Her hair was blowing in the wind. She was getting some air and staying off my back. I had the radio on loud so we could hear it as we zipped along. This peace and quite (by Valerie) would be short lived.

About thirty minutes after she settled into the middle of the back seat, a little yellow bird flew into the car and hit the rear window on the passenger side. My wife let out a scream. She almost scared the shit out of me. Before I could blink an eye she was in the front seat again. I tried to get her to get in the back seat and get the little bird and throw it out. She adamantly refused to do it. There would be no more sitting in the back seat with all the windows down ever again. I had to retrieve the bird an hour or so later when we stopped for gas. At lease she forgot about being hot for a while. She wanted to raise all the windows. I refused this request, at least on my side of the car. It was just too damn hot and this car's air conditioner was NOT coming on.

I filled up the gas tank while she went to the bathroom. I paid the attendant and went to the bathroom and we were on our way in less than fifteen minutes. This is just the way I liked it. It did not hurt my miles per hour average to much on this stop.

After driving for a while we started smelling something that smelled like shit. We checked our shoes, clothes and the car seats several times. My wife even looked under the seats. The gas station was all cement that we had stopped at and neither of us thought that we stepped in anything while there. We drove over one hundred miles with this smell off and on. I was following a number of eighteen wheeler vans. They were moving at a good clip and I saw no reason to pass them. The truckers are the best drivers on the road. I liked driving with them. I worked with many truck drivers in my job and I knew that they were well trained and very capable of handling these big rigs. I just kept a good distance between us. They all seam to know where the cops were. This was before CBs were so popular, but some of the guys may have had them. I don't know. When they slowed down, so did I. Sometime they would go just to fast for me to keep up. I would back off and let them go, and ride along with those that did not go to fast.

After having to deal with this smell off and on for two hours, I finally noticed what it was. We had been driving behind a long line of eighteen wheeler vans. As time went on, each van in front of us would pass this one van that was not driving as fast as the rest of them.

When I got within about one hundred yards from this one van, the smell really got bad. This is when we notice that we were following a cattle van. We was smelling SHIT all that time. We just could not see where it was coming from. Somewhere in the Florida Panhandle we passed this smelly trucker. I wished that I had a bucket of shit for Valerie to throw on his windshield as we passed.

We made it home in one piece.

CHANGING OIL ON MY SPORT FURY

After a big trip such as this one, it was time to change the oil and oil filter again. In these days it was recommended that the oil be changed ever one thousand miles. I usually changed the oil filter every other oil change. But after this trip of about fifteen hundred miles I wanted to change my oil filter too.

I parked the Fury under the carport to be out of the sun. I jacked up the front end of the car. This made it easier for me to slide under the car. I placed my oil drain pan under the oil drain hole and the filter. I unscrewed the oil drain plug and drained the oil from the engine block. Then I started working to get the oil filter off. Michelle was a huge man with very big arms. The sucker had really tighten this filter on. The best position to change the filter on this model car was from under it. I was on my back or side trying to remove this oil filter. I had several oil filter tools. The one with the loop clamp on it would slip and I just could not get a good grip. I tried a very large monkey wrench. This was a big mistake. I did not have much room to position the wrench. I did get the jaws on the wrench around part of the filter and when I pulled on the handle hard, the filter crimpled in a bit. I tried to reposition the wrench on the back side of the filter. I finally did after many minutes of anguish. I pulled the handle hard and it crimpled in some more. Oh shit. During this process I dropped the different tools that I was trying to use into the oil pan with drip oil in it several times. I had to fish out my tools and try to wipe them off so they would not be so slippery. I had a mess on my carport under the car and on places not under the car. I was also getting full of oil.

The oil filter had crimpled so much that the filter removal tool could not clamp down on it at all now. I went to a smaller monkey wrench and crimpled the filter even more. This was not working. I will have to do something else.

I decided upon another plan of action. I will drive the car over to that damn Michelle and have him take the oil filter off. I put the plug back into the oil pan. I put a couple of fresh quarts of oil into the engine, remove the jack, jump into the car and started it up. What a stupid idea. I was brain dead or something. I was so piss off at Michelle because he tighten the oil filter on so tight that I could not think straight. I had been messing with this oil change for over two hours now. As soon as I cranked up the engine the low oil engine light came on. Oil was spraying on the brick wall and kitchen door and everywhere else on and around my house and yard. It only took me a couple of seconds to realize how stupid I was and cut the engine off. But those two seconds made a mess under my carport.

I got out of the car, got to my knees in some oil splotches and oil was running out of the crimpled up filter. I still had the pan under it- thank God. This was the only good thing I did right. I got some old bath towels and started cleaning off the carport area and under the car where I had to crawl again. After jacking up the front end again, I was ready to go back under the car. I wasted another forty minutes cleaning up the oil mess.

The crimpled oil filter still needed to be removed. I tried using a screwdriver. I braced the crimpled filter as best I could and place the end of a standard screwdriver about two inches from where the filter screwed into the block. This was as close as I could get to the base of the filter. I used a hammer to drive the screwdriver through the filter. Then I tried to pull on the handle of the screwdriver. I thought It moved it a little. I was happy for a very short time. I tugged again. Yes, I moved it alright. It was splitting the filter apart. I pull out the screwdriver. It came out rather easy after I split the filter a bit.

I started thinking about getting a chisel and cutting the oil filter at the base of the block where it screwed in. But before doing that, I decided to try the very small monkey wrench one more time. The filter was now a little over one inch in diameter. It started out about five inches in diameter. I put the small wrench around the back part of the filter. I gave a tug and it moved a little. I slid the wench off and got another grip and pulled again. It moved some more. I was home bound. I finally removed that damn filter. After putting the new oil filter on the car, I came out from under it. I jacked the car down, removed the jack and put five new quarts of oil into the block. I started the car and backed it out from under the car port. I still had a mess to clean up. About two hours later the area looked pretty good.

I cursed Michelle for everything he was worth. His ears must have been ringing. That's how much I cursed him. I vowed never to let him change my oil and filter again. I was positively sure that he tightened my oil filter on this tight to make me take it to him to replace when time for another oil change. Well I showed him. I replaced my own damn oil and oil filter and it only took me five or six hours, including clean up, to do it. I only ruined one shirt and had to throw away several cleaning rags and a couple bath towels and use up some chemicals, washing powder, gasoline, etc., to clean the brick on my house and my carport and door to the house and utility room. I showed him, I really did.

Within a year of the date, I got in a hurry again and had to have Michelle change my oil and oil filter again. But when my car needed the next oil change, I did not fool around with the oil filter. If I could not unscrew it with my oil filter unscrewing tool after one try, I went to Michelle for the oil change. I tried unscrewing the oil filter BEFORE draining the oil from the pan.

Did I tell you about the time I put ten quarts of oil in my Satellite? No? Well that is a story for another time. I could write a book on what not to do when doing maintenance or minor repairs on your autos. You know about the shocks and this one time oil and oil filter change. There were other times when I replace the intake and exhaust manifolds, and gaskets changes, fuel filter changes, alternator changes, carburetor kits, a week to change a water pump, trying to replace mufflers and tailpipes, changing out head lights, brakes, etc., etc.

I did some really stupid things working on my autos over the years. The money that It cost me for doing the work myself, I could have purchased a Cadillac. I paid a very high cost by doing the work myself. I should have taken the autos to mechanics and just pay them to do the work. I did learn on many occasions what NOT TO DO.

I am not all the way stupid. I did learn after making a mistake. I never did make the same mistake twice. At least I don't remember doing the same thing wrong more than once. But I could have what is called "selective memory". Anyway, I am happy that much improvement were made to autos and rules and laws on what to do with drip oil and old oil filters and old batteries and old tires, etc., that I don't try and work on my autos at all today.

Barry Raffray and 1965 Plymouth Sport Fury

FIRST SON BORN, TWO MORE TO COME

We had pretty much settle in our living style in Baton Rouge. My wife was working full time and I had almost two years in at Foster Grant Chemical. One day after arriving home from work, my wife told me that she was pregnant. This was a happy day.

The largest event in my life was when my son, Kent Steven Raffray was born. Up until his birth of my son, the kidney disease was the largest event in my life and I picked my marriage as the second largest event. You may ask why did I feel like this. Well, I will tell you. The kidney disease shattered my life. It took six years to get rid of it. It never was the same afterwards. It changed my life course and created another history for me. Perhaps all for the better. I have no regrets now, but I do not know what would have happened if I had not come down with it. I may have gotten killed in Southeast Asia- who knows. As for putting my marriage number two. There were other girls who would have married me if I would have asked them. I thought that

Valerie was the one. As it turned out, she was not, but that is another story.

Dr. Venard had given us a date to expect the baby to be born. When the time came, we went to the hospital. Kent was a full term berth and now was the time so Dr. Venard gave Valerie something at would induce labor. After some time, I was ask/told to leave the room that the nurse was going to move Valerie to the room that the mothers to be are in.

I went to wait in the daddy's to be waiting room. While in the waiting room, I notice Gary Guillot. Gary was a sugar cane farmer from White Castle and he graduated two years before me. His wife, Linda, was having a baby also, I think. We visited for a couple hours when I got the call to meet Dr. Venard near the delivery room. Gary came with me. The doctor said that everything came out alright and I could see Valerie in about twenty minutes and here was my son. He told me that it was a little girl and right at the last minute the thing popped up at the bottom and the baby became a little boy as he pulled the small blanket off of him. I was on cloud nine. I looked at Kent and said "man, he is well hung". Gary laughed and told me that I was crazy. Dr Vernard just smiled then wheeled Kent to the baby section. I was not around when Gary's baby was born. I do not know if they had a boy or girl. I am not really sure that Gary's wife was having a baby.

Kent was born October 12, 1970 on the real Columbus Day. He was a beautiful baby and looked just like me. No wonder he was so pretty.

We were very proud of Kent. We showed him off to everybody. People were giving us money for him as I gave out the "it's a boy" cigars. I started a saving account of him with the money and added to it over the years.

Kent went through one Christmas before Lane was born but he could not remember it because he was only two and a half months old.

Valerie dressed him in this little red Santa outfit. He sure was cute. A chip off the ole blockhead.

We went through all the excitement of him scooting on his belly, then crawling, then walking, then running. As an infant, Valerie could not feed the sucker fast enough. When he emptied one jar of baby food, he would scream until more food was place into his mouth. He was a very healthy baby. He had only one medical problem. He would go into convulsions just as I did when I was a baby. On the first occasion, we had to rush him to the hospital in downtown Baton Rouge. The first time it happened was very traumatic especially for my wife. When he was about sixth or seven months old, Valerie went to check on him in his crib. She started screaming. I ran from the kitchen to see. She was jumping up and down in the full size bed that was in the room and screaming and pointing toward the crib. I saw Kent trembling/shacking. I looked in his face very closely. I placed my hand on him but could not stop him from trembling. I knew what it was. I put one finger in his mouth. I had to pry it open. I knew I had to keep him from swallowing his tongue or he would smother/chock to death. I was shouting at Valerie to quit what she was still doing and go get help. About this time, Wallace Price, our neighbor came into the room. He was outside his house and heard Valerie screaming. She was still doing it. Wallace took over for me with Kent. I grabbed Valerie and tried to settle her down. It worked. I pulled her off the bed. Wallace said he would get his car keys and we would take Kent to the hospital. Wallace gave Kent to Valerie. I again put a finger into his mouth to hold his tongue. This action showed Valerie what to do. Wallace had on an under shirt, long pants and no shoes. I had old short pants on. I ran and got my wallet. Valerie, Kent, Sabrina (Wallace's daughter) me, and Wallace jumped into his four door sedan as we were dressed and took off. Wallace forgot his wallet, but drove fast but careful the seven miles to the Baton Rouge, General Hospital. He was flashing his headlights and blowing his horn to move traffic over. Sabrina and I were yelling out of the back windows that we needed to get to the hospital.

Kent convulsed until we were about two miles from the hospital. We arrived at the emergency entrance. We went inside while Wallace parked the car. We talked to a nurse and Kent seamed to be out of trouble now. Wallace and Sabrina waited for us in his car. We saw a doctor real soon. He did a blood test. He knew as I did that he had convulsion but did not know why. He told us what to do for the next several days. Several days later, we received the results of the test and may have changed his diet a little. The doctor did say to not let the baby swallow his tongue during convulsions and that is all you can do at the time. I think it took this to convince Valerie that I knew what I was doing.

Kent only convulsed one or two other times after this. One time on the kitchen floor. Valerie was in the kitchen phone and I was in the breakfast area. I heard her tell the person on the phone that she had to go because her baby was having convulsions. I jumped up and again put my finger into his mouth to be sure he does not swallow his tongue. The little sucker sure could bite hard - even without teeth - thank God. If he had a full mouth of teeth, I would have nubs for fingers today.

Kent outgrew this very quickly just as I had many years before. He may have inherited this from me. When I was a baby, I had convulsions. After trying several doctors, Momma took me to this old doctor in Plaquemine. He told my parents to take off of coke and popcorn. After they stop letting be have that stuff, I stopped have convulsions. I believe that we did not give certain foodstuff to Kent and he stopped having the convulsions also.

One other problem was the Kent was not the baby for a very long time. Before long, Valerie told me that she was pregnant again. I had no idea why this had happened again. What is going on here? Our plan was to try and have another child after Kent in two years or so. A coil was inserted after Kent's birth two help make that possible. The coil got shot to pieces in no time at all.

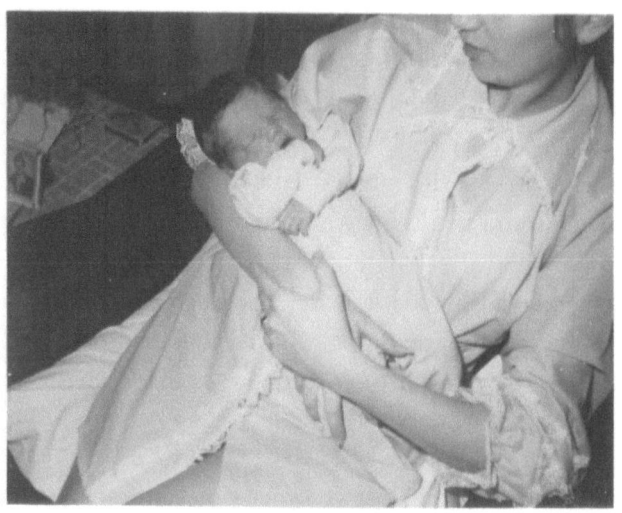

Kent Raffray 3 days old

LANE'S EARLY ARRIVAL

It was just before Christmas in 1971. Mr. and Mrs. Stoltz were visiting us for the Holidays. We were all setting in the den watching television when Valerie said " oh, oh, my water just broke". Her mother got a bath towel from the bathroom just across the hall and gave it to her. She assured us that she was not kidding which is something that she did not do.

Valerie, her Dad and me, headed to the hospital in her dad's car. Her mother stayed to look after Kent who did not know or care what was going on. We had told him that he would get a little brother or sister in the next couple months, but did not think that he really understood what we were talking about. He was only fourteen months old. We did not think the addition to our family would be this soon. This was sooner than we were planning on. That just shows to go you - or something like that.

I walked Valerie into the emergency room while her dad parked the car. Someone had called Dr. Venard before we left the house so we knew that he would be there soon. We got a room in a hurry. I stayed with Valerie about twenty minutes when Dr. Venard said that they will induce labor because her water broke.

They took her into another room where there were pregnant women everywhere. I went into the waiting for babies to be born room. I filled my father-in-law (who was already there) in on what was going on. In the waiting room was Dennis Daigle, whose wife, Marilyn, was having a baby also. Dennis graduated from White Castle High two years before me. Marilyn and I graduated together in 1962. Her maiden name was Simoneaux.

We did not talk very long when I was called to meet with the doctor. It was less than an hour after Valerie went into the mothers to be room. Dr. Venard said that she was doing fine. Lane was very tiny and looked to have a hard time breathing.

Lane was born on December 23, 1971. He was two or more months early and weigh in at only four pounds and one ounce and had to be put under a lamp for several weeks. Two days after he was born, he was transferred to the Baton Rouge General Hospital, which was known for their premature baby ward. He had to stay in intensive care until his weight got up to five pounds before we could take him home. This was very hard on us. It is really tough not to take your baby home with their momma when she is discharged. We would try and visit him every day. Lane was in the hospital a total of thirty one days. Two days in the Baton Rouge Women's Hospital and twenty-nine in the Baton Rouge General Hospital. Valerie was released the morning of December 24th. at nine in the morning. Lane was born a couple hours before midnight on the 23rd. This was a very easy birth for Valerie. She was released within twelve hours after giving birth but refused to leave until they transferred Lane to the other hospital. She slept two nights in the hospital for this reason.

All of my boys were born at the Women's Hospital in Baton Rouge. Lane was the only one to have an extended stay in a hospital. To help pay Lane's hospital bills, I started giving blood at the two hospitals. We got credit off our bill for doing this. Several of my friends and family members gave blood for our account also. This helped me out tremendously. It knocked several hundred dollars off our bills.

Valerie had quit working before Kent was born. We did not have any insurance from her end. I had Foster Grant insurance which did not pay much at the time. When we decided to try and have our first baby, I knew my insurance left a lot to be desired, so I purchased an extra policy from Blue Cross that covered child birth. My Foster Grant insurance only paid two hundred fifty dollars for child birth. The baby doctor cost more than this amount. We paid Dr. Venard each month during the pregnancy. By the time of the birth, we usually had him almost paid off. I think we paid a little extra for the boys to be circumcised. He did three of these for us. I was always hopeful that he did a better job on my boys, than I believe Ole Dr. Tomney did on me.

Blue Cross handled a lot of the hospital bills for my sons, but would not pay for Lane's long stay in the intensive care premature ward. Back at Foster Grant, my friend and co-worker, Annis Petters, who handled employee insurance, told me that she thought our company should pay under major medical care. She was able to get the paperwork done and we finally qualified for it and my company insurance paid for about eighty percent of the Baton Rouge General's baby bill. This really cut into the several thousand dollars that I owed. This helped be greatly since I was not even making five hundred dollars a month. I had been at Foster Grant for over three and one half years now.

Lane was the baby for a little over three years. Now that we had Kent and Lane, we had to buy everything in twos. We had this stroller that has two seats. It worked out great and lasted through all of our sons. When they finally outgrew it, we put it in storage and several years later gave it to Randy Zammit to use for his growing family. Randy and Susie Zammit may have gotten the ply pen, feeding table, and a crib or two also. If they did not get these items, I do not remember who did. But we tried to help people in need as we were helped so much.

Randy/s mom and dad, Walter and Geneva Zammit were very good friends of the Stoltz family and became Valerie's and my very good friends also. They sort of looked after us for Kay and Al Stoltz, who lived in Texas, then moved to Oklahoma before moving back to Louisiana.

We showed Lane off to everyone, I again gave out "its a boy" cigars to everyone who would take one. We were just as proud of Lane as we were of Kent. Lane had a little harder time because of being born earlier than normal but he held his own after gaining some weight and getting to a normal size.

I now started a saving account for Lane. The monies we collected after his birth and one half of the coke bottle deposit money and one half of the grocery coupon money was going into his bank account. The other half went into Kent's bank account. My goal was to still see that I put at least one hundred dollars a year into each savings account.

About two and a half years after Lane was born, Valerie started getting fat again. I did not know how this was happening, but another bundle of joy was on the way.

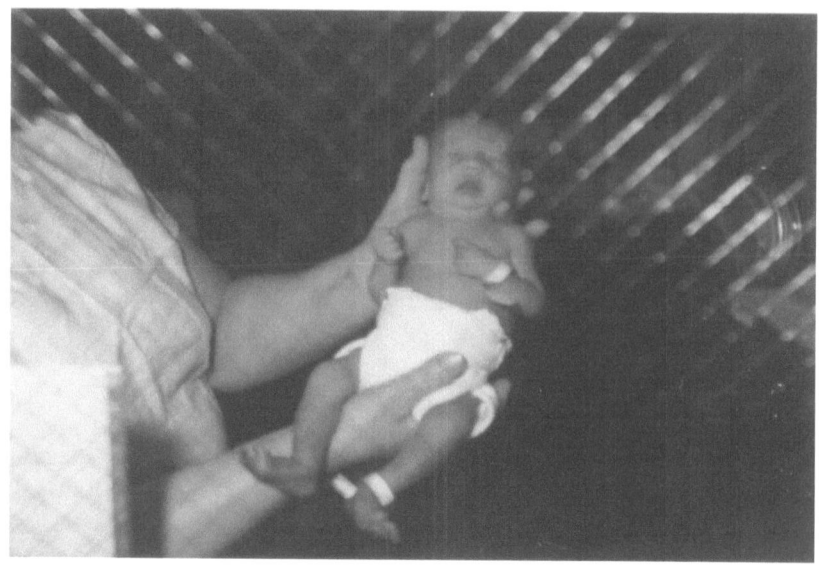

Lane Raffray 3 days old

STILL WORKING FOR FOSTER GRANT CHEMICAL COMPANY

I had been working for Foster Grant for several years now. I thought that I would tell you a little about the product we produced and sold and our department makeup and what we did.

I worked for Harvey Bourgoyne who was our Supply and Distribution Manager. Margaret Arceneaux worked for Mr. Sleeth our Vice President of Sales and Marketing and also helped Harvey and me a lot. We had two sales guys on the road selling our product. They were Lars Steib stationed in Chicago and Bob Simon stationed in New York.

A year or so after I started working there, the Company started to work on expanding the production, and we than started to hire more folks for our department. First to be hired was Greg Galloway, than later Cherie Theriot, Nickie Delapasse, and still later Harold Spencer was hired. It took a number of years after Greg's hire to get up to this many folks within our department. More folks were hired later as we kept expanding the production at this location and accruing product from other locations.

The first six or seven years that I worked there we had two loaders from the Union that worked out of my office. They were Reggie Landry our Head Loader and Jimmy Smith our Assistant Loader. Every pound of product that was shipped from this location was loaded by these two guys – except for the time that one or the other was on vacation. They did it all.

At Foster Grant Chemical Company we produced styrene monomer. Stryene monomer is a clear water color liquid. Styrene monomer means "plastic liquid". We shipped most of our production to our sister plants and sold the balance of our production into the domestic and foreign commercial markets. Our sister plant were polystyrene plants which produced many different grades for polystyrene of course. Polystyrene means "solid plastic". Poly means solid and styrene means or is plastic.

We shipped the liquid to our sister plants and customers via barge, rail tank cars, highway tank truck trailers, fifty-five gallon drums, containers, five gallon and one gallon cans and in tank ship parcels for export. During these days the tank ship parcels were not loaded at our dock. We exchange styrene with other producers that were located on deep water ports or docks. They would load tanker parcels for us and we paid them back by loading barges at our dock in Devils Swamp.

Our polystyrene plants would cook the styrene down into a taffy like form. Then pressure the product through small holes in plate steel in their processing units. This is referred to as extrusion. The pure D white product came out of the extrusion section in long strings and went into a long water held trough to harden the plastics. It looked liked very long spaghetti coming out of the water bath. It was cooled enough to then go through a set of choppers. The choppers cut the long strings into smell pieces or pellets as they referred to them as.

They also ground some into powder. During the process different formulas were added to make plastic beads or pellets or powder into different end products. The products was then bagged or boxed or loaded into hopper cars for use internally or shipment after being sold into the merchant market. Polystyrene is sold by the pound as is styrene monomer.

At one time, I believe the sunglass business was the largest user of polystyrene. The polystyrene division also had many merchant market customers such as Gillette Razor Blade for the small blue and clear plastic container that their razors were sold in. This was before Bic started producing razors and ball point pens out of the stuff. They also had Borden Milk Company as a customer. Many toy manufactures were customers and a huge volume of product was sold to companies that produced the picnic plate, bowels, knives and forks, styrofoam ice chess, insulation and clam shells- these are the containers that keep hamburgers/hot dogs hot. Many are used in fast food restaurants.

Styrofoam may be a Dow Chemical trademark name. Most polystyrene producers made it and refereed to it by another name. This is the light weight product that is produced by inducing air into it at certain point in the process to make it expand. Hence expandable polystyrene was born. It is referred to as EPS.

There are many hundreds, if not thousands of usages for these products today. You should know of what is refereed to as styrofoam cups sued for coffee and other drinks. Yes it is produced from expandable polystyrene. This product was a sensation when it first came out on the market. Here you had a cup or other type container which would keep hot liquid hot for longer periods of time and the same cup would keep cold liquid cold for longer periods of time. How in the hell does the cut know? It is a puzzle to me, but it knows to keep hot stuff hot and cold stuff cold. What a product!!

This is a very brief description of the process. It is a very detailed and delicate process for producing all the different grades for polystyrene products that is used internally and/or sold into the world wide merchant market. Our polymer plant ship their finished product via hopper rail cars, in one thousand pound box and different size bags in box cars and hopper trailers for highway delivery by trucks. They have a number of special packages for delivery to their customers in the United States and abroad.

The headquarters for Foster Grant was in Leominster, Massachusetts. Why you ask? Because that is where Mr. Samuel Foster lived and started the company in 1919. Sam started making plastic in his garage. He made/manufactured combs and barrettes for ladies to use in their hair. After becoming proficient in this, he branched out to other products. Leominster, Massachusetts was the location where the world wide famous Foster Grant sunglasses were produced. Besides the polystyrene plant that extruded the plastic pellets this location it where folks assembled the sunglasses. There were many shapes and designs.

There were several thousand people working to make the parts and assemble them into the finish product – sunglasses. Each and every part of a pair of glasses was made of plastic. The rounded frame that fit over the nose, the right and left piece that went over the ears, the left and right lenses and the very small pins that connected the ear pieces to the eye pieces – all plastic part produced from small amounts of pellets/powder placed into molds and heated to temperatures that would melt the beads into the shape of the mold. When cooled down, the molds were broken apart and the pieces taken out and placed in bins that would be delivered to the assembly department.

The process of putting the pieces together was all done by hand labor. This is why there were so many workers at the Leominster location. As many as three generations from one family worked for Foster Grant at the same time.

When I worked for Foster Grant, Sam's son Joe Foster was the Chairman and President of the company. He became the leader in the 1940s until his death in 1971. I can still remember in 1969, when he came to a ground breaking ceremony at our plant, he came into my office and shook hands with me and told me what a good job I was doing. I KNOW – I KNOW . He did not know me from Adam or Eve, for that matter. But it sure in hell made me feel good. I could tell that he was not feeling good and in bad health. I was very sorry that Mr. Joe died less than two years later.

THE 1973 HIGH WATER ON THE MISSISSIPPI RIVER

The 1973 high water on the Mississippi River gave us big problems. The majority of our finished product, styrene monomer, was shipped by water in tank barges. The barges ranged in size for ten thousand barrels (3,000,000 pounds) and twenty thousand barrels (6,000,000 pounds). A little after 1973, we contracted for twenty-five thousand barrel barges (7,500,000 pounds). Still a little later, after the Chesapeake, Virginia polystyrene plant started production, we contracted for an eighty thousand barrel barge (20,000,000 to 22,000,000 pounds), to start a regular run from our Devil Swamp dock to the Chesapeake Bay. All of the styrene monomer produced throughout the world was and still it sold by the pound.

During the 1973 high water, we had a very difficult time keeping all the polystyrene plants running. The high water came each year. I am referring to the water level of the Mississippi River. The May/June raise came because of the winter snow and ice melting as the weather warmed up North. Up North is anywhere above Shreveport, Louisiana. Actually parts of thirty-one states and two Canadian Provinces contribute to the runoff of water going into the Big Muddy and passing through Baton Rouge on the way to the Gulf of Mexico. The current flowing down the River is very fast and dangerous as well as is the raising water that damages land, homes, farm crops and everything else that it touches.

We also received one-half of our raw- material (benzene) by water. Ethylene, the other raw material, came one hundred percent by pipeline. Much of the benzene came in various size barges from up river locations and Texas via the Intercoastal Waterway. We did get some benzene via pipeline also. During high water, the river traffic was severely curtailed and much slower in transit time to get to its destinations. Much planning and work had to be done to continue an adequate supply to keep our plant running twenty-four hours a day, three hundred sixty-five days a year. All Chemical/Petrochemical, Oil Refineries etc., etc., are not designed to run and stop, run and stop. They are all continues operations. Some industry production plants run for several years before having to shut down for what is referred to as turn-a-round. Some turn-a-rounds last a month or more to make repairs, change catalyst, replace equipment, etc., etc. It depends upon the type of product that is produced and how large the plant is. Most styrene monomer plants could make a normal turn-a-round in thirty to forty days.

We loaded/unloaded barges at our dock located on the Baton Rouge Industrial Canal. Everyone except the political folks referred to it as Devil Swamp Canal. It is a cut off of the East Bank on the Mississippi River that went about a mile or so. It ended several hundred yards past Uniroyal's dock which was forty or fifty yard past our dock at the Agway Systems dock or nearby it. There was a Port of Baton Rouge small dock located down there also.

The 1973 high water was over thirty-five feet above the mean level of the Mississippi River at Baton Rouge. Our dock and walkway and valves for opening and closing the flow for loading and unloading normally was about thirty feet above water level. This time the water level was not only over the walkway and valves, but three to four feet over the hand rails along the walkway. The hand rails were about four feet high over the walkway. To load or unload a barge, the dockman had to go under the water to turn the big wheel that controlled the valve for starting and ending the operation. It was a really scary situation and very, very dangerous. There were not any Coast Guard laws preventing us from doing this during these times. That change within a year or two. One of my jobs, was to notify the Coast Guard each time we had a transfer across our dock. I did this by teletype.

We were very lucky that we did NOT have any leaks or spill during this kind of operations.

There were times during high water that the Port Allen Route, which is a short cut from Texas on the Intracoastal Waterway to Baton Rouge, was shut down for traffic by the Coast Guard and or the United States Civil Engineers District. This was because of wave/wake damages to citizen homes and erosion to shoreline. This meant that the boats had to traverse the Intercoastal all the way to New Orleans then come to Baton Rouge on the Mississippi River against all that current.

NOTE:
Using the Port Allen route from the West would cut off four or five days in transit time. When coming from the West, one would cut off near Morgan City, Louisiana to get onto the Intracoastal for a direct shot to Port Allen/Baton Rouge. This is the way that all the push boats heading above Baton Rouge would come and go. If the delivery was to New Orleans, the boats just stayed on the Intercoastal all the way there.

You may have noticed that Intercoastal and Intracoastal or spelled differently. That is because Inter is between different states and Intra in within one state.

During normal river levels, moving a barge from New Orleans to Baton Rouge would take about two days. But during high water it may take four days and sometimes- two push boats to move it up river. The current coming down river is so strong, one canal boat could not move it. If you happen to have loaded barges in Baton Rouge and heading for New Orleans, you make it there lickety-split. The big problem for the pilots was to just keep it straight in the river. Empty barges moving down river were even more dangerous. I would not want to be a pilot heading down river during this time of year. It is like a runaway train. The current is moving you forward at a very fast clip. My guess is that the pilots kept the engine in reverse the whole way to try to keep control of the boat and barge and used the reverse to slow it down or make corrections in the direction headed. During this time of year, there was much more debris than normal on the river. Debris such as huge trees, lumber, parts of houses and other large objects that float down the river. The large objects could capsize a push boat, so the pilots had to be on alert every second.

As a kid, I lived across the gravel road from the Mississippi River. During high water, I would see all sorts of debris floating past. I saw trees over forty feet long and up to two feet in diameter go into a world pools and never come up for as far as I could see. This is another thing to be aware of and steer away from when traversing the Mississippi River during the melting of the snow and ice up North.

TIMES OF LOW WATER ON THE MISSISSIPPI RIVER

There were times that we had extremely low water on the Mississippi River. Since the River is so deep it did not effect water travel much from St. Louis, Missouri to New Orleans, Louisiana. But it did create problems on the Upper Mississippi and tributaries, such as the Illinois, Missouri, Ohio, etc. and channels off the River such as our Devil Swamp canal.

The natural flow of the River would make a silt buildup at the mouth/entrance into the canal from the river. During high water, the silt buildup is washed away with the strong current. Times when the North Country had a mild winter, not much ice and snow, there was less runoff coming down river to flush the canal entrances out and the buildup would restrict the draft amount we could load on barges and also the draft of benzene barges being delivered to us. These low levels at the entrance into our canal would catch us by surprise. No one could tell if and when it will happen and before we realized it, a barge was stuck in the mud at the entrance of Devil Swamp Canal. This changed our whole way of operation until we could get it dredge out.

First I would notify the Coast Guard about the same time as notifying the Corp of Engineers District in New Orleans that the entrance into Devil Swamp has silted up some and needed to be dredge out so we can keep all of our plants running. They would send a team out by boat and verify the depth of the water with measuring equipment. Usually rods/long sticks throughout the mouth. They make a report for their headquarters and put this section on the wait list. They did notify us as to results of their gauges. Whenever this happened, there would be areas all along the Mississippi Rive and the Intracoastal Canal that needed to be dredged out. Also the Intercoastal Waterway would have low water problems. The Mississippi River feed all the other waterway connected to it in one way or another. The Corp of Engineers District would have a priority list. We would call several times a day and yell and scream to no avail. They will get to us when they get to us and not any sooner no matter who calls.

Styrene loading

This low water was a really costly situation for us. To get our tows and barges loaded, we would have to hire folks to come by water and measure the entrance for depth before the barge company would try to deliver a barge for loading. This was a daily occurrence since the River goes up and down continuously. We also check the depth of water at our dock. We had a deep drafted dock area and only had to have it dredged out one time in many years. Since we were located about a mile from the entrance into our canal, we did not experience silt build up as all of the mouths of the channel entrances did at the River.

As a matter of explanation, when I refer to A TOW, this means that several barges arrive at one time, sometimes as many and four barges. They all must be loaded as soon as possible. The power unit, a four story, five or six thousand horsepower push boat will wait for these barges to be loaded and head back up river. We had a certain amount of free time to load these barges before demurrage came into play. Demurrage is the penalty we paid, after free time, in money, if the huge boat had to wait for them. You cannot miss the tow, because the plant (s) waiting for the loaded barge would shut down. Also our barges help make up the configuration of the complete tow. There are other company's barges in the tow also. When I refer to the barge or a barge, it is usually one barge with a dedicated small canal push boat with it.

To keep our plant running, and our sister plants, and customers that we ship barges to, we had to keep loading barges no matter what. We could not load enough rail tank car or tank trucks to keep a plant our size running- and the cost would have been prohibitive. We could only supply a very small portion of their daily usage. Sooooooooo- this is what we had to do.

After having the water depth checked when our tow arrived to Baton Rouge, we would order one barge to our dock to be part loaded. The carrier moving the barges back and forth sometimes had to hire smaller shift boats than normal to be able to get into the canal through the mouth. The normal loading draft for all inland waterway barges is eight feet and nine inches. The tankerman that loaded the barge would look over the sides of the barge for the draft markings which were located on each corner of a barge. This was a routine thing and any tankerman with a Coast Guard Tankerman's License was very good at hitting there mark. In the case of low water, we had to have the barges short loaded and shuttle it back and forth to the river for trans-loading into other barges. After having the entrance depth measured before having the barge shifted to the dock, we knew how much draft to have the tankerman load to- to make it out into the river.

This is the way we loaded a tow - for instance:
We have a three barge tow that had to be loaded as soon as possible. All barges had to be loaded upon arrival to make the big river tows

headed back up river in time. These tows may push thirty or forty or more barge at one time and was not going to wait for one barge unless it had to have it for the configuration of the tow. And that happened several times. We had to get them loaded and moving up river. We would order the first barge to be loaded to the dock. If the entrance has a water depth of five feet, we would have the first barge loaded to four feet eight inches. Have it shifted to the holding area on the river. We ordered the second barge to the dock. Loaded it to a draft that we could pass through the entrance to be placed along side of the first part loaded barge. We had to make all the arrangements ahead of time and hire many extra people and have some of them on standby. It took many folks to complete these tasks. The second part loaded barge would unload into the first part loaded barge. If that did not fill the first barge to the required draft, we would have to do it again. We had to load the whole tow of barges this way. It was very time consuming and costly and dangerous. All of this trans-loading was one in the middle of the Mississippi River and we worked around the clock, twenty-four hours a day, seven days a week including holidays. It had to be done as quickly and safety as possible. We were very lucky as we never had a spill or water contamination with our hazardous materials, styrene monomer or benzene for that matter.

LOADING THE OCEAN GOING CHESAPEAKE, VIRIGINA BARGE

What I described above was simple when compared to what we had to do to load our ocean going barge for the Chesapeake plant. The barge was huge. It was ninety seven feet long, twenty-two feet deep and about two hundred eighty feet long. While under our contract, all it did was load at Baton Rouge and make runs to Cheapeake and back. It would take about twenty-two days to make a round trip. We averaged about fifteen trips a year during good polystyrene business years. The big headaches were during hurricanes season and low water time on the Mississippi River.

During the low water loadings, we had to do the same procedure as stated earlier, but make many more shuttles back and forth from our canal into the river to get the amount loaded to keep the Cheapeake plant running until the next trip. After sounding the entrance into Devil Swamp,(during low, we had to have this done for every barge that came to our dock), to find out the depth of the water at that time, a smaller flat bottom push boat would push or pull the barge and place (spot) it at our dock. Usually the tug attached to this big barge would do it. But during low water this tug could not get into the canal. Ocean going tugs have a thirteen to sixteen foot draft. This means that there is that many feet under the top level of the water. This in needed to traverse the Gulf and ocean waters. The depth is what kept the tugs afloat. It need to have this much boat under the water for balance and buoyancy to take the wave action in the ocean. The largest river push boats that are three hundred feet long and could handle fifty or more barge traversing the rivers of America have only about four or five feet draft under the water level. They are flat on the bottom and would not last an hour in the ocean. The tugs that traverse in the ocean have V shape bottoms. Any flat bottom boats could not handle this work.

After the big barge was spotted at our dock, we loaded it to a draft that we could get out through the mouth of the canal. We would hire smaller barges to shuttle back and forth from or dock, part loaded, to the river and off load into the big barge. We would have to make eight or more trips to get this big baby loaded. The logistics of getting this done was a nightmare. The barge was so large and so high out of the water that many lengths of hoses needed to be connected from the small barges and lifted up to be connected to the loading manifold on the big barge. All of this was accomplished in the middle of the Mississippi River. All of the barges in the river service had good pumps on them. The barges may be small, but the pumps we powerful. This was because they were always pumping up hill. The water levels of all river/canal loading/unloading locations is always lower that the storage tanks. Many times the storage tanks were over a quarter mile from the dock. That is what the situation was at our dock and tank farm. So the pumps on the barge were powerful and designed to pump up hill.

For the transfer of product on the River, we had to have many folks on hand to hook-up and disconnect the hoses, handle the lifting up and lowering down of these same hoses after each trans-loading and also for gauging both barges before and after each trans-loading, taking samples, tankermen, supervisors, transporting workers from river docks to the trans-loading site, etc.,etc. What you just read about the high water and low water operation problems is a, believe it or not, brief description of the work and activity that had to be preformed to keep all of our plants running. It was just part of the job. If you are wondering, I did NOT get a nickel extra for all the extra sleepless hours that I put in during nights, week ends and holidays. I was hired to work eight hours a day, five days a week. I did not become a twenty-four hour a day Manager, until I relocated to the new Bayport, Texas plant in 1980.

The ocean going barge, the Hugh, and its power unit, the tug (I forgot the name), was married together. The barge had a V shape at the aft end. The tug, which is a V on its forward end, fit right into the barge V. It is tied together with line/cable. When the equipment is in the River, the tug is connected to the barge and pushes it forward. Although the tug had fifteen feet under the water level, the pilot house is high up and some even have a hydraulic system that can lift the pilot house higher to be able to see over and past the front of the barge when empty.

After loading, the tug pushes the barge out of the River and several miles into the Gulf of Mexico. They disconnect from the back of the barge and go to the front and connect it to a towing line/cable. A large wench with the cable is connected is located on the aft end of the tug. The tug gets underway and unreel the cable out for about a quarter of a mile or more. The Tug then pull/tow the barge. They go direct across the Gulf and past between Key West and Cuba, being sure not to stray into Cuban waters, then head up the Eastern Seaboard. The whole unit is as far out as one hundred miles from the American Coast. At times, I contacted the pilot, by marine telephone, to get updates, eta, and conditions, when we were worried about arrival into Chesapeake because of their inventory getting low. The crew on the tug goes days without ever seeing the barge because of the swell of the ocean and the distance that the barge is behind them. They could not have it to close because the conditions on the ocean would push the barge forward several hundred yards in one swell and swamp/sink the tug. They can tell that the barge is still there by the pressure indicator on the wrench and radar on the tug.

When they get near Chesapeake Bay, they wrench up the barge, disconnect it and relocate the tug behind it for pushing up the Elizabeth River to our dock at our plant. This is how every trip it made. On the way back to us after getting out into Chesapeake Bay they do the same procedure as getting out of the Mississippi River and tow it back toward us until they get close to the River and then again get behind the barge and pushes it up the River to us. Our dock is located two hundred thirty-five miles from the mouth of the River.

BENZENE UNLOADING DURING LOW WATER

Benzene would come to us by barge from numerous locations. Upon arrival, much of what we did for styrene barges going out had to be dome for benzene barges coming in. We had the carrier, the barge company moving the benzene, arrange to have an empty benzene barge on the River near by. When they arrived into Baton Rouge, all arrangements had been made to call out all the folks needed to transfer one half of the cargo into the empty barge then push it to our dock for unloading. Afterwards they moved the now empty barge to the river and connected to the other part loaded barge and pushed it to our dock for unloading. The benzene barges were usually ten thousand barrels (3,000,000 pounds), and would only need two barges to complete the task.

For any transfer of product at a dock or on the river, I had to notify the Coast Guard Office in New Orleans of the Transfer of Product. I did this by teletype at least twenty-four hours before the operation is scheduled to begin. This was the LAW and I followed it to a tee. Again, I made all calls and arrangements for this dangerous operation on the River. We had to have cargo inspectors to gauge and sample the barges and our shore tanks loaded or unloaded, on land or on the River, for every operation. When working with two barges, you had to have two tankermen. One for each barge- this is a LAW also. We had to have extra hoses and tools if need to connect hoses, hire boats to shuttle inspectors, gaugers and tankermen to do the trans-loading to the site, etc., etc.

I tried to sleep on my kitchen floor near the telephone when these off time operations were going on- which was most of the time. We were suppose to be at work for only eight hours a day, so there was sixteen hours a day that you were probably not at work. Yes, that is when most of the activity happened at our dock. It is the Law of Average. Most of the transferring of cargo was during off hours. I would get called all during the operation because of this or that or to do this or that or to call someone else etc. I did have a telephone in my bedroom, but I unplugged it so my wife and kids could sleep. I only use the phone in the kitchen when these operations happened. Cell phones- what in the hell is that? There was no such thing. They had not been invented yet and if they were, the Big boss was to damn tight to let us have one.

When loading/unloading at our dock, we had to have a dockman to open and close the valve on the pipeline and to assist the tankerman in case of emergencies. We also had to have one of our loaders, that worked out of my office, open and close the tank valve at the tank in the tank farm. He also started the pump for a loading operation at the dock. For benzene, he opened the valve leading into the storage tank. This is called lining up the tank to receive cargo. After the loading/unloading operation, the loader had to cut of the pump and close the valve at the tank for styrene and close the valve for benzene. Our loaders were union men and only worked eight hours per day. Everything that needed to be done by them after seven a. m. and four thirty p.m., Monday through Friday, was on overtime. If one came out to open a valve or start a pump, we paid him for four hours. Every time one came out, it was four hours pay. If it was for pushing a button to start a pump and took only ten minutes to punch in the clock, walk to the tank farm, call the guy to see if he was ready to receive, than push a button to start a pump, he got four hours pay. To cut off the pump and block the valve and the tank after the transfer, the next guy was called out and got his four hours for doing that. After he punched out, if you needed one to come back to cut off the pump because of a problem or whatever, it was another four hours pay. A lot of the union workers wanted to be a loader and work our tank car and tank truck loading rack.

In the early days that I worked for Foster Grant Chemical Company, we had a very good transportation and distribution crew. Starting with Mr. Charles Sleeth, who hired me, then Harvey Bourgoyne, who trained me, Margaret Arceneaux, who worked for Mr. Sleeth and helped Harvey and me, and two of the very best union men that I know, Reggie Landry, the head loader, and Jimmy Smith, the next head loader. These two guys loaded every damn truck, tank car, drum, barge, and can of styrene that left our plant for many years. They were the best. Sometimes I had to take some shit from them and for them, but they would get the job done. These guys were the greatest. I might say something behind their back, but would not allow anyone else to berate them. They did it all. After I learned the job, these guys were MY men and worked out of MY office.

As we expanded the plant and made more production, we add more folks to our crew and still continue to have the best loading and distribution group in the industry. Am I prejudice? Yes, you are damn right I am. After me came Greg Galloway, a good man, then Nicky Delapasse and Cherie Theriot, two good women and another good man for the loading rack crew named Larry Songy from the union. We had a very good crew. This was the main crew until we started building the Bayport, Texas plant. We started hiring other folks to train them for Bayport and replace any folks in Baton Rouge that may transfer there or leave the company for one reason or another.

SELLING OF FOSTER GRANT COMPANY

After Mr. Joe Foster's death, his family sold their shares to United Brands Company. United Brands was the new name of the old United Fruit Company which owned Chiquita bananas, A and W Root Beer and several other Companies. The Foster family owned 35 percent, the Goodman family owned 30 percent and the public owned 35 percent of the Foster Grant stock.

A few years later, United Brands ran into financial trouble. A hurricane in Central America damaged the banana plantation of Chiquita and they were losing money-big time. They could not provide the investment funds that the Foster Grant folks felt were needed to buildup the chemical and plastic and sunglass business. What happened was that the Chairman of United Brands, Mr. Eli Black, the guy who built the United Brands Corporation up to what is was then, got into trouble with the Securities and Exchange Commission over bribes and kickbacks given to Honduras generals where the Chiquita banana plantations were located. United Brands was losing value and the high-up rats within the organization was jumping ship and leaving Mr. Black to face the charges. Mr. Black started selling off part of the company that was making money to pay the lawyers and for government fines and to try and keep other companies afloat. Well, this got to be too much for Mr. Black to handle. He was looking at millions of dollars in fines and jail time. On February 3, 1975, Mr. Black took the elevator up to the 44th floor of the Pan Am Building in New York. He went into his office raised the window blinds and shattered the glass with his briefcase then jumped out of the opening. He was 53 years old and truly was a big wheeler-dealer in New York City in his day.

Sooooooooo, here comes American Hoechst. With all that was happening to/with Mr. Black, to get more money, he was selling Foster Grant to American Hoechst. American Hoechst, being a subsidiary of Hoechst AG of Germany, had to buy all 100 percent of Foster Grant. I do not remember if that was a law on American books or if the Germans wanted it this way. American Hoechst did acquire the Goodman family shares and tendered offers to all the public shareholders for the other 35 percent. They finally purchased Foster Grant on December 31, 1974. With Foster Grant came companies and parts of eight or nine companies that Foster Grant owned.

I remember one time looking up the share price of Foster Grant on the stock exchange. The stock was running just over $15.00 per share. I am not sure how much the shares were going for at the time of the purchase, but I do believe that they were paying more than the share value as printed in the papers. They needed to get it all. The folks with shares made out really good – folks like Mr. Sleeth, my big boss. All the time that I worked for Foster Grant, they did NOT have any employee stock purchase plan. If you are wondering, NO, I did not even have one damn share to sell. I did not make enough money to even try to buy any shares of stock.

TODD CAME A CALLING

Todd was born on February 3, 1975. He was a relative easy birth for Valerie. I guess that she was used to it by now. She could just pop them out. We thought that three was enough so Valerie had her tubes tied by Dr. Venard while he was in there helping to get Todd out. I was afraid of having a vasectomy. If the doctor would make a slip, like Dr. Tomney did when he circumcised me, I would not have anything left. It really scared me. I always felt badly about Valerie having to go through this after just having a baby. I did not step up and be a man and have the vasectomy when I should have. Instead, I put her through the ordeal of having her tubes cut and tied. I guess in this case, I was the pussy. This term was used for guys that were afraid of something.

So here we were with Pete, Repete, three Pete and me. This was more Raffrays than you can shake a stick at or this is more than a piss pot full of Raffrays.

Todd looked and acted very much like Kent did when he was a baby. He was almost a carbon copy of Kent. After a couple of years, he found himself and went his own direction. He did not need to be led by his brothers nor would he allow them to lead him. As Lane did before him, Todd marched to his own tune.

We again went all around showing off Todd. Like Kent and Lane, he was very cute. I did the "its, a boy" cigars again. People at work and other places was wondering when we were going to stop having boy babies. It was costing them money or gifts. Like Kent, Todd went the distance and was born after the usual nine months gestation period. He was seven pounds plus as Kent was. Valerie came out of the hospital the second day. She had that down pat too. Each time she gave birth, she came home the second day.

I set up a saving account at the bank for Todd. All the cash we received for him went into his bank account. The coke bottle return deposit and coupon money savings got divided three ways now. Life was good. In 1975, I was making something over six hundred dollars a month. We were paying the bills and trying to save money. We got plenty of help from Valerie's parent. She was an only child and her parents want to help us out all they could. And they did. Her parents Christmas presents to us were something that we could use around the house. Like a two-seater stroller, a dish washing machine and the cost of having it installed, a repaired like new Maytag clothes dryer, a repaired like new Maytag washing machine, - you know, things like that. That helped us out a great deal. We used our money for baby food, clothes, baby this, baby that and other household bills.

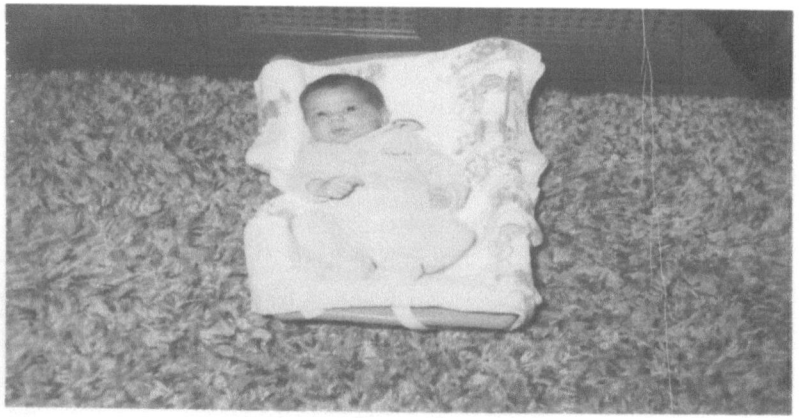

Todd Raffray 20 days old

I DONATED BLOOD

After Lane's birth, I kept on donating blood to the three hospitals in Baton Rouge. The Lady of the Lake was the third hospital. I became a regular donor. I also would give for our company blood drive and any other request for blood. I did this for several years until one time, the Baton Rouge General Hospital almost killed me. I usually go in, wait my turn, and in fifteen minutes after getting into the chair I was out of there. This time, I went in and got somebody different who stuck me several times before finding the correct vain. I lied down and waited but the blood bag was not filling. This was very unusual for me. She was not in my vain properly. I call her over, she said that it was alright. I told her that I am usually out of there by this time, something is not right. She was irritated with me and ignored me. Some minutes later, I got the attention of another nurse. I had been on the table for one half hour. I started to feel really bad. They called a doctor in to check me. I was passing out. I lost all my color. They pulled the needle out of my arm and tried to set me up. I could not sit up because I was really feeling bad. I fainted. Just before I went out, I heard "we are losing him". After a short while I stated coming around again. They made me lie there for about another half hour. They gave me a Delaware Punch which is what I usually drank after giving blood at all the location that I gave at. I do not think they got a full pint of blood after all that time and all I went through.

After an hour or so, I felt good enough to leave there. I arrived there before nine a.m. and it was well after eleven when I departed for home. I drove home the six miles or so and after arriving home, I started feeling very bad again. I had diarrhea and also started throwing up. I got into bed and only got out to throw up or when I had the flying shits. I was in bed the whole weekend. I could not get out of bed on Sunday either. By Monday morning, I was feeling better so I went to work. I was not in great shape but work always came first with me. I will regret this for the rest of my life. Your family should always be first in everything you do.

About ten days later, I received a letter from the Baton Rouge General Blood Bank advising me to go see my doctor and have my blood tested because I have a problem. They also enclosed a twenty-five dollar check for my blood. I had never accepted money for my blood before. My first thought was to send it back because I had always told all the blood banks that I do not want any money for my blood. That I was making it a donation of it. If I took money, then I was selling my blood and I did not like the idea of that. But in this case I decided to keep and cash the check for what they put me through.

I went to my doctor who worked at the Baton Rouge Clinic. This was the doctor that gave me the physical for pre-employment at Foster Grant several years before. After I found out from Mr. Sleeth in his backyard meeting that their test showed no trace of my kidney disease, I went back to this doctor and had him do another urine test. Which he did and it was also negative. Since I did not have a personnal doctor in Baton Rouge, he became mine. After the blood donation ordeal, I did a blood test with my doctor at the Clinic. The results were that I developed some Asiatic blood strand or virus and it was not anything major for me to worry about. The only problem was that I could never donate my blood again. This happened in the mid 1970s.

KENT'S MAGIC THAT DID NOT WORK

When Kent was about four years old he used to love to watch the magic acts on television. He really got a kick out of them. After some time showing this interest, he was given a gift of a magic set. It had a billfold that made a dollar disappear, plastic eggs that came in two parts, a magic wand, magic finger rings, a scarf to lay over items, a magician's black cape and other items. He would play with them from time to time but showed no special interest or excitement on his part. Then one evening as we watch television a magic act came on. He sat on the floor in front of the TV and just soaked it up. He especially liked the part when the magician tapped a large egg like container with his magic wand and spoke some mumbo jumbo while tapping his wand on it and - presto - the egg broke open and out came a bird. Kent thought that this was great. He jumped to his feet all excited and ran out of the room. When he came back he had his cap on, some plastic eggs and his wand. He dropped an egg or two on the floor before he placed one egg on the coffee table in front of the sofa where I was sitting. He glanced back at the television then quickly returned his attention to the egg on the coffee table. He placed the egg in the center of the table then covered it with his scarf and with his wand tapped the egg and said "Abbra Kadabba". He lifted the scarf and waited a couple seconds and repeated the whole routine again. After several seconds the egg had not done anything. He grabbed the egg and threw it on the floor and picked up another egg and did the complete procedure again. Still nothing happened. Not even a bird peep. He threw this egg on the floor also. He picked up the third egg and looked at it closely. He opened it to look inside. It was empty. He threw it on the floor with the others then walked out of the room very disappointed that his magic supplies did not work. He took off his cape and threw in on the floor too.

KENT'S FIRST WAIST WATCH

About the same time that Kent was into magic, he received a gift from his mom's parents. It was a plastic wrist watch. It had a plastic band and plastic time piece. It had plastic minute and hour hands and plastic knobs to wound and set the time and a plastic crystal. In other words this watch was completely plastic. The timepiece itself was a little over a quarter inch thick. It was kind of bulky. This toy watch kept real time for two hours before needing to be re-wound.

Kent did not care very much for the watch. I tried several times to get him to wear it. I wanted to start teaching him how to tell time. I showed him my watch on my arm thinking that he might like to wear a watch just as this dear ole dad did. He still did not care to wear it. One Saturday I decided to make him wear this damn watch. I strapped the watch on his arm. He struggled with me because he did not want it on his arm. He really did not like this watch attached to him. A few minutes later I noticed the watch on the floor. I picked it up and put it on his arm again and explained to him that he should wear it to get used to it. A short time later, I found it on the floor again.

I put it back on his arm a third time then went into the kitchen. A few seconds later I notice Kent come into the kitchen from the television room and go straight to the trash basket and jam the watch into it. Our trash basket had one of those swinging lids on it. You know the kind that goes down into the basket when you place something in it. After he threw the watch into the trash basket he then rubber his hands together and said THERE. Then he went back into the den to play. I went and retrieved the watch from the trash and did not bother to try and get him to wear it again. I gave up, Kent won.

CARS THAT I OWNED BY PURCHASE OR GIFT

My first car was a 1953 two door Chevy. I purchased it in 1963 from either Mattie or Margie. They are the twin sisters that I never could tell apart. Before they married, their last name was Ponsano. They were nieces of Uncle Charlie Ponsano who was married to Nan Noon who was my momma's aunt on her daddy's side. We all call Charlie, Paran. Paran Charlie was one of the brothers of Uncle Andre (as we called him). Uncle Andre Ponsano was Mattie and Margie's daddy. He was incapacitate and living with one of his daughters in White Castle and could not drive any more which is why his car was sold. The car was still in very good shape even after being laid up for almost two years. It was a two tone colored car. It had a brown top and the rest of the car was tan. After washing and waxing it looked really good. It was just old. There was no rust spots on the car.

A couple years later, I sold the Chevy to Lynndale Sciortino and purchased a 1954 four door Plymouth from Dixie Sales and Service in White Castle. This was the dealership that the Dirion brothers (cousin Fred and cousin Steve) owned. This car was black and had a small rusted spot on the rear fender on the driver's side.

In 1966, I purchased a 1965 Sports Fury from Dixie Sales and Service. This had been a lease car and was in a hurricane in New Orleans. It was in an auction yard with more other Chrysler products to be auctioned off to the dealer with the highest bid. I pick out this car before the auction. Pee Wee Dirion (Steve Jr.) actually purchased it and resold it to me. It cost me three thousand dollars. This was more then we thought it would be. Pee Wee told me that he got into a bidding contest with someone else who wanted the car and that was why it cost so much. I could have purchased a 1966 white two door hard top Chrysler for five hundred dollars less because it was not bided on as heavily. Sam Boudreaux, who later married Joy Acosta (one of my classmates at White Castle High), ended up with the white Chrysler. It looked gooooooooood.

My car was a two-door hardtop with a black vinyl top and maroon bottom. It had black interior with bucket front seats and had an automatic on the floor gearshift. The radio had a reverberator which was the forerunner to stereo/surround sound. I loved this car. It had low mileage but had many very small pecks on the body because of the hurricane it was in. A good compound polish job made it look much better.

The only problem with this car was the gas mileage. It had a V-8, 383 cubic inch engine with a two-barrel carburetor. I really thought that it would be good on gas mileage because of the two-barrel carburetor. But that was not the case. On regular gas, I got nine miles per gallon. On premium gas, I got twelve miles per gallon. This was not good gas mileage at all.

Later that year, Herbert Hebert purchased a car that looked just like mine but he had a four-barrel carburetor and got over eighteen miles per gallon. He also had the take off power that my car did not have. Everybody with smaller engines could out run me from a stand still. This was all right with me. I did not buy this car to race, but I would have liked better gas mileage. I loved this car. Did I mention that already?

After I got married in 1967, my wife brought her 1964 Dodge Dart to the union. I sold my old 1954 Plymouth during harvesting season to a black guy who worked on Cedar Grove Plantation that my daddy knew. The dart was a smaller car. It was a two-door hardtop with push button drive on the dashboard. It was cream color with a black strip the length of the car on both sides. This car was a gift to my wife from her mom and dad when she graduated high school in 1964. They let her keep the car when we got married in September.

In 1970, my in-laws gave us their second car. It was a 1968 Plymouth Satellite. We only had to pay the last two notes to get the car. It had a 318 cubic inch V-8 engine. This was a very good car. I really liked the Chrysler 318 cubic inch engine. It is the right size. It was beige in color. This was a four-door sedan with automatic transmission with the gearshift on the steering column. The car came with Sears steel belted radial tires. I did not buy these type tires because they cost too much. I always purchased the cheap may pop tires. I was always having a flat fixed. My experience with this car and these tires changed my outlook on tire purchases for the rest of my life. In short, we went six years before I had any tire problem on this car. The problem I had, I caused because I ran off the street and on a curb. I had over 20,000 miles over the stated tire warranty amount and there was still seven tenths of the ten-tenths thread left on the tire. I purchased a new forty-dollar tire for about ten dollars because of the warranty- that is the thread still left on the tire. When I finally replaced the other three tires they had almost seventy thousand miles on them. These were forty thousand mile tires. I really replace them because they were dry rotting. Cracks started showing up in the sidewalls. I only purchase high mileage radical tires after this experience. Wouldn't you?

We sold the Dart to Harold Spencer's sister. Harold and I worked together at Foster Grant Chemical Company in Baton Rouge at the time. In fact we shared the same office.

In 1974, my in-laws gave us their 1970 Oldsmobile 98 Luxury Sedan. I sold my Sports Fury to Eric Allen from White Castle. He worked for Dixie Sales and Service at the time and loved my car also. I knew the Allen family and knew that they were good people.

The Oldsmobile was a big four-door car. It was a good car. It had an automatic transmission and was all power. This was our first car with power windows. It was light brown/tan in color. The roof had vinyl covering on it. This was a good family car and was the right size for our growing family. Kent born in 1970 and Lane in 1971 had more room in the back seat to play or sleep. It also had a huge trunk and new steel belted radials from Sears all around.

In 1976, we purchased a 1974 Oldsmobile Custom Station wagon from Coleman Oldsmobile in Baton Rouge. This was a two tone blue car and it was loaded. It even had a built in CD, which we enjoyed listening to on trips. Since Todd, born in 1975, was added to our family, we felt we needed more room when traveling. We sold the Satellite when we purchased this car. I started using the 98 to go to work every day. It started needing work on it. But the tires never needed repair or another set.

During 1977, I made several thousand dollars on stock I purchased in 1973. After meeting Charlie O'Brien a Vice President with Matlack Trucking, I was so impressed, I went out a purchased several hundred shares of Rollins Leasing Corp (who owned Matlack) at three dollars per share. I sold for over thirteen dollars per share in 1977. The stock went to over sixteen per share shortly after I sold. But I did all right. In late 1977, I purchased a 1977 Chevy Chevette for cash plus the one hundred dollars trade in I got for the 98 Oldsmobile. The Matlack stock paid for this car and I invested in two other stocks with the balance.

The Chevette was a small car. It was light blue and had an automatic transmission with the gearshift on the floor between the bucket seats.

It was a hatch back car. I got very good mileage. I wanted to get a standard transmission but my wife refused to learn how to drive a standard shift car, so I purchased this one. In late 1979 we moved to Texas with the 1974 Oldsmobile wagon and the 1977 Chevette.

In 1981 I traded the Chevette in on a 1978 Dodge standard cab pickup truck with a camper shell over the bed. It had a small V-8 engine. It was blue with a cream-colored six-inch wide strip from front to back on both sides.

In 1984 we traded the Olds station wagon on a 1984 new Oldsmobile Custom Cruiser station wagon. It was a very nice car with powered everything. It was a two tone brown very nice riding family car.

In 1986 I traded my truck for a 1982 Cadillac Biarritz with a stainless steel moon roof. It was a fine looking dark blue car. My wife was pissed off at me and did not come with me to look and shop for a car. She did not even want to drive it. I wanted it for her. Her attitude on the car went back to the 1984 station wagon. She wanted a sporty car, but I FORCED her to settle for a wagon (which we needed for our growing family). Since I had a standard size pickup, she wanted a sporty car. This is when I found out that she did not like or want the pickup. When I purchased the pickup, I should have purchased a station wagon or something else according to her. I just didn't think that two station wagons made a lot of sense. Anyway, more was to come.

When she moved out of the house in 1988 and we divorced in 1990, she took the 1984 station wagon. I still had the 1982 Cadillac.

In 1989 I got a company car to drive from my employer, Huntsman Chemical Corp. I had been promoted from Manager of Supply and Distribution to Director of Supply and Distribution and took the company car in place of a raise for that year. The car was a 1989 Ford Crown Victoria. It was a white four-door sedan with all power equipment. It had a V-8 engine and got over 26 miles per gallon. On a long trip, it averaged almost 30 miles per gallon. This was just great. I really enjoyed the size and the mileage of this car.

I sold my 1982 Cadillac to Mike Kersman a friend of mine for less than half of what it cost me in the divorce settlement and he did not even pay me that much. I did get him to replace a water filter at my house for one hundred fifty dollars toward his car bill. It took over two years to get anything out of him. For eight hundred dollars toward the car, he put together a piece of shit computer, which was out dated, when I got it. I just gave up trying to collect my money from him. Mike was a good guy, but don't ever sell him anything unless you get the cash up front. He still owes me for one of his checks that bounced that my bank charged me twenty-five dollar for. You learn as you go along.

In 1990 my Uncle Nolan in Louisiana died. My brother, sister and I were the only airs.

My brother and sister gave his 1986 Dodge 600 K car to me. It was a four door dark blue sedan. My two older sons who were living with me at the time would take turns driving it. Also in 1990, I purchased a 1987 Ford Ranger standard cab pickup to have a third vehicle available to drive. My youngest son moved back with me after his mom moved to Louisiana. We did not have enough vehicles to go around. The truck was red with a tan strip along both sides. It had a very powerful V-6 engine.

In 1992 I was sent another company car to replace the 1989 Ford Crown Vic. It was a 1992 Mercury Grand Marque. It was a car that went to another company that did not take it. The car lease company offered it to Huntsman. I would not normally qualify for this type car, but they made Huntsman a good deal and I was next in line for a replacement car. When it was offered to me, I said "yes". This car arrived by truck carrier from Kansas City, Kansas. I was on vacation at the time so the car was parked in the plant near the guard house. When I came back to work the next week, I was informed that Huntsman was canceling the company car plan for some employees to save money. This was very upsetting. They made an offer to sell the car to me at a discount. I had six to eight weeks to make up my mind. I had already told Violet Marsh that she could purchase my company 1989 Ford and I did not want to go back on my word. I could have purchased it for less than six thousand dollars. The Mercury stayed in the plant for about six weeks. I took all the time allowed to make my decision. I purchased the car outright for twelve thousand dollars. This was a very good deal for a brand new car with a twenty three thousand dollar sticker price. I raised some hell before purchasing it but was very satisfied with this car. What pissed me off was that I gave up more than a thousand dollar raise three years before to get the first company car. This took money out of my pocket then and every year since then. It really cost me many thousand dollars in the end. It also cost me to get a lesser amount of retirement. What made me so upset was that I turned down the first company car because of the cost to me for the rest of my life and was talked into taking it by our corporate comptroller who was my good friend, Mike Ringwood. He told me that when Huntsman gave you a company car they never took it away. Now that they did, I looked at it as a ploy to screw me and sixteen others in the company out of our raises and the percentage increases on that money for every year afterwards as well as the final retirement amount we would get upon retirement. I let Mike Ringwood, Brent Turkington (Vice President and my boss) and Tom Wood (General Manager/Vice President), know how I felt. It was not a good time. I was very obstinate, vocal and said some things that should never be said to superiors. If I was any of these guys, I would have fired me on the spot and be done with it. Thank god, they did not.

This large car got very good mileage also. Not as good as the 89 Ford, but in the mid twenties on a trip. I was well pleased with the performance of this car. But I am still not over the feeling that I got screwed by Huntsman - yet.

In 1993 I traded the Dodge 600 in on a 1993 Mercury Tracer. It was a small car. It had four doors and was light blue or gray in color. I now had the 87 Ford Ranger pickup the 92 Mercury Grand Marque and this car. My three sons shared the usage of the pickup and the Tracer. I was the only one to drive the Grand Marque.

The Tracer ended up going to Austin/San Marcos with Lane and Todd. Over a two or three year period, it had two engine replacements. Todd eventually traded it in on the Honda he purchased in Austin in about 1997. I signed for Todd to purchase the Honda.

In the Mid 1990's I put down half on a used car for Kent. He paid the balance in notes. It was a 1986 foreign made Ford sporty car with a turbo charger. I paid for a transmission replacement and about fifteen hundred dollars in other work to try and keep it running. I finally gave it to the mechanic working on it in Austin for the bills that he ran up trying to fix it. They blew the engine up and wanted more money to fix it. I refused to pay any more to get this car running. I co-signed for Kent to purchase his 1994 Trackor.

JUMPING WAY AHEAD OF MY STORY BECAUSE OF CARS

I remarried in January 1997. With Sarah came her 1990 Buick Skylark. I helped her pick out this car after she was paid off by her insurance company for her older Skylark that was totaled in a wreck.

In May of 1997, we purchased a 1997 Toyota T-100 extended cab pickup. It was off white in color and had a V-6 engine. About this time we gave Lane Sarah's Skylark. He was in graduate school at Southwest Texas State University in San Marcos, Texas.

We now had the new 97 T-100, the 92 Grand Marque, and the 87 Ranger pickup, which I used mostly to haul junk from "the Place" to the dump in San Jacinto County. I purchased "the Place" in June of 1996. The old guy that lived there was a junk collector and had accumulated quite a bit of it at the time of his death in 1994. I moved over twenty-five truck loads to the dump and still have more to haul.

In early 1999 we purchased a 1997 Mercury Grand Marque. I did not trade in anything. This was a white four door and looked good from the outside. We ended up replacing the automatic transmission while the car was still under warranty and got screwed by not having a Ford/Mercury dealer do it. We kept this car about fourteen months. At the time of this purchase, we gave the 1992 Grand Marque to Sarah's mom and took ownership of her 1980 Ford Crown Vicgtoria which we gave to Nathan. He is Sarah's youngest son and was living with us at this time. We spent over eight hundred dollars repairing the old Crown Vic. Nathan went through cars pretty fast. He sold this one a year or two later.

Between 1999 and 2000 we purchased a 1990 Chevy standard cab red pickup for Sarah's oldest son, Jacob, who was a senior in high school near Forth Worth, Texas.

Later, we purchased a 1994 black extended Ford pickup for Nathan who was now without transportation after selling the older Crown Vic.

Sometime after Jake and Nate had there trucks, they wanted to swab them with each other. We let them do it. The type trucks now seamed to go with the personally of the boys. After some months, Nate traded his nice looking red pickup for a piece of shit sports car and eventually traded the car down to a motor bike which he sold for nothing and was without transportation again. We decided that we would not buy any more vehicles for Nathan.

Sometime in 2000 we sold the 87 Ranger to a friend to get it out of the driveway. We had four vehicles for three people at the time we sold it. It would not have been smart to hold this truck for Nathan because he would have ruined it in less than a month. He is just hard on vehicles.

In mid 2000, we traded the 1997 Grand Marque for a 2000 F-150 extended cab (with two small extra doors) white Ford pickup. It is a standard transmission with five speed drive and all power equipment pickup. It has a V-6 engine and is a nice looking truck.

Also in 2000, Jake totaled the 1994 pickup. We purchased a 1981 pickup for him. We also purchased a 1996 Mercury Sable four door sedan at a public auction in Pasadena, Texas. We spent over a thousand dollars trying to get it in better running condition. It was light brown in color and had a lot of power equipment. We let Nathan use this car until it would not run any more. It was getting more beat up every day and we would not put any more money into it so we donated it to Volunteers of America in early 2001. It was a mistake to buy this car. I got caught up in a bidding war for this car and paid way too much for it. The only good thing about buying this car was that I found six Susan B. Anthony dollars in the car.

At this time, late December 2003, Sarah and I drove the 1997 Toyota and the 2000 Ford pickup. Jake sold his truck because he married in May 2002 and will share his wife's car. Nate has his Grandmother's car that his dad gave to him in early 2002. It is a 1984 Ford Crown Vic. It was sort of yellow in color. This car was donated to a charity because Nate did not/could not put more money into it. Nate has had two other vehicles since.

BACK TO MY STORY

CARS FROM THE STOLTZS

In the early 1970s, Al Stoltz decided to keep just one car. Even though Mrs. Stoltz did not drive they always had two cars all the time that I knew them starting back in 1964. They had two cars into addition to Valerie's Dart when she lived with them. Mr. Stoltz was a federal bank examiner and worked for the Federal Deposit Insurance Corporation better known as the FDIC. He did not ever want to be late to get to a job so he kept two cars in case something happened to the one he was driving. Working for the FDIC meant that he was on the road a lot. Each week he would receive a letter in the mail telling him where his next assignment was. This was all top-secret stuff. He could not let on where he was going. When the Federal guys showed up to examine a bank, they wanted to pop in and surprise everyone. It was against their rules to notify the bank ahead of time. The Feds did not want to chance that the bank folks might try and cover up something if they found out that an examination was about to take place. When he had to be in a bank when the doors opened at nine in the morning, if the city was more than two hundred miles away, he drove on Sunday and got a motel/hotel room near the town that the bank to be examined was in. He kept two cars just in case one broke down. This way he could use the other car while his number one car was being repaired. They did send some bank presidents and officers to jail and had to take over the operation of a number of bank because of shady/crooked operation by the owners while Mr. Stoltz worked this job.

They gave us a 1968 four door Plymouth, Satellite. It was a very nice and clean car and in great condition. This allowed us to sell my gas drinking 1965 Sports Fury. Now we had the 1964 two door Dodge, Dart that my wife had when we got married and the four door Plymouth, Satellite that was more of a family car than my Sports Fury. I used the Dart to go to work and the Satellite stayed home in case Valerie needed to use it. It was easier getting the boys in and out of it because of the four doors. We really enjoyed the Satellite. It was just over three years old when we got it. It was in very good shape and had an engine with guts. It had the 318 cubic inch engine with a four-barrel carburetor. It had much more get up and go than my Sports Fury that had the 383 engine but a two-barrel carburetor. That car could not get out of its own way and I burned much more gas than this one did. I believe the two-barrel carburetor was the reason it burned so much gas. Before I purchased the car, I thought having a two-barrel carburetor would get more gas mileage. I was wrong. The 383 cubic inch block was a good engine and would not reach maximum operation efficacy with a two-barrel carburetor. It just had too much restriction on it.

Alfred (Al) Stoltz - Valerie's dad

CHANGING SHOCKS ON THE DART

Sometime during 1970 it was time for new shocks on the Dodge, Dart. I always did as much maintenance on my cars as I could. I changed the oil and oil filters on all my vehicles. I could also change out alternators, fan belts, water pumps, exhaust manifold gaskets, fuel pumps, brakes, and do some very minor repairs.

For some time, our Dart needed new shocks. I decide that I would do that job. I went to the closest auto parts store and purchased four shocks designed for the Dart. I told the man that I wanted light duty shocks. As least that is what I ordered. He also had medium and heavy duty available.

I had a bumper jack that came with the Dart so I plan to jack up one wheel at a time, replace the shock and go to the next wheel and do the same until I got all four shocks replaced. I did not have jack stands at this time (I did purchase some soon after this job), so when I jacked up the front driver's side wheel first, I placed an old galvanized bucket under the center of the car to the rear of the engine where the chassis was. I jacked up the wheel. I had to get the tire off the driveway to take the wheel off to get to the shocks. When I got the tire off the driveway, I placed the bucket under the car. I thought that this might help if the car fell off the jack after I took the wheel off. This bucket might give be enough time to move my legs out of the way before the car crashed all the way down.

I had the front wheel off and was sitting on the driveway straddling the hub and checking out how the shock was screwed on. My legs were under the car. A neighbor across the street, Eddie Gallagous had been watching unbeknown to me. I heard this noise coming from up the street. I looked over that way. Here was Eddie pulling a large car jack. This was the kind of jack that the automotive places use to replace tires on a car. Eddie was upset that I was doing this in a very unsafe way. He worked on his cars and had all the tools you could name. I knew this, but I hated to borrow anything from anybody. He placed his jack under the front end of the Dart screwed the handle and started pumping the handle up and down. This big jack lifted the whole front end of the car off the driveway. I had a piece of four by four chocking the rear wheel already so the car would not roll backwards. Eddie told me to use his jack as long as I want to. He locked it in place and showed me how to unlock it when I was ready to let the car down.

This jack was a God send or at the least an Eddie send. I know now that I would be able to do this job in one day and not the whole weekend as it was beginning to look like.

I replaced both shocks on the front end, replace the wheels, got everything secured than unlocked the jack and let the car down. It only took me about three hours to get the front shocks replace. I dragged the jack to the back end of the car. I placed my four by four chocks in front of a front wheel and behind of the same wheel. This would prevent the car from rolling forward or backward. The jack lifted the whole rear end of the car off the driveway-no problem. I locked it in place. I removed the rear wheels and replaced the shocks without any problems. After removing the jack and the chocks, I stepped back to admire the car. I walked up to the driver side front wheel area, put one hand on the fender and pushed down. The car did not budge. I put both hands on the fender and put my weight on it to push downward. The car still did not budge or move in the slightest. Oh no I thought- what is this. I tried it again. I turned around and jumped up on the fender. Ouch, I hurt my butt bone and the car still did not move. I ran into the house cursing and told my wife that the parts man sold me the extra heavy duty shocks instead of the light duty which was what I ordered. I was hot. I did not want to take all these shocks off the car. I did a good job and it did not take me all day. That bastard that sold these to me probably would not take them back because they were now used. What a shit-head he was to give me the wrong shocks.

I had said my piece. I took a couple of deep breaths and headed back outside. As soon as I got under the carport and looked down the driveway at the car, I noticed something. What is this? I went to the car, shoved down on the hood again. It still did not move. I got on my knees and looked under the car. There was my little galvanized bucket. It was from this position that I noticed that my front tires did not have that little bulge in them that they suppose to have when the weight of the car in fully on them. I got the big jack and jacked the front end up again, removed the bucket then removed the jack. I again stood over the right side bumper, placed both hands on it and pushed downward. The car moved as it is supposed to do. The movement was not as bouncy as it was before I replaced the shocks. The shocks were working fine.

I had solved this problem all by myself. I was happy. Then I looked around to see if any of my neighbors were outside. I was afraid that they were watching when I removed the bucket from under the car. I know that some of them must have heard all the co-motion that I was making when I thought I was sold the wrong shocks. I did not notice anyone watching me. I felt relief.

After moving all the tools, chocks, jacks, etc. under my carport, I took the Dart for a ride to look for pot holes. We found some and the new shocks preformed well. This was a job well done and it only took me about six or seven hours to complete. I felt really good. I brought Eddie's jack back to his house late that afternoon after wiping it down in case I put any grease on it. I thanked him again for the loan of it. He told me that I could borrow it anytime. Eddie would have been a good man for me to pattern myself after. He had the two best looking and running vehicles in the whole subdivision. He and his wife was always washing and cleaning their autos. They must have cleaned their cars at least twice a week. They would even come out and wash them after a rain. Now that is something.

IN-LAWS MOVE TO OKLAHOMA

In 1971 or 1972, my in-laws were transferred from Austin, Texas to Oklahoma City, Oklahoma. This was a completely different division of the FDIC. They had different states to keep an eye on than the Texas division had. Austin was an eight hour drive from Baton Rouge. Oklahoma City was a twelve hour drive. Four more hours of road time driving. At least following this family around I was seeing parts of the country that I would never have seen otherwise. I did my share at helping the oil companies make money with all the gas that I was buying. A twelve hour drive is a hard days work when, just two adults do it. You can add a little more stress when it is done with two kids and then three kids. Oh boy what fun that was. I did all the driving because I was just that kind of guy. I could not rest if my wife drove. I do not know why. Perhaps, because I wanted to tell her how to drive or something but it was better for me if I drove. So I did- all the time while on a trip with my family. We would pack a lunch and some snack, bring water and or cold drinks and an empty mayonnaise jar or two. The jar was for my boys to pee in when they had to go. When I got on the road, I only wanted to stop for gas. While getting gas, I expected everybody in the car to go to the bathroom rather they needed to or not- because I am not stopping again to pee or poop. I wanted to set a new traveling miles in an hour record each time I made a trip.

Every time we made a trip, an argument started about peeing in the jar. My boys could be convinced/threatened to do it, but their Momma would always bark at her having to pee in the jar. She just adamantly refused to do it. She was definitely not setting a good example for her boys. If she needed to go to the bathroom she would stay on my back in between gas stops. In over twenty year of marriage I never could break her out of her habit of having to use a toilet to pee. When I would gas up I hurried up and paid the attendant and used the bathroom rather I needed to or not. It seamed like most of the time nobody in the car needed/wanted to go. We would not go fifteen miles down the road when I would hear "I need to pee pee". I would reach down to my right side, grab a hold of it, and hand back the JAR. Then the auguring would start.

I believe that I was the average dad and husband. I think other dads and husbands did the same thing that I did and had the same problems that I did. I know for a fact that Louie Anderson's dad did what I did. He told the whole world about it on this Special on television some years ago. I am not a monster. I just wanted my family to use the bathroom on command. I wanted them to use it when I was ready for them to use it. After all, I was supposed to be the boss. What the boss says, goes. RIGHT? That may have been true in other families, but not in mine. Years ago, Pee Wee Campesi told me that while in the Marines, they had to shit by the numbers. It was like, 1- 2- 3, strain your guts out and shit. They did it. I just could not run my house-whole like the marines.

I was just an old softie. Sometimes I would even stop to let my wife use the bathroom when there wasn't a gas station in sight. I did this many times on many trips after a lot of bitching and begging and ready to start a fist fight right there in the car when I was driving- that is. O K maybe I was/am a monster. I am sorry for making everyone pee in a jar. Even me. Yes, I could and would pee in a jar and drive if I had to. Doing the other number in a jar was a problem, put peeing, that was nothing. My wife just did not want to squat down in the front seat. I was confident that she could pee in the jar without even a drop missing it. She was very good at everything she did. If I would not hit a pot hole, she could have done it. I have no doubts about that.

OKLAHOMA- A HOT/COLD PLACE

Sometimes we would make two trips to Oklahoma City a year. Once during the summer and another at Christmas time. Until 1994, the hottest temperature that I had ever been in was one hundred nine degrees Fahrenheit in Oklahoma City. I cut my in-laws grass that day. It was really hot but I did not sweat as much as when I cut my grass in Baton Rouge. When I passed under a tree or the shadow of their house it was not that bad at all. I would actually cool down a bit when I stayed in the shade from the sun. It was not nearly as bad as I thought it might be. There was actually a small breeze blowing. I just could not feel it while in the sunlight.

As for the winters, they were something else. One winter the temperature did not warn up above minus seven degrees Fahrenheit for a twenty-four hour period. The wind chill for that time period was a minus thirty-five degrees Fahrenheit. This IS the coldest temperature that I ever remember being in. They say that it is a dry cold there. Well, all I know is that it was damn cold, dry or not. My boys would try and play outside building a snowman during the cold snap and would get nose bleeds. I would laugh at them and call them little sissies. One day after Kent and Lane came in from the cold, I decided that I would go out and finish the snowman. In about fifteen minutes, I came back inside with a nose bleed. My in-laws, my wife and my boys really had a big laugh and got a big kick out of the big sissy laying on the couch with his head back and a hand full of tissue to try and get his nose to stop bleeding. They got a lot of fun at my expense for a long time. I enjoyed them having such a good time making fun of me. It was funny. Needless to say, I did not call them sissy any more- at lease not on this trip.

Barry, Lane, Todd and Kent Raffray

OKLAHOMA'S CROSSROADS MALL

Over the years on trips to Oklahoma City, we visited many places and sites. Among them were: The Will Rodgers Museum, The Cowboy Hall of Fame, Old West Frontier, many parks and the Oklahoma City Zoo which is one of the largest in the country.

My father-in-law and I went to a couple baseball games to watch the Oklahoma City 89ers play ball. The 89ers was a triple A - Minor League team in the Houston Astros organization. I watched John Mayberry playing first base for the 89ers. Several years later after I was transferred by my company to the Houston area, I watched John Mayberry playing first base for the Major League Houston Astros.

One of the joys I had on our trips to Oklahoma was going to the large three or four story mall with the huge ice skating rink in it. This mall was on the outskirts of Oklahoma City. It was called Crossroads Mall. It was the largest shopping mall that I had ever seen. We made a number of trips to this mall to shop and browse around and spend the day. This mall was some distance from my in-laws house in Oklahoma City. One thing about the people who lived there is that they do not let snow, ice or very cold weather stop them from doing what they want to do. When we went out together, my farther-in-law usually drove and I always rode up front with him. The in-laws usually had a large four door sedan or a station wagon. There was always enough room for all of us to sit in comfort.

On this winter time visit, we all went shopping at Crossroads Mall. We had to park some distance from the entrance, so my father-in-law drove up close to the entrance to let the family out before finding a place to park because it was very cold at the time. I wanted to show him that I was tough like him so I opened the doors and let the women and kids out. I then got back into the car to ride with him to find a parking place then we could run back to the entrance together. This time the closest parking space we could find was about one hundred yards from the entrance. So be it. I almost froze before we got back inside the mall.

We spent the day shopping, had lunch there and the kids had visits with Santa Clause. Lane, who was about three years old, was asked by Santa Clause what he was going to get for Christmas. Lane replied "reindeer pooh pooh". Santa could not understand him and asked the question again and Lane said the same thing. Santa nodded and said that was good. He apparently did not understand what Lane said which made us happy. Lane had been told by his Grandpa- Al and his Grandma- Kay, that if he was not a good boy, Santa Clause would give him reindeer pooh pooh. We were the only folks around who knew what Lane was saying. For that, we were grateful.

We were at the mall all day and it was getting into evening time now. When the sun goes down it gets even colder there. We got to the entrance where we came in to make our exit. I told Al that I will go get the car but he thought that I could not drive in this kind of weather I guess because he said that he will do it. I told him that I will go with him then. We went through the double set of doors and started running in the parking lot in the direction that the car was parked. Man, it was really cold. I did not have a hat or any gloves on. My hands were not in my pockets because I needed them out for balance while running. I sure did not want to fall with my hands in my pockets. Finally there was the car. The way the car was parked meant that I would get to my side of the car first. Al used his key to open the driver side, than hit the switch on the door to open my door. I noticed blood dripping on my over coat. My nose had started bleeding again. After getting my handkerchief and holding my nose with my right hand, I reached for the door handle with my left hand with two of my fingers stretch out, I hit the door just above the handle and I felt a sting. My fingers were almost numb from the cold. I pulled my hand back to look at it. Al had the car running by now and I was still outside. The finger nails on my trigger and middle fingers on my left hand had cracked and split all the way to the cuticles on each finger. I just could not believe it. My fingernails had frozen from the mall entrance to the car. They did not hurt much at this time. We backed out of the parking spot and drove to the entrance and Al got out and opened the car doors and everyone scrambled into the back seat. On the way back to my in-laws house, my nose stop bleeding and my fingers started hurting. Man did they hurt. I am lucky because my fingernails grow fast. Each day I could see the growth. I did not go outside very much for the next several days. I was what you call gun-shy of the cold weather. The next time I went to Oklahoma City in the winter time, I had a good pair of winter gloves and a cap that had flaps to cover my ears. So did all my sons and their momma. Enough is enough.

KENT AND LANE IN PRIVATE SCHOOL

A number of years went by. I can remember a few noteworthy things that happened. Kent started kindergarten then Lane started a year later. Valerie spent some time with them at the Lutheran Kindergarten where they went near our house. This was at the church that we attended. Kent tried the first grade in a public school just around the corner from us. But he just could not make it there. He was a momma's boy and when she tried to leave after bringing him there, he would pitch a fit. We took him out and placed him in First Lutheran private school near down town Baton Rouge. His momma would drive him and stay there as a teacher's aid. The next year, Lane went to First Lutheran also. Their momma would stay there and help out and I believe she also took Todd with her. They had a day care at this church school.

LANE IS ABOVE AVERAGE- WE HAVE THE PAPERS TO PROVE IT

When Lane was in kindergarten, his teacher thought that we should hold him back a year. He did not seam mature enough to compete with the others. He acted silly and was kind of clumsy also. He marched to a different beat. You might say that he made his on beat and marched to it when no one else could. When Lane went into the first grade at First Lutheran, the same thing came up. We were advised to hold him back a year. I did not want to do that. My idea was that if he could not do the work, let the teacher hold him back but if he did the work, he should not be held back because he acted different in any way.

Valerie and I finally felt compelled to have him tested at The LSU Center for Testing Adolescence. After making appointment and filling all the paperwork that you must do to proceed, we got Lane approved for testing. For several days we dropped him off and picked him up later that same day. I believe that this went on for a week or so. They compiled a huge file on him. Afterwards the specialists did their test and evaluations we had a big meeting.

What we found out was Lane was better than average for a six year old. In some categories he scored at levels for an eight year old and older. His knowledge of things was several years above his age level. They told us that he did not have any learning impediment. He was a little immature because he was much younger than everyone in his class was but his knowledge was way above average. Lane was born December 23, 1971. He was two months (at least) premature. Most kids in his kindergarten class and the first grade was seven months to a year older then him. In Louisiana, you can start the first grade in August if you would become six years old before January 1 of the next year. Lane was a little over five and a half year old when he started the first grade. If we would have lived in Texas at that time, Lane would have been over six and a half before starting the first grade. In Texas you must have already become six years old before starting the first grade.

Although he seamed slow and marched to his own band, he never failed any class in school. He graduated high school when he was seventeen and a half. He received his bachelor degree in Political Science from the University of Houston when he was twenty-one and a half. He went on to get a Masters' degree in Public Administration at Southwest Texas University in San Marcos, Texas several years later.

Kent, Lane and Todd were all cute little boys. They went years before their first hair cuts. Many folks would congratulate us on the pretty little girls we had. We had this stroller with two seats for whenever we went shopping. Kent and Lane were fourteen months apart and did not look alike at all. Kent was always larger than Lane, so folks knew that they were not twins.

Todd came along four years after Lane. His baby pictures remind me very much of Kent when he was a baby. I think until the time Todd was about two years old he look like Kent did at that age. After this age, Todd started developing his own looks.

I have many stories to tell about Kent, Lane and Todd growing up. I will save them for when I write about my sons early years sometime in the future.

IN-LAWS MOVE BACK INTO BATON ROUGE AREA

In early 1978, my father-in-law was transferred back to the Baton Rouge District. He was still working for the Federal Deposit Insurance Corporation and still a bank examiner. He stilled checked the books of the Federal Banks to see if any crooked things were going on. The FDIC was the only branch of the Federal Government that earned its own way. They made money for the Federal Government instead of costing the tax payers money to run their agency. They put money back into the system. It is this agency that insured all deposits up to one hundred thousand dollars. This is why they had the right to go into and investigate the books of the Federal Banks. Banks paid them for the insurance coverage and also paid them to check their books. The crooked bankers went to jail. Several times, bankers, when they realized that the FDIC was in their bank to check the books, committed suicide. The inspectors would show up unannounced. They did not want the bank president to know that they were coming to his bank. This agency actually took over ownership of badly operated banks. They ran the bank until they could reorganize it than sell it to private enterprises usually at a profit for the agency. All hours and manpower and time spent while taking over and operating a bank was repaid by the bank assets to the FDIC. They got their money spent back and that is why they were a self supporting agency of the Federal Government. No other government agency does that today. They all and I mean all run on tax payers money. They operate on the backs of the folks that work in private enterprise. Many government employees will contend that they pay tax too. Yes they do, but they would like to forget that their salaries are made up from the folks paying taxes that work in the private sector. I have never come across a person at any level of government who pays enough taxes to pay their own wages. Have you? If you have, you are a DAMN LIE, and I am here to tell you that to your face. We have to damn many leaches on the government payroll. These leaches are in all local, state and federal branches of government. They are starting to out number the folks working in private enterprise. When this happens, this country will collapse.

Al moved back to Louisiana to run a pioneer audit program. This was the forerunner to the FDIC official program that would come out a couple years later. It was a minority lending audit for blacks and women. The FDIC would look into discrimination in the lending of money to blacks, women and other minorities. You had better have a very good reason for NOT lending money to those mentioned above. This was supposed to stop the bankers from discriminating because of race and gender under penalty of federal law. If a black had the collateral to pay a loan back, they should get the loan just like any white person. I truly believe this. It was way past the time for programs such as this.

Valerie and I found a place in the country for her parents to live. It had twelve acres of land and a three bedroom brick house. There was a one acre stocked pond on the property. This was OUR dream place. Only we could not afford to buy it. It was the place like I always wanted. I did not care for the redneck Parish that it was in, but the taxes was lower than in East Baton Rouge Parish. I guess that was the only bright side.

They purchase the place and move onto it in 1978. About a year later, I caught a five pound ten once bass from this pond. This was the largest fish that I had ever caught up until this time in my life.

This property was about fifteen miles from our house in East Baton Rouge. It was great to be this close. Any closer would have become a problem for my wife at this time. She was an only child and very much over shadowed by her parents. They had strong personalities and my wife would cow down to them

I really enjoyed the year plus that we had being this near to my in-laws. The kids loved to go to the country and fish or just run about and play in the large front yard or very large back pasture. My in-laws purchased ducks, geese, donkeys, chicken, banty chickens, peacocks, etc. They even came up with their own breed of banty chickens by cross breeding hens of one breed with roasters of another breed. In one of the floods that happened while they lived there, they lost most of their animals. It was really a sad situation. I really hated to leave all of this but when opportunity knocks, I had to listen and we made the move to Texas.

Barry, Kent, Valerie, Todd and Lane Raffray

PLANT UNION HELP US REGULAR OFFICE WORKERS

Working for Foster Grant Chemical was one of the joys of my life. I learned that I did not have the kidney disease anymore and got a job much closer to home and saved fifty-six miles driving each day and over one hour a day traveling time. It was just great being alive and having a future. I saved two gas fill ups a week at the station. This was money in the bank.

I worked two years before I got my first paid vacation. After two years working, I got two week paid vacation. After five years you get three weeks paid vacation. After ten years you get four weeks paid vacation. After fifteen years on the job, you get five weeks paid vacation. During the years that I work there, the union bargained for and got six weeks vacation after twenty years of service.

After fifteen years on the job, I would have gotten five weeks paid vacation, but I transferred to Bayport, Texas after twelve years. American Hoechst purchased all of Foster Grant the last day of December 1974. They decided to build and new nine hundred million pound styrene monomer production plant at Bayport. The vacation time was different at Bayport. Your paid vacation time did not accumulate as quickly. In fact you topped off with four weeks after twenty years of service. This is because this was not a "union" plant. We got additional vacation in Baton Rouge because we had a "union" plant. The union had to bargain for everything. Besides wages, they bargained for vacation, sick leave, insurance coverage, personnel day off, holiday off and holiday pay, seniority on the job, advancement, etc., etc. The union members had to pay for everything that was in the bargaining agreement. Whatever extra benefits that they received, they paid for. The office workers, of whom I was one, would get the benefit of some of what the union bargained for. From the Vice President on down, whatever the union workers got, we got, except wages of course. But things like medical insurance, additional vacation time, days off with pay, extra holidays, we got them too. I cannot say anything bad about the union. The union at this plant worked. I don't think that it was right that they did all the paying for and we got the benefits. But I also did not think that it was right the way I and other office personnel got paid either. After three months, a new hire in the union would get their first raise and make more money than I did after working there for over twelve years. This is just not right. Because I was not in the union, I feel that I got shafted along with most of the other office workers. I feel that I worked damn hard for the company. I made money for them. If I did not do a good job, they should have fired me. I felt like shit knowing a stranger being hired in the labor gang of the union will be making more than I did in three months. You can say that I was upset. So when the transfer opportunity came up, I jumped at it. It did not concern me that I will eventually lose one or two weeks of paid vacation. I was not taking all my vacation anyway. I just gave it back to the company.

This transfer opportunity came at a very good time for me. In 1978 I went to Mr. Sleeth and outlined the many jobs that I was doing and told him that the raise he had given to me just was not good enough. I told me that he had been working for forty years and never asked his boss for a better raise. He said that he would just quit and get another job. Well, he was telling me to not let the door hit me in the ass on my way out. I started calling around checking on jobs. When I got my next paycheck, it had an additional fifty dollars in it as did the one after that, and the next one and so on. He had given me an additional fifty. It was not enough. As we got into 1979, I was looking at two possibilities for job with two different inspection companies. It was during the time that I was talking with them that Mr. Sleeth mentioned I should take a trip to Bayport where the new plant was being built to see if I liked the area. I have gotten ahead of my story. I did not take one of the other jobs offered.

I worked for almost thirty years without missing a day of work for being sick. I did have some health problems. I got sick. I even went into the hospital in Baton Rouge in 1977 for three days one time. I always used my vacation time for this purpose. Call me STUPID- because I surely was. All this got me was making less money than when a new unskilled person came into the union. My work ethics in the twelve plus years at the Baton Rouge plant did get me the chance to transfer to the new location. Although I lost four weeks vacation in 1979, which was the year that I transferred, I was still happy to be in Texas. I just did not have the time to take the vacation.

After five years or so in Bayport, they added the one paid week of vacation and so after thirty years of service, I started getting six weeks paid vacation. I never did take all the vacation time due to me. Jon Huntsman purchased our plants in 1986. When I worked for Huntsman for thirteen years, the last three years, I sold some of my vacation back to the company and we could carry forward two weeks. This was a good deal for the employees who did not take all the vacation due during the year. I still did NOT take all vacation time due to me. After NOVA purchased the business, they stopped the buying back part of our vacation. We had to take it or lose it. I lost it. This was the same policy that existed at J & L Engineering in the 1960s.

WOMEN DOING "A MANS" JOB ???

During the 1970s and early 1980s, I saw several areas that were considered "Man's Work", where women came into the work place. It was a great time to be where I could see and help these women during their struggle for equal job rights.

TANK TRUCK DRIVER-EIGHTEEN WHEELERS

In the very early 1970s, while working at the plant site in Baton Rouge, Louisiana, I saw my first woman eighteen wheeler tank truck driver. I was still doing the bills of lading and paperwork for loads leaving the plant site. We had this load of styrene to be delivered up the East Coast. I set up the load with Matlack Trucking of Baton Rouge. The dispatcher there set it up as a back haul by a Yankee team. This means that a Northern driver team, two folks, had made a delivery into the Baton Rouge area. So instead of sending a Southern team to dead head one way, they used my order as a back haul for the Yankee team to get them back toward their base area. All good trucking companies tried to get back hauls with team heading that way so as not to return to their home base empty. Running these big tractor trailers empty was a costly situation and cut into profit. So the Central Dispatcher was always looking for a team to make a loaded back haul instead of going back empty. It was just good business to do so.

When the driver came into my office after coming into the plant, I checked his paperwork and notified the loaders and gave him directions to the styrene loading rack. About forty-five minutes later, he drove up from the loading rack, parked his truck, and came into my office with the loading papers that our loaders gave to him. I was working to finalize the bill of lading when all hell broke loose.

I heard the guard yelling outside my door. My office was the first that you entered coming from outside the building. It was set up this way so the truck driver would not be walking around in the office area. The guard had contacted Mr. Bob Capin, who was a boss in charge of something and they burst into my office and started chastising the truck driver. The driver was a bearded guy, well over six feet tall and about two hundred seventy pounds. It took a minute or two to find out what our guys were upset about. It seamed that the co-driver had been in the sleeper when the truck arrived at the guard house and drove into the plant area to be loaded. As the driver parked outside my office to get the bill of lading for the load, the co-driver got out of the sleeper and into the front seat and was brushing HER hair. That is right, HER hair. By God, this truck driver had snuck a woman into out plant. This was against plant rules. In fact it was the number ONE rule. NO WOMEN IN THE PLANT. The big truck driver said that the woman was his co-driver and his wife. And that they were a team and drove all across the country. Mr. Capin did not believe him and kept accusing his of sneaking a women into our plant.

By this time a large group of office and in plant workers were gathering outside the door of my office. The two loaders had come up from the loading rack to watch the action.

The truck driver started getting upset. I could see his face and part of his neck that was not covered by his black beard getting redder and redder. I saw a vein in the side of his neck getting larger. I stepped in. I out shouted Mr. Capin and the guard. I got everyone's attention. I told them if the driver's wife was the co-driver, she had every right to be in the plant. The driver went outside and got her CDL and showed it to everyone.

Capin and the guard left my office still upset. I still had the office crowd hanging around. I ask the driver if he would let his wife (co-driver), drive the rig out of the plant. I told him that none of us had every seen a woman driving an eighteen wheeler. He had calmed down and said "sure".

I apologize for all the commotion and explained again that we had never seen women tractor trailer drivers in this business. He told me that his wife was one of the first women to get a license.

He took his paperwork and headed toward his truck. We had about eight or nine on lookers now. We all went outside to watch her drive out of the plant. The guy went to the driver side and got in. My shoulders slumped down and I thought that he was pissed off and will not let her drive. He cranked the rig up and looked around. He saw us all standing there. He said something to his wife. He than got out of the driver seat. While he was walking around the tractor to get into the passenger side, his wife slide over into the drivers seat. We all got excited. She took off. She hit about four gears while still on our long entrance road before she got to Scenic Highway. Several of us ran through the gate to watch as she turned right onto Scenic Highway and heading toward Scotlandville. We could hear her change gears as they headed away.

After they left, Reggie and Smitty, the loaders, came into my office which is where they hung out when not loading something or otherwise doing their work. They had seen the woman get out of the sleeper just when they were finish loading the trailer. They knew that there would be fireworks when the driver got to the front of the plant. They did not mention anything to the driver. They said he was just too damn big. Anyway, it was not their job, so they hurried up to get to the front to watch the fun. They, just as the rest of us, did not know the woman was a driver.

Years later after moving to Texas, a lady named Mary Lloyd was my sales contact with DSI Trucking in Houston. Mary and her husband, K. D., were a husband/wife tank truck driving team in the early days when it was a novelty for women to drive these huge eighteen wheelers. Mary had a lot of great stories to tell us about when she was driving. She should write a book.

WOMEN WORKING IN THE PLANT

I still remember when the plant hired the first woman to work in the plant. This opened the door for women to come into the union as pipe fitters and carpenters. They later got jobs in operations, utilities and the plant laboratory.

I was very happy for women to see this happen. I was sad for our plant site because the management team in place could not/would not do this on their own. Our location was ordered by the EEOC to hire women and minorities. We should have done it on our own. Because of restrictions place on hiring practices, this location went about four years before we could hire a white man again. This was a disgrace. God knows that the Foster family who owned Foster Grant Chemical Corporation with headquarters in Leominster, Massachusetts, being Jews, would not discriminate against others. This was done by the local folks in charge.

FIRST WOMAN DECK HAND

Before transferring from baton Rouge to Bayport in late 1979, I saw the first woman deck hand who worked on a barge enter our plant through the guard gate to meet a tug and barge at out dock. Again the guard did not want to let her in and called me to the guard office. When I got there, Harris Chermie was jumping up and down because he was upset with our guard for not letting his worker into the plant site. Harris Chermie owned a number of tugs and worked for Arthur Smith Towing, Hollywood Marine, Alamo Barge Lines and others. This deck hand just happened to be Harris's wife. I told the guard to let him take her to the tug to work. Harris and I became good friends after this. When his boats were pushing barges headed to us, he would call me and give me the estimate time of arrival to our dock. He did not have to do this since he was contracted to the barge company that was supposed to call us. The updates by Harris really made it easier for me to plan our dock activity. He always had better updates than our barge contacts in Houston.

I had great times hunting ducks and fishing with Harris and his family members on several occasions in the Golden Meadow, Louisiana area. In fact he almost made me swim for my life one time in the mash of South Louisiana. After a morning duck hunt from a blind in the marsh, Harris had picked up Chuck Sweeney in a pirogue then came to pick me up. I could see with the two of them in the pirogue that it only had about one inch of freeboard. I told Harris that we would sink if I got in. He did not want to make two trips and told me to get in the damn pirogue or he would leave me there. I stood on the very edge of the blind, handed my empty shotgun to Chuck and put one foot in the pirogue. As I lifted the other foot to get into the pirogue, it went under water. Sweeney yelled. I placed my foot back on the blind and my other foot missed the blind and I went down to my crotch in the water and silt. Harris decided that we better not put three people in the pirogue and said he would come back for me.

I had one leg wet from my toes to my balls, but the other leg and the rest of me was dry. I was happy- sort of. I found out what looked to be the bottom of the marsh was actually just black silt. It was about four or five feet deep below the two feet or so of water. It looked like solid ground- but it surely was not.

MORE FIRST- MARINE, RAILROAD AND RAIL CAR LEASING SALES WOMEN

During these years, I met the first women who worked in sales for a large marine company, and the first women that called on me for a railroad company and a rail car leasing company.

Doloris Delsing was the Sales person for National Marine Barge Lines. This was a very large company at the time. Doloris had worked many years in several areas before taking over the U. S. sales responsibility. I had a lot of respect for what she accomplished. I believe she worked almost forty years for this company.

I also had a lot of respect for Mary Crotheris who made sales calls on me representing the Louisville and Nashville Railroad which was to later become part of the Chessee System Lines. Like Doloris, May had paid her dues holding down several jobs before getting the sales job. She did well in the sales position for many years.

I also had the privilege of doing business with Wanda Hall of General American Tank Car Leasing Corporation. Like the other two ladies above, she worked her way up through the ranks into a sales position. We did several contracts for new tank cars into our service with her. She did a very good job and retired after many years of service with GATX.

During the 1980s, more women became involved in distribution, transportation logistics, traffic scheduling and sales and services while working for major chemical corporations and manufacturers. Many other women worked in responsible positions in trucking, barging, railroading, petroleum inspecting, and container operations. For many years these were considered "jobs for men". These babes finally came a long way. And they had to work for it all the way. I know this because no man will give up "his" job to a woman. All these women had to have something on the ball.

A friend and business associate, Joy Lloyd, who is retired from Lyondell Petrochemical Company and now teaches at the University of Houston has a daughter who is an airline pilot for one of the major airlines. The women have come a very long way in business and the political world.

I believe there is still discrimination against them in many areas. But they are doing better in this country than any other place on this earth. This goes for all the other classes of minorities also. We should all work to stop discrimination wherever we find it.

MY MOVE TO TEXAS

In late 1979 I took a transfer to the Houston, Texas area. American Hoechst had purchased Foster Grant Chemical on the last day in 1974. They changed our name to American Hoechst in 1978. I think it took them a long time to decide to make the name change because of the Foster Grant sunglasses. Nobody every heard of American

Hoechst sunglasses. They had set up the sunglass division as a separate company then changed the name of the chemical company. In 1979, they were ready to expand our plastics business and purchased over three hundred acres in the Pasadena Industrial Development District near Seabrook, Texas. The area was referred to as Bayport Industrial District. Bayport was a developed deep water port for hazardous materials on the Houston Ship Channel route. It had a forty foot deep channel and could handle large barges and tankers.

I transferred there to set up our distribution system for product to and from this location. I became Manager of Supply and Distribution for the Bayport Works working with the Manger of Supply and Distribution for product from all production locations who worked in Baton Rouge. I needed to hire my support group which I did in late 1979 and early 1980 while the plant was still being constructed.

It had been decided many months before I arrived that this plant location will not have our own dock facility. I inherited a contract with Anchor Tank which became PetroUnited Terminals before we even started up our plant. Anchor Tank went bankrupt in mid 1978 and the company that started PetroUnited bought this location in 1979 and operated it under this name for many years.

My responsibility was for all transportation of our product by rail, truck, barge, containers, tank ships, and drums. I also was responsible for terminal operations and hiring inspectors, or anyone else that we needed services from. I was responsible for scheduling in all raw materials by barge/ship and coordinating all pipeline transfers between our plant and the public terminal. I had my department organized and set up when the plant started operations in April of 1980.

We started out with a great crew. I had Nell Davis, Nancy Hall, Joy Beadle and Tommye Jo Pennington. Thats right- four women. We had a good team and accomplished a lot of impossible things. As my friend for Shell Chemical, Mr. Bill Noak would say "the impossible take just a little while longer". My team had the know-how and the get up and go to make it happen.

BETTER SCHOOLS

My sons would have a much better education in grammar and high school thus creating more opportunities for them. Louisiana was home and I loved the state very much, but the state schools of education left a lot to be desired. My state was something like forty-eight ranked out of fifty states. I believe only Arkansas and Mississippi was below us in education. Texas on the other hand, was in the top ten states in the country and the Clear Creek Independent School district was in the top ten in the state. It was a very good area to be in. The NASA Space Center was less than a mile from my house. When there is an installation such as this in the area, it brings in educated professionals and the whole area benefits from it. High school teachers in this area had Master and Doctorate degrees. Not just education degrees that allowed them to teach. It was a great place to raise my sons.

My only regret was that they each were raised with a silver spoon in their mouths. If we would have been in the country, they may have learned what good old hard farm work was all about. If they were raised in a location where they had to get their hands dirty and put their backs into the work, they may have taken the opportunity for a higher education a little more serious and got the college degrees that I was willing to pay for.

I started going to night school in early 1977 in Baton Rouge. I took the world renowned Chicago School of Traffic course. It was a four semester transportation course. These classed were taught by Mr. Ralph Ware who worked for the Missouri Pacific Railway Company in Baton Rouge. He was the sales representative for our area. Ralph taught this course for about twenty years. He was very good with the rules and regulation of the transportation industry.

After completing this course in late 1978, I took two semesters of Interstate Commerce Commission courses. This was on ICC rules and regulations. The ICC rules were in the process of changing at the time because the United States Congress voted to de-regulate some of the transportation industry. So the rules and regulation were in the process of being changed. It was a very challenging course at the time I took it to say the least. Our instructor was Mr. Med Hogg who was a director with the Baton Rouge Port Authority. Med was an ICC Practitioner and being such could present cases before the ICC. Only a lawyer or and ICC Practitioner can present a case before the Commission. Med later became the number one guy in charge of all activity for the Baton Rouge Port Authority.

I received my diplomas and headed to Texas. I finished the ICC course one month before being transferred with my family to Texas.

After the plant start up and settling into the job in the first half of 1980, I decided to go back to night school. I went to night school in Louisiana and Texas for seven years. I was working full time and on twenty-four hour call seven days a week. I finally received my Associate Degree of Applied Sciences in Domestic Traffic and Transportation from Houston Community College in May of 1985. I was hoping that my boys, seeing what I was trying to accomplish, would be serious about trying to get a college degree when they got out of high school. Well, one of them did. Lane not only got his Bachelors Degree but have a Masters to go with it. I am still hopeful that Kent and Todd go back to college and get a degree in anything.

GOOD TIMES WITH MY TEAM

During the early days of my team in Bayport, We had some great times. We all became friends and went out together when away from work. With my wife and their husbands, we went to dances and dinners as well as Houston Oilers football games and Houston Astros baseball games and Houston Rockets basketball games. We did outings with our families as well. One time we organized a gathering to meet at Eddies Country Ballroom in Manville, Texas. We called business associates and co-workers to meet us out there for a big dance. We had fifty-two couples show up. Everybody had a great time. One of the girls husband brought some brownies which I just loved. After eating several of them, I was informed that I should stop eating them because they were laced with marijuana. I had never heard that term before so It had to be explained to me. I didn't know if they were or not, because I could not tell the difference. I know I had a very good time.

On another outing, a number of us took buses to a Louisiana horse race track a couple of times and had great fun there. These were chartered buses and usually two or three made the trip. Most of the folks on the bus were strangers to us. Tommye Jo Pennington's husband, Big Tommy Pennington was a great joke teller. On the bus ride to Louisiana, I believe Tommy told one joke after another for the two hours it took us to get there. I was his straight man. He and his wife were sitting towards the back of the bus and me and my wife was in the front of the bus. He would should out, "hey Barry do you know why such and such" and I would say, "no Tommy why such and such," and he would let the whole bus have the punch line. We had one hell of a time. Word got out of all the fun we had on the way to Vinton, Louisiana because after the races were over and we were boarding the buses to head back to Houston, almost everybody there was trying to get on our bus to head back. The driver had to get folks off the bus and tell the crowd that they had to ride back on the bus that they came on. Many people were pissed off. They had heard of all the fun we had on our bus and wanted to be a part of it. We had just as much fun going home as coming even though some of us lost our shirts at the track. The laughing made it a little easier to take. If you were on this bus, you were going to laugh. There was not doubt about that.

We made a second trip a couple months later and had even more couples coming along with us because they a heard of the great time had by all. We were all disappointed when Mr. Tommy had to cancel at the last minute because of an out of town trip. This trip just was not the same. Although I tried to fill in with some jokes, I could not take the place of Tommy Pennington.

In the early years, our gang consisted of Nell and Dexter Davis, Joy and Pat Beatle, Nancy and John Hall, Tommye Jo and Tommy Pennington, and Valerie and Barry Raffray. All the ladies except my wife, worked with me at the office. When we went out dancing, Putt and Harry Schneider and Chris and Carl Moran joined us or maybe we joined them. That Carl Moran was the dancing machine. He is still going strong at sixty-six year of age and still working full time at the styrene plant now owned my NOVA Chemical Company. Carl was one of the group who came over from the Baton Rouge plant in late1978 or early 1979, when the Bayport plant was being built. What a piece of work the guy Moran was. Note: Carl worked for forty-nine years for our company. Some folks wanted him to make fifty years. But Carl had had enough. After all, he was in his seventies when he finally retired.

Over the year the team members changes as did the name of our company. I was hired by Foster Grant Chemical Corp in the late 1960s. United Brands owned most of the stock in the early 1970s. American Hoechst Corporation purchased us in the mid 1970s. Huntsman Chemical Corporation purchased us in the middle 1980s. And NOVA Chemical Corporation purchased us on January 1, 1999 or December 31, 1998. I sort of went with the business. After each name change, I was asked to stay on and continue to do the job that I was doing. It would have been great for me to have all my years with one company. If I did I would be better off today. But the other side is, I was very happy to keep my job after each new owner took us over. My salary was never cut and I was able to raise my boys and give them as much education as they wanted at the time. I know many folks that lost their jobs after being sold to another company. I was very fortunate indeed.

THE BOONDAGGLES WERE JUST GREAT

Being the boss of a department that contracted for transportation needs was just great. Since I controlled a lot of business I had more than my share of invites. Like invitations to lunches, dinners, boat rides, plane rides, hunting of all kinds- birds, deer, hogs and fishing. There were many Major League baseball games, basketball games, football games (until the Oilers left town) and golf outings. About eight or nine golf outing a year is all that I allowed myself to attend. I just had to turn down the rest. I had to work exceeding hard to get the time to do these things. After a couple years in Texas, I had a trained crew that I trusted to make the right decisions if they could not get a hold of me. As I got older, I learned to count on my folks more and more to do there jobs right. In our business, transportation of water white hazardous liquids, one little mistake could cost millions of dollars. So believe me, there was pressure to see that every little thing always went smooth.

Over the years, the team members changed as did the name of our company. I was hired by Foster Grant Chemical Corp. in the late 1960s, United Brands owned the majority of stock in the early 1970s, American Hoechst Corporation purchased us in the mid 1970s, than Huntsman Chemical Corporation purchased use in the mid 1980s, and NOVA Chemical Corporation purchased us on January 1, 1999 or perhaps it was December 31, 1998. I sort of went with the business. After each sale and name change, I was asked to stay on and continue doing the job that I was doing which was distribution logistics- keeping all plant running with product. It seams like I just said that. Well, I just said it again.

It would have been great to have all my years with one company. I would be better off today if I did. But on the other hand, I was very happy to keep my job after each new owner took over. My salary was never cut and raises were slow in coming at times, but I was able to raise my sons and give then as much higher education as they wanted at the time. I know many folks that lost their jobs after being sold to another company. So I was very fortunate indeed.

I had to work exceptionally hard on the job to be able to do all these other things. No matter how much time that I was away from the office, I stilled averaged well over forty hours in the office per week over the thirty-three years plus that I worked for these companies. I lost many, many months of vacation time because I just could not take it because of the workload. Since I was a "hands on" guy, and planned everything on the computer, I just could not do this job from home, on the road, or by telephone. There was just no way.

Top: Barry Raffray in Breckenridge, Colorado playing in the snow
Middle: Barry with Grahm Schooley and George Mays
trying to hold him up getting off the ski lift
Bottom: Grahm to the left, George to the right,
Barry in the middle after being let go

Barge carrier fishing outing

Top: Barry Raffray and Micky Bell of Hollywood Marine with fish from Lake Guerrero, Mexico Bottom: Bob Dooley, Barry Raffray and Micky Bell with mess of fish the 2nd day of fishing

Home of the Mexican lady who cleaned the fish for us in that area

Ladies Golf outing in Houston. The guys were
the caddys - Barry have the red cap

AFTER RAISING SUGAR CANE | 181

Top: Deer hunting in West Texas with Hollywood Marine
Bottom: Hollywood Marine Golf Outing in 1993

Deer hunting with CXI Trucking group. Ernie Kenzina Mgr. is 3rd from left

BIG CHANGES OVER TIME

The communication devices made it possible to participate in more activities away from the office. The pagers and several years later, the cell telephone were great additions to helping remain in contact and staying on top of our business activities. It was a great time to be working.

We came from having a telephone and telex and twx in office and using sixteen column pads to plot our inventory and barge movements with the aid of pencils and erasers (which we used a lot), to the computer for inventory and barge movement and e-mail for notifications and pagers and cell telephones to be available twenty-four hours a day. Man, what a time to be working in this industry.

I witness railroad tank cars growing from ten thousand gallons (75,000 pounds of product) to twenty thousand gallons (150,000 pounds) to twenty-five thousand gallons (190,000 pounds net capacity), which was the maximum weight because of rail track limitations. I also witness capacities for tank trucks come from fifty-five hundred gallons (40,000 pounds of our product) to sixty-five hundred gallons (55,000 pounds of product). Again, this was the maximum amount set by

DOT and highway weight regulations. I was there when our barge movements changed from ten thousand barrels (3,000,000 pounds) of product) to twenty thousand barrels (6,000,000 pounds) to thirty thousand barrel barges (7,500,000 pounds of product). Many other changes occurred over the years that I worked in that industry.

The Federal and state governments got more involved in the business of transporting hazardous materials. This created new departments in all companies that produced and shipped or handled hazardous products. This created thousands of new jobs and continuous training for safe handling, packaging and transportation of hazardous materials. The rules and regulations were constantly changing. I am happy that I am not in the business anymore. It had become harder and harder and costlier and costlier to do business. More folks are losing their jobs because of cost at a time when more folks should be hired to do all it takes to safely ship the hazardous materials these days.

MOMS PASSING

Easter of 1980 was a terrible time. My family had been in Texas less than a year when my momma died. Momma had medical problems for the last twenty or so years of her life. She maintained a very good sense of humor during all this time. Besides the many major operations she went through, she had heart problems. On one of my visits while walking in the yard showing my wife the flowers, she stepped in a hole and broke her ankle. This added to her health problems and it took several years for the break to heal completely.

My mom was only sixty-six years old when she passed away. I did not believe that it was only her heart that did her in. But we will never know for sure. Daddy refused to let the Corner do an autopsy because she had been cut on so many times while she was alive. He did not want her to be cut on any more. I was concerned because all of my adult life until this time, I had heard about the Correl Curse. The "Curse" came into being because most of the women of this family died younger than normal. Both of momma's sisters died in their late fifties or early sixties. Her two brothers died when they were seventy-two years old. My Momma's momma died in her twenties. She and my Uncle Nolan were very young at the time. Her daddy remarried her momma's best friend, Maude Flemming and had two more girls and a boy. Momma's daddy died in his early fifties. The Quantrivez side of the family lived longer than the Correl side, except for my momma's momma. Just before momma passed away, we had spent several days in Louisiana and visited her in the hospital in Baton Rouge several times. She died the day after I got back to Texas.

I remember sitting the waiting room at the Baton Rouge General Hospital with daddy and my brother. There were several other folks there to visit a relative. The subject of crawfish came up. These folks had never eaten crawfish and could not understand why people from Louisiana did. Daddy and my brother was telling them how good they were and that they should try them just one time. If they did, they would like them and continue to eat them. After stating that, daddy turned to me an said "ain't that right Barry"? I said "NO". Daddy was shocked. I told these people that crawfish taste horrible. They taste like mud. If they liked eating mud, they would like crawfish. I could see by the way that they nodded their heads that they were agreeing with me. Daddy and my brother could not believe that I was saying this. I also mentioned to these folks that they should only use crawfish for fish bate. Use one at a time on a fish hook. They nodded in agreement. Then I stated, " every time we get somebody who had never tasted crawfish before to try them, the price I pay for them goes up". I continue with, " I have to pay more for them because the new crawfish eating folks started buying them and getting other new eaters to try them and that put pressure on the supply and the price went up and I had to pay more." I did not want any more non-crawfish eating folks to try them. If they use them for fish bate, there would be more available for me. You see, people eat more crawfish than fish do by feeding them one at a time.

My daddy and brother got the message. The folks in the waiting room did also and promised that they would NOT eat any crawfish while in Louisiana or any other location either. I was happy. I saved the price structure for this season.

We had arrived home late in the day. We all went to bed early because it had been a tiring week-end. My brother called early the next morning. The telephone awoke us. He told me the news. He was crying and so did I. This was on April 8, 1980.

Several of my friends that I worked with in Baton Rouge attended momma's funeral. We got several beautiful reefs from a number of folks from my old office and different companies that I worked with. I appreciated seeing Annis Peters and Margaret Arceneaux at the funeral. It was good of them to come. We laid momma to rest. I spent several days with daddy and then returned to Texas.

I talked with daddy a couple times a month. He was very lonely. He would cry on the phone. He really missed momma. When I went for a visit, we played bingo at several locations in and around Plaquemine, Louisiana. There was a bingo game going on every night of the week somewhere in the area. It was a good way to pass the time. Many older folks went to play bingo and visit with friends. They got a chance to catch up on gossip and maybe even win a buck or two.

DADDY REMARRIED

About two years after momma died, daddy met someone at bingo in Plaquemine.

Daddy met a number of ladies at the bingo games. One of them finally caught his eye. Her name was Fernna Judice of Plaquemine. I remember when he called me and said that he wanted to get married again. He asked if I would be all right with it. I told him to go for it. After all you are over three times seven, I said. Daddy had this saying when someone wanted to do something. Three times seven is twenty-one. At twenty-one years old a person is all grown up and old enough to make decisions for themselves. Right or wrong, they should make the decision then be man enough to live with it or pay and consequence because of it.

Daddy got remarried about two and a half years after momma died. He was seventy. Fernna was fifty-five. She had four adult children. He and Fern, as he call her, visited us in Texas a couple times. We had fun when they came over for a visit. Before daddy got remarried, he came over for a visit. While he was visiting, one of my sons had their annual after baseball banquet. We all went to a pizza place and had a sit down dinner and gave out awards afterwards. All the kids on the team received awards. Daddy was sixty-nine then. We ordered pizza. Daddy ordered a pasta dish because he had never tasted pizza. We got him to take several bites of pizza during the meal. After we finished eating and the awards were handed out, I asked him how did he like the pizza. "Well", he said, "it is o k, but I wouldn't order it in a restaurant". This meant that he did not care for pizza and I am sure that he never tried any again.

After daddy remarried, Fern went to work on him every day trying to get money out of him for her kids. She was very successful at this. My brother had daddy's journals where he wrote down everything that happened ever day of his life for over forty years. Fern's kids owed daddy many thousands of dollars that they borrowed from him as did other folks in the White Castle area. When daddy died on December 14, 1984, not one person came to us and said that they would pay back what they owed. Not even one. They thought that their debt died with daddy, I guess.

I was in Texas the two years that daddy was married to Fern. I thought that he was happy. I did not know what that women put him through.

My Uncle Nolan (momma's brother), continued to live with daddy after momma died. When daddy remarried, He and Fern lived mostly in the newer house trailer he and mamma had purchases some years before. Uncle Nolan lived in the older trailer. They had a trailer complex under the big live oak tree on Cedar Grove Plantation.

In the late sixties, because momma was in bad health, daddy purchased a two bedroom house trailer and moved it under a one hundred year old live oak tree on the other side of Cedar Grove store on the River Road. This was supposed to be a smaller place to live and get out of the ten room house. Momma would have less to take care of although I remember them always having a black lady helping momma most of my life on the plantation. First was Ida Washington who worked for us until she was too old to work. Then Sister Link worked for many years. I remember that Sister Link did all the ironing for us. Anyway, after the trailer was installed, daddy built a shed over it with a tin roof. He added a room to the back door and place a washer and dryer, deep freezer and closet was located there also. He also built a large screen porch on the front of it. It was about ten feet wide and over half the length of the trailer.

I lived in Baton Rouge at the time, so when we came down we stayed for the day and went back home at night. There was not enough room for my family to sleep over for the night which was the idea behind buying the trailer in the first place. Momma did not need to be doing for a bunch of people all the time. She was supposed to take it easy. My brother, sister and I supported them living in a trailer for this reason.

In the late seventies or very early in 1980, daddy had to buy another house trailer. He had to because momma wanted another one. The older trailer was still in very good shape, but momma wanted more room for family and relatives to sleep overnight.

They placed the new trailer in front of the old one in such a way that it looked like a T. The wall that enclosed the porch on one end was removed and an entrance was made and attached to the new trailer. We would still use the same entrance unto the porch. After getting on the porch, we went straight forward to get into the old trailer or went to the right the length of the porch to get into the new trailer. Momma had built her complex to a four or five bedroom, two bath, with a couple of living areas. Now family and friends could spend the night if they wish to because room was available.

Momma and daddy still slept and lived in the old trailer with Uncle Nolan. Daddy slept in the old trailer after momma died. When he married Fern, they moved into the master bedroom of the new trailer and lived there for two years until he died at the age of seventy-two.

It was during sugar cane harvesting time that daddy died. He was still working for the Plantation owners who were headquartered in Sulphur, Louisiana. There were two tenant farmers farming the plantation. They were Kenneth Hernandez who basically farmed Cedar Grove Plantation and Davis Callegan who basically farmed the White Castle Plantation. They had about three thousand acres between them. Daddy looked after the landowner's interest and worked with both of these guys. Kenneth was a pain in the ass and always wanted something for nothing. He was a good farmer, but you had to keep an eye on him. Davis was my best friend from the eight grade onward. He was raised in the cane field and was an excellent farmer. I cannot think of anything negative to say about this guy. Daddy like him very much. He was straight forward, honest and hard working. He did new things and raised crops in low land on White Castle Plantation where non was ever successful before. He also won best farmer awards for tonnage on a regular basis. Daddy knew that Davis would do right and respected the landowner's right.

JULY 1984- TUBING ON THE GUADALUPE RIVER

Why tubing? Why on the Guadalupe River near Canon Lake, Texas? Well, because Lane went a time or two with the Kimble family who lived down the street from us. Lane and David Kimble were friends. David invited Lane to go with them a year or two before we went. He really enjoyed his time there and told us all about it. I gave this some thought for some time. I decided to take some vacation time in July of 1984 to make it happen. At the time, Kent was over fourteen years old and Lane was over thirteen years old. Since this vacation called for pitching a tent and cooking outside and sleeping in the tent, their mother did not care to go. This is not her idea of what a vacation is suppose to be. She did not think our youngest son, Todd, should go either. He was nine years old then. I do not think he wanted to go either. If we were going to be in the Holiday Inn, they both would have probably tagged along.

I found out from Mr. Kimble the name of the place where they camped out. I even got the campsite number and the telephone number of the Meckels from him. The place was called The Meckel Ranch and was located on River Road. River Road ran along side of the Gradulupe River from near Canon Lake for about fifteen miles down river toward the town of New Brunfelds.

I made arrangement with Mrs. Meckel over the telephone to rent a site at their Lazy R and R campsite several months in advance. This area is so popular, that you must make arrangements months in advance if you expect to have a campsite available when you arrive there. I made our arrangements to arrive there on a Monday afternoon. This was on purpose so that the very large weekend crowds would have departed before we arrived. This way we would have the whole place to ourselves and just a few others during the week. We planned to stay there for three days. This would give me three plus days to rest up at home before going back to work

I had to plan for the time we were going to spend camping out. I purchased a five gallon plastic container for fresh water. I wanted to bring water from home because we probably would not like to drink the local water. Bottled water was not as popular as it is now. I would not have purchased bottled drinking water anyway. The boys knew that. Since I had all of the camping gear, such as tents, cots, folding chairs, table, stove, lantern, eating and cooking wear, ice chest, etc., I only needed grocery's and sodas. I never cared to drink alcohol when I went on picnics or camping or any other outing with my family- when I was driving. It is something I just did not do. I have seen other do it. They put the life of their families at risks. I was not going to do that with alcohol. The only other supply I needed or at least thought I needed was a couple of large inner tubes. I purchased two large truck tubes from Academy. I had them inflated and placed in the back of my pickup with all the other camping gear. I had a camper shell over the bed of my pickup that I could lock. I had this sucker loaded down.

We departed our house in the morning for the four hour trip. The New Brunfelds area is between Austin and San Antonio. It is much closer to San Antonio. We took NASA Road one and went West about five miles then took a right on I-45 and headed North to Houston. Just past downtown Houston, we took I-10 West and stayed on it until we were about fifty miles from San Antonio than headed North to the Canon Lake area.

We arrived early in the afternoon. We found the Mechel Ranch and the Lazy R and R on River Road. I paid for the three days camping. The spot we rented had someone in it still. They had until five p.m. to pull up camp. I was hoping that they leave a little early but those bastards stayed until five. We parked at the campsite next to them and waited for several hours. I should have gone back to the office and requested another site so we could unpack and set up camp. There was a lot of site available. But that just never occurred to me. I keep thinking that these folks would leave soon and that was the site Lane told me about. It had a little pier on the water. It was site number thirty-one.

The Mechels must have about a half mile of river frontage. The camp sites were toward the back one forth of the place. There was dust everywhere. The road to the site was about four inches thick with very loose dirt. Every time a vehicle past by the dust would fly everywhere. The campsites were on the river bank and the dirt was hard there. There was also a pasture area with grass on it on the other side away from the campsites. It was not used. There were no trees at all there. All the trees were along the river bank. Every fifty yard or so was an outhouse. They were located on the grassy side of the entrance road and away from the river.

After about fifteen minutes waiting there we could tell that these folks were not going to be leaving soon so we piled back into the truck and went for a ride to look about. Upon our return about an hour or so later, those bastards were still there just sitting around. At about five minutes to five, they started taking down their tent and loading their car. I could have bitten the heads off of ten penny nails I was so pissed. As they took off I was backing up my truck into their spot trying to get as close to their car without actually hitting it. I had some problems getting the tent set up. I was afraid that I would run out of sunlight before getting it all set up. This was a very large tent. It was over twenty by twenty feet and took some time to set up. The ground was so dry and hard, I had trouble hammering the plastic spikes into it. We got it just before darkness overtook us. This was before daylight saving time and the tall trees along the river and the hills in the distance made it get darker earlier. It got darker along the river before it did in the pasture. We set up our lantern and stove and made our beds up for the night.

Early the next morning I fried some bacon and cooked eggs for breakfast. We had a good hot meal. I just always seam to taste better when you are camping out than it does in your house for some reason.

I made the boys wait an hour before getting into the river. While they sat around waiting, I washed the dishes and cooking utensils.

As I was checking out our supplies I found out that one of the inner tubes that I purchased did not hold air. This was a pisser. When we road about the day before, I found out that you could rent tubes everywhere on the river for a couple of bucks a day. I rented two tubes at the office near the entrance. After getting the tubes, we walked over to the river which was only about twenty yards from the office to have a look at the river from this vantage point.

As I mentioned earlier, the river ran along Mechel's property for a half mile or so. It was straight from the River Road entrance to just past our campsite than it made a left turn and there were rapids just before exiting this property.

We walked back to our campsite with the two tubes that I rented and got into the water there. We drifted toward the middle. The Guadalupe River is not very wide. Less than twenty-five yards in some places. In South Louisiana where I was raised, this would be a large canal, not a river. We drifted around the bend and toward the small rapids. In the area of the rapids were a lot of tree roots that came about the water level. Just before exiting the Meckel's property, we paddled toward the tree roots and caught hold of them and pull ourselves toward the bank and then exited the water. This area has been used for this purpose for many years. We walked back to our campsite and got into the river again. We did this throughout the rest of the morning. We only stopped to eat sandwiches and drinks sodas for lunch. The ride on the river from this spot was about fifteen to twenty minutes. After an hour passed we went back at it until it got dark. We were tired that night and looked forward to a good nights sleep.

One of the problems that my sons had was using the outhouse. I used them when I was a kid when visiting and spending nights at Nan

Noon and Paran Charlie Pansano's house on Richland Road. So this was no big thing for me. You just have to hold your breath as much as possible. Get in and do your business and get the hell out. Kent had never seen a usable outhouse. Lane saw these the time that he was here last year. They did use it but they did not like it at all. When we were in the water, it was easy to pee without any body noticing, but doing the other, the outhouse had to be utilized. At night and during the day also, if nobody was nearby on land or on the river, we pee peed behind a tree. I almost got caught several times by folks floating quietly on the river.

The next morning during breakfast we planned what we were going to do. We decided to each carry a tube to the front of the property and get into the river there. This would make the river ride much longer. It did. It took thirty-five or forty minutes to make a run. This was much better but the damn walk in the hot dust to get up there was a bitch. After the first trip, I decided to drive the truck and park it at the front of the property. We placed the tubes in the bed and put towels on the seat and rode to the front. We had to walk again after all the other runs. We took a break for lunch. An hour after lunch we continued this routine for the rest of the second day.

When you are camping in this fashion and in the water and away from the campsite so much, you have to do things to try and guard and protect your personal property. For instance, we would put all the chairs, stove, lantern, pots and pans, ice chess and everything else inside the tent. I would zip close the tent. I had a small lock and key set that I used to attach the three separate zipper tags together. Of course a person with a knife would have cut my canvas tent open. But if a thief was lurking around I was hoping that they picked an easier tent to get into. We always tied down the window opening from inside during the day. We opened them up at night when there was not any traffic to stir up the dust.

Another thing you do is not leave any valuables in the tent. I kept my wallet with me in a zip lock bag in by buttoned down pocket. I kept my truck keys in another zip lock bag in another pocket. I did not worry any loose change. We also locked some thing in the cab of the truck.

One of the things that Lane had told us about was to ware long pants and tennis shoes and a tee shirt. You did this to protect yourself from the rocks in the river. When the water was running low, the rocks could cut you up pretty bad. We wore old blue jeans and tennis or canvas shoes. In late afternoon after finishing tubing for the day we put on shorts or swim suits and another tee shirt. We place the wet ones to dry overnight on the picnic tables. We put them back on for the next days tubing.

During this trip we went to Canon City to buy supplies. We drove on the River Road from one end to another. We checked on the prices for tubing and floating trips at various places. We also drove up to Canon Lake Dam Park. We walked on the levee holding the water in the lake from flooding the Guadalupe and all the folks and business places that lived and worked on the river. It was awesome.

The top of the water in Canon Lake is about seventy or eighty feet above the River. A certain volume of water is pumped from the dam into the river each day. This is the water that we tube on. In the middle of July and August, the water temperature is sill about fifty degrees Fahrenheit or below. It is very cold. You really have to get accustomed to it each time you get into it. The water is this cold because it is taken from about seventy feet below the surface of Canon Lake. The Canon Lake surface water is over eighty degrees Fahrenheit at this time of year. I wish the Guadalupe was eighty degrees. If it was, I would still be tubing in it. But as I've gotten older, I've gotten colder. This river is just to damn cold for me now-a-days.

The next day we departed for home hours earlier than our normal check out time. I wanted to get home while it was still daylight. I do not like driving at night. The day after we arrived home, I returned the bad tube and the good one back to Academy and got a credit on my account for the full amount. I knew that we could rent them for just a few bucks each day on the river. We had such a good time we decided that we want to go back in the future. And we did.

DADDY'S PASSING

I spent six days with daddy and Fern in early December 1984. Daddy was a little under the weather and was seeing Dr. Connie Major in White Castle. We played bingo at several locations at night and roamed the plantation during the day when I was not visiting with other family members or friends.

Two days before he died, we were again visiting with Davis Callegan in the field where his workers were hauling sugar cane. They were burning sugar cane across the road and daddy was being bothered by the smoke. He went sit in the cab of his truck while I visited with Davis. I told daddy that we could leave to get out of the smoke but he told me to continue visiting with my friend. This was a Saturday and I was leaving the next morning to drive back to Texas. I said so long to Davis and got in the truck. I asked daddy how he was feeling. He said, "pretty good". He just could not shake the cold he had and the smoke outside was bothering him. The next morning I said my good bye and departed for home. Monday morning I went to work early. My wife call me about seven forty five in the morning and said to come home and hung up. I rushed home, she was crying and the three boys had not gone to school and all had long faces. She told me that my daddy was dead. I just could not believe it. This was December 14, 1984.

I am thankful to God for many things. Two of them are that I was able to visit with my momma and daddy for some time the day before they died. Many people do not get that chance and regret it all their lives. I regret that I cannot remember if I told them how much I loved them.

Sometime after my daddy's funeral, my brother moved the old house trailer to his house for our Uncle Nolan to live in. He had the other trailer moved to a trailer park in Plaquemine for Fern to live in. We gave her the newer trailer and daddy's new car. Daddy had her included on some of our inheritance from my momma's Uncle Charlie Pansano. She must have pressured him into this. This account had been in the bank for many years and had nothing to do with Fern. This was momma's side of the family.

As I made each trip back to Louisiana to visit my brother and sister and their families, I learned more and more each trip about Fern and some of her actions while married to my daddy. I did not like any of it and had no idea of the hell she put him through. I thought that she was taking car of him and treating him good but that turned out not to be the case. I will not go into any details about her. She was not worth me spending any time here and bringing back memories that I don't want to recall. She even took my momma's coin collection, and ------- oh shit----enough already.

Newton Sr. and Josie Raffray graves in the White Castle, La. cemetery

IN 1985 A CHANGE WAS GONNA COME

Going into 1985 my momma and daddy had passed away. Going back to Louisiana for visits was never the same. When I had the time to go, my wife and kids did not. They were doing something else. It went longer between trips to visit my brother and sister and their families and my friends there. We were dwelling on ourselves more and more.

I was still going to night school trying to get an associated degree in the early part of this year. This took up much of my free time during the week. I even had a course or two on Saturdays during one semester but that was the only time I had a Saturday class.

Kent was 15, Lane was 14, and Todd was 10 and they all still were doing well in school. They had their friends and were having fun as far as I knew.

During June of 1985 is when I first heard that American Hoechst was really trying to sell our business. They had denied this in meetings and speeches made at our plant. The Baton Rouge location shut down production in 1982 and Brian Parsons and Harvey Bourgoyne (my boss in Baton Rouge), had transferred to Bayport in 1983 or 84. After restructuring our department, Harvey was my boss again. This was fine with me. Harvey was a good man and taught me so much in those years that I reported to him in Baton Rouge. I looked forward to working for him again. We soon heard that the name of the company that wanted to buy us was named Huntsman Chemical. I only knew one thing about them. They were very slow in paying their bills. Our corporate polymer folks did business with Huntsman several years before and it was reported that some problems occurred trying to get payment from them. It was very difficult keeping all the plants running during this time. Each month we were told that the sale to Huntsman was to happen within thirty days. Three of the ladies that worked for me were trying to be transferred into other departments. Two of them did transfer. This left me very short handed. We still had our internal plants and customers to supply. None of our plants were shutting down and need product to keep them running.

These were the hardest working times that I faced during my career. American Hoechst had laid off Brian Parsons but told him if he left the company before the sale to Huntsman was final, he would forfeit his severance pay which was a significant amount of money. Brian missed out on several job opportunities because of this action taken by Hoechst representatives. Brian had more than eight years of service with American Hoechst so the severance money due him was something he did not want to lose. He stayed and helped me throughout this horrendous ordeal. What a mess we had.

My boss, Harvey Bourgoyne, had retired. As soon as the heard that Hoechst was selling the Company, he put his name in for retirement. Harvey had more than 35 years in and was ready to move back to Brusly, Louisiana.

TUBING THE GUADALUPE IN 1985

Hear we go again. I made the reservations at the Lazy R and R several months before hand. This time Todd was ten and he decided to come with us.

Because there were four of us and we did not bring any truck inner tubes or nearly as much groceries, I used the station wagon instead of the pickup. We had a really comfortable ride to the Mechel's Ranch. It had not changed at all in the last year. There was still the dusty main entrance road onto the property. Just as before, once a day a water truck would come and wet down the road to help keep the dust down. Also just as the time before, Mr. Mechel came in the afternoons and spread lime in the outhouses. This helped very little to alleviate the smell but acted as a disinfectant for the body waste. Or in other words, the shit and piss. After signing in, paying and getting our pass card, we found our campsite. We unloaded everything and set the tent up. We locked up the tent, made sure that the ice chess was in the car and drove the five or so miles to the Canon City grocery store for supplies. We ate hamburgers while in town for supper so I would not have to cook this evening. Todd had looked at the outhouses while at Meckels. He went to check one out. He did not use it. He did his business while we were in town. The whole time there, Todd would not use the outhouse. He did get stomach cramps and I had to drive him to town once to use the toilet. I told him that I would not do that again. He never asked me again but still did not use the outhouse. Maybe he shit in the river- I do not know for sure. We all would find someplace to pee instead of using the outhouse. There is almost nothing better than peeing outside for a male. It is like being free and the world is yours to do what nature calls for.

It was still early when we got back from town and the boys got into the river in front of the campsite and played there. They did not ride on tubes because we did not have any yet. They played until almost dark. Oh, by the way, snakes are not a problem on this part of the Guadalupe River. This close to Canon Lake the water is just too damn cold for snakes.

The next morning, I cook a good breakfast. We all like to eat. At about ten a.m. we loaded into the station wagon and headed for River Road. I had decided that we were not going to waste our time walking from one end of Meckel's Ranch to another. We could spend that walking time riding on a tube somewhere else on the River. We went to a place close by.

You can rent inner tubes that have a section of three eights inch plywood tied to the center or for a dollar less get just the tube. The plywood tubes are set up so you sit on the plywood. Our butt will not scrape on any rocks in the low water areas. Some folks use them to tie their ice chess on. Others use them for their three or four years olds and a little older to sit in. They are really sturdy. I rented two with bottoms and two without. At the place where we rented the tubes, we paid a few dollars each for this company to ride us and the tubes to a starting point up river. We would get off the truck there and go into the water and float until we see their sign on the river and get out of the water at their shop. They had several large trucks and as their paying customers got out of the river and back into the truck they would again drive to the starting point and everybody does it again. Their beginning point could be two miles or so up river. It depends upon how fast the water is flowing as to how fast you get back to their location. They ran the trucks all day. When you pay for the tubes and trips, you make as many runs as you can or want to until the cut off time late in the afternoon.

Kent had his tube and would float ahead of us. Then I came next. I had a rope from my tube to Todd's tube and also a rope from Todd's to Lane's tube. We were tied together with about four feet between each of us. I wanted to keep us all together in this manner. Kent would have no part of it. He went on ahead. I did not like it because sometimes he wanted too go far ahead of us and sometimes I could not see him. Most of the time he led us to the shoots over the water falls. There are many areas that are very dangerous on the river. You cannot be too careful. Kent usually found the easier passage ways by watching the tubers in front of him. We tried not making the mistakes they made.

We floated down the river for at least two hours and did it again. It was much more fun being in the water for longer periods of time and then not walking to get back into the river again and again. We saw more of the river scenery also. We broke for lunch. We went back to our campsite and made sandwiches. After the one hour sitting time to let our lunch go down, we headed back to the same location to do the river again. After all, I paid for the whole day and we were going to get my money's worth. That evening, we again made sandwiches for supper, drank our sodas and listened to the radio or played games until it was time to go to sleep. We all slept good that night.

The next day after breakfast we headed out again. We wanted to try another place this time. We stopped at a small jobber this time. They advertised really good prices and were just getting their business started this season. The guy and women there were fixing up the little brick building that was to be their office. The guy was the helper. He was a retired Pasadena, Texas fireman. He was not much older than me. He was very young to be retired. But he had put in twenty years. He must have been in his very early forties. The lady and her husband owned the business. She was a nurse from Pasadena and was on vacation running and fixing up the business. Her husband was a doctor in Pasadena. She looked to be in her late thirties or early forties also.

I rented four tubes and paid their fee. We piled into the back of a truck with our tubes and off we went. This was a different area on the river than where we tubed the day before. We were further upstream. The boys did not want to be tied together. So much to my chagrin, I did not use the rope this time. We followed the same procedure as before with Kent in front than me then Todd followed by Lane. I did not want Todd to get more than ten feet from me at all times. We floated for about two hours the first trip. We did it again. The second trip I sort of got caught in the middle of the river and could not get to the right bank where the water was flowing without a waterfall. Kent had made it to the section and I could see Todd and Lane heading there also. I went over the waterfall. It was only about an eighteen inch drop. My tube stayed upright. I was happy that I did not tip over. I tried using my legs to kick me away from the waterfall, but could not. As the water was coming down from the higher lever, it caused a vacuum or sort of suction all along the waterfall. I tried kicking and using my arms to back stroke but to no avail. I was directly in the middle of the river. I thought that the river was over my head where I was. I was right. I kept trying to kick away by pushing on the edge of the rocks with my feet at the same time as back stroking my arms. I was getting tired and moving nowhere. I notice that all three of my sons were holding on to tree limbs or roots waiting for me to join them.

I gave a big kick and pushed away as hard as it could from the waterfall a couple of feet. But the vacuum sucked me back very hard and my tube got under the waterfall and I tipped over. I had a very nice pair of sun glasses on with a tie on string attached to it that I purchased just for this occasion. When I went under the water, my sunglasses disappeared never to be seen again. I had my eyes open under the water but could not see anything because of all the bubbles. I was deep all right, very deep. I reached my left arm/hand above my head out of the water and just happen to feel my tube. I kicked my legs and came up and grab hold of the tube with both hands. I got my head above water and took a deep breath which I was very thankful for. I was really tired now. While holding on to the tube with my left arm, I use my right arm and legs and feet to pull and kick in the water. I was finally moving toward the far bank and away from the deep part of the river. At last, I can touch bottom. I crawled to the shallow area and sat on my tube in the rocks to get my wind and some of my strength back. I sat there for several minutes than got on my tube and drifted toward the middle then right side of the river where my sons were still holding on a waiting for me. I do not know if any of them saw what just happened. I tried to act cool. But the truth is I could have drowned right there. It was just fate or divine providence that my hand hit the tube when I was under the water. I do not think I would have made it without that inner tube. Until this day, I still have the sunglass case and two extra lenses that came with those nice sunglasses that I will never see again.

We continued on down to our getting out of the water location. We went to Canon City for burgers for lunch because we was closer to town than our campsite. A little over and hour later we were back. We made two more trips on this section of the river. The third trip we made in about an hour and a half. I was racing with Kent and the other boys tried to keep up too. We were back stroking and getting more speed than the current was taking us. Todd stayed at the office for the fourth trip. We again made in record time. I know it was a record because the owner told me so. We made four trips and had time to do one more. She said we tied the best efforts of other folks and if we made another run we would have done five trips. Nobody had ever done five trips there yet. I was willing but I did not whine when Kent said "no mas". He was ready to head back to the campsite. Lane had already decided that he would sit it out with Todd if we did another trip. So we settled for a tie with a number of other folks.

The next day we headed to New Brunfelds to go to the Slitterbaum. It is a huge water park with rides, pools, concessions and the Comal River running through it. It is fairly expensive. We spent the day there. I went down the big water slide several times. But I really enjoyed the inner tube shoot and rode the tube down it many times. At the end of this ride was the Comal River. The wonderful green warm water of the Comal awaited you as you come flying off the fiberglass shoot/slide. The main trick here was to stay on your inner tube as you went airborne and landed in the river. Over fifty percent of the riders were thrown from their tubes. I had a great time just watching the people hit the water. The expression on their faces when they hit the little rise at the end of the shoot that lifted them into the air was priceless. All of the first time riders did not expect this. I seen some females get the tops of their swim suits pushed down as they flew head first into the river. When they came up for air, they were struggling to pull their tops back up at the same time as trying to get a hold of their tubes. Some of the smaller kids came flying off the tubes with their arms and legs waving in the air aimlessly. Some of them were trying to run in the air.

How did I do, you ask? I did very well. I came off my tube only one time. That was my first time on the ride. This is not bad because I made this run many times. I watched the action here for a long time before I tried it. The trick to staying on the tube when it hit the Comal

River was to lift the front end of your tube slightly just as you are coming off the shoot. This made for a much smoother landing. The time that I flew off my tube I was spending around in the shoot and I come off it backwards and could not lift up the landing end before I hit the river. This is the other trick to this ride. You have to try and right yourself to coming down the shoot feet first before you get to the end of the shoot. After your tube hit the river, the current moves you toward the bank where you have to get off your tube. The workers collect the tubes and you can get back in line (if you want to) and do the ride again. The workers keep a supply of tubes going to the top of the tubing shoot which is the starting point for this ride. There must be over one hundred fifty steps to get to the top platform starting point. This ride is so popular that you usually get in line and move up one step at a time and wait your turn at the top of the steps. It goes fairly fast. There may be a fifteen to twenty minute wait before it is your turn again I really liked this ride.

The Comal River is pretty. It flows slower than the Guadalope and the water is warmer also. The Comal River is off a shoot of the Guadalope River. Many people spend their vacation on the Comal River tubing and canoeing and such.

We headed for home the next day feeling refreshed and clean. With all this water how could we not feel clean? These rivers in this part of Texas are very clear with rock bottoms. You can see your feet in three feet of water and also see fish under the surface.

1986 A BIG BAD YEAR

Going into 1986, my wife had her career and I had mine. We were headed in different directions. She could/would not take vacations when I did and would not let me know her vacation plans until the day before she left. I could not make arrangements to get off that soon to accompany her and the kids. I guess I should have figured something was up but I didn't.

We drifted more apart and just stop communicating with each other. The kids surely noticed something was up. We would bump into each other in the hall of our house and say "excuse me", and go on about our business without saying another word or involving the other person.

This built up to such a state that my wife would recall things from twenty years before that was so trivial at the time but she dwelled on them so much her memory became something terrible and twisted. Of course her recollection was all about my actions when our kids were born or not wanting to go out to dinner with the family or not wanting to replace the shitty carpet in the house or not wanting to buy the kind of expensive car that she wanted, or about this, or about that, etc., etc., etc. She blew all these and other things out of proportion. This showed her mindset and how she must have spent much time brooding at this time. She twisted my comments and changed the context and manner of statements that I made in the past. She would not accept the fact that I went to the doctor and was on medication when I did not feel like going out to dinner when her parents were visiting us one time. It was Lane birthday and I should have gone anyway and thrown up all over everybody. I did visit my doctor that very day. She refused to acknowledge that I told her I would buy new carpet when she stopped letting the Old English Sheep dog and the other dog sleep and use the house for their bathroom. My thoughts were why buy new carpet that will become shitty in three to six months. Besides she was making thirty-five thousand dollars per year. She could have purchased new carpet anytime she wanted to. She was making money and became independent but surely did not want to spend any of HER money on the house. I wonder if she had other plans, huh. I guess she was socking HER money away and wanted me to spent our (my paycheck) money on new carpet and other things.

We lived on what I made. I paid all the bills. Her income was suppose to be extra, except I did not see it. I even purchased IRAs to the maximum allowed by law in her name each year because she refused to use HER money to do it. This was when you could deduct two thousand dollars per person from your income tax. My income was our money. Her income was her money to use as she liked. I purchased the IRAs with our money for each of us as long as it was an allowable deduction from our income tax. I built her account to over twenty thousand dollars before we split up.

We put up with each other as long as we could and then some. She had her friends at work and I had mine and never would the two meet again. This is how she wanted it to be. You should keep in mind that I am telling this story and this is what I remember. For balance you would need to ask my ex-wife her thoughts on this subject.

THE SALE OF OUR BUSINESS TO HUNTSMAN

The sale finally happened during May of 1986. I started doing work for Huntsman while still on the American Hoechst payroll in February of this year. I was in charge of all the distribution of products during what was call the transition period which was part of February, March, April and the first week of May. I began working for and being paid by Huntsman on May 6, 1986.

I received my Associated Degree in Applied Sciences for Domestic Transportation from Houston Community College in May also. After being hired by Huntsman Chemical, I never went back to night school to get a bachelor degree. I just did not have the time to do so. Huntsman spread their workers thin. It was exciting to say the least. Harvey Bourgoyne took retirement from American Hoechst in September of 1985. Brian Parsons stayed to work with me for Huntsman. The other ladies on my team transferred into other jobs before the sale transpired. Some of the other folks retired or were laid off by American Hoechst.

The deal was, if Huntsman offered you a job, you had to take it or receive no severance pay from American Hoechst. You only got severance pay if Huntsman and Hoechst did NOT want your services.

In other words, you were forced to go to work for Huntsman if you wanted to or not if offered a job from them. This was the deal. This deal really stunk. It did not set well with many folks. I found out years later that several folks sued Hoechst individually and received settlements because of the company's action. Of course this was not publicized at the time or I would have filed against them also. I believe the settlement made by Hoechst was on condition that the person never divulged that they received anything. Some of my best friends did not mentioned a thing about this to me. They knew how I felt about the whole situation. But nary a word. I later re-evaluated who would be my "best friends" after finding out about how that all came down. I was pissed-off. The way I looked at this was that Hoechst did not want me and using the severance plan that they offered to others, I would have received just over twenty-five thousand dollars in severance pay. They still owe me and I guess always will.

I was working from sixty to seventy hours a week for Huntsman to try and keep everything moving. We came down from five in our department to two. It was really stressful but I hung in there and kept all the plant and customers running. I was just elbows and assholes the rest of the year and from then on.

1987

Some of the Christmas holidays my family went through from 1986 thought 1989 is a blur. I just do not remember if I went with her and the kids to her parents, stayed home by myself or went and visited with my brother and sister in Louisiana. The kids would usually go with their mother if she went somewhere. Lane was the only one to come with me on several occasions.

During 1987, I worked and worked and worked. Kent and Lane were in high school. They were attending Clear Lake High. As far as I knew they were doing alright in school. Their mom and I were still not communicating very well. We were sleeping in the same bed but not much was happening between us. I was not having very much fun at home. We made it through this year in the same house. I went to work in the dark and came back from work in the dark. It was not unusual for me to spend twelve of more hours at the office each day Monday through Friday. I usually went in for five or six hours on Saturdays or Sundays. If any of the boys were playing sports on Saturday, I usually worked with the coach at the game and went to the office on Sunday to do some catching up.

As far a working was concern, I thought that I had to work sixty to seventy hours a week to make everything go right. I always felt like I was a little slow so I needed to work more hours to make up for what I could not accomplish in forty hours. I tried to make good, un-rushed decision that would not cost us later. I worked on getting things right the first time-so it took me longer to do a particular job. My door was always opened for everyone who came by with their problems. If someone visited with me for an hour or I had a meeting for two hours, I felt compelled to make up the time by working over. I felt this way when I went out to lunch or golf outings or any function away from the office. I worked past quitting time to pay the company back for the time that I was away from the office. I did not want anyone to say that I did not put in my forty hours per work for any reason. I even kept up with the hours that I worked past the usual quitting time at the office each day. I have these records for almost a twenty year period. No, I never got paid for overtime. I just kept a record of it for me.

During my thirteen years plus with Huntsman, I spent more overtime at work than ever before. For a number of these years, I put in more than six hundred hours a year above the forty hours per week. I usually loss vacation time during these early years when working for Huntsman. One time I figured my time on the job when working for Huntsman. When counting a work-week as forty hours, in my thirteen plus years, I worked over seventeen and a half years. My eighteen plus years with Foster Grant/American Hoechst would equate to over twenty-five years of service. What a stupid thing to do.

All this working overtime without pay is what I am talking about. I stayed away from my family to much time. I was caught up in building a career that me and my family could live very well on and be proud of. I did not want to be remembered as a person who just wanted a paycheck. From my very first day, I rolled up my sleeves and dug in. The only problem was, I never stopped to catch my breath or to smell the roses- as the saying goes. Even after my boys were born, I never slowed down at work. I should have taken more time off and helped my wife out more around the house. But I was the bread winner. I thought that I had to keep working like a dog to show my bosses that I was a worker with more mouths to feed and they should think twice about laying me off. They would have to hire three people just to get the work done that I do. This worked great for thirty years, until Nova Chemical purchase our business. Nova Chemical - now that is another story that I will not go into and this time except to say that they have a great severance package. I believe Nova has the best package for a person loosing their job than any other company in the United States.

BIG CHANGE HAPPENED

During 1988, my wife moved out and got her own place to live. She had been working since we arrived in Texas in 1979. She started working full time a couple years later. She had her friends and was making very good money and became independent. She did her thing and I did mine with my friends at work. At the time she moved out, we had not had sex in over a year and a half. She had not touched me in an intimate way in over six years. When I state that we did not have sex, I mean with each other or anyone else. I did not have sex with anyone else and I believe that she would not do such a thing either. We did sleep in the same king size water bed, but never touched each other all this time. Was it hard? You bet it was hard. Every damn night it was hard.

When she moved out, the boys continue to live with me in our house. I cooked four or five nights a week. I learned about that cooking in a bag in the oven. It worked out really well. I could do pork chops, beef roast, chicken, meat loaf, beef with potatoes and carrots, pasta dished and much more. We ate a lot of vegetables from cans also, and also a lot of rice from box dishes, and pasta from a boxes as well. We had pizza from a box and home made poboys and sandwiches on weekends. We did not go hungry.

I kept the boys in school, fed them, and clothed them. I washed and dried the clothes and bed linens on week ends with their help. I did all the yard work. None of them could do it to my satisfaction. All these things I had done throughout my marriage except the cooking. I just had not done it all. I was used to washing all the clothes in the house and cooking some meals and cleaning, and vacuuming and dusting, etc. etc. I guess I can say that I did most of the cleaning inside the house and all of the yard work outside the house and all of the maintenance on the cars. I used to change the oil and filters myself until about this time. Kent and Lane were in high school and Todd was in the eight grade. Todd was as big, I should say bigger than his older brothers at this time.

We went on like this for over two years. We were separated with no hope of getting back together. I had a lot of hope but it was one way hope. I still do not know what her problem was. Anyway, she did not want to come back. I do not know what she did or with whom she did it with over those two years. We were both on our own. I do know that I had a fling or two or three that kept me going for a while. Than I sunk into a deep depression as time went on.

THANK GOD FOR RON AND REGGIE

Soon after my wife moved out, I withdrew from after work get together and just socializing with co-workers and friends. I was working seventy hours per week on a regular basis. I did not ever seam to catch up. I would work to nine and night on Fridays, stop by Whataburger for dinner and go home. Generally I was in bed by ten thirty every night. I was still living in the big house. My sons were living with me. I was just withdrawing from society. I could not make myself go out. It was like everyone would point and say "he could not keep his wife happy", or "what is wrong with him, he was married for twenty years and his wife moved out". It was really hard. It is the only time that I was glad that my momma and daddy were not alive to see this happen to me and my wife.

Ron Gedye worked for American Hoechst at Bayport where I worked and Reggie Hurr worked there as a contractor. Ron's wife of thirty years or so had a crippling disease and died. It was really a sad situation. They had two grown daughters. Ron lived two blocks over from me in Clear Lake Forest subdivision. We had worked on a project or two. He was an engineer and we really did not spend a lot of time together. We both knew many of the same folks that worked at different facilities for Hoechst because we both had been with them so long. Before coming to Bayport, Ron worked at the Peru, Illinois plant which was one of the locations that I kept running with our product.

Ron had a very different personality than mine. He was really outgoing and after a time, He would invite me out on Friday nights to cruse the NASA Road One night clubs. I would say "no, thanks". He started coming over to my house after I was in bed on Friday and Saturday nights. He would pester me until he got me out of bed. I would get dressed and we would go out. We would meet up with Reggie Hurr who had been divorced for some time and would become a three sum. I met a lot of ladies because of Ron and Reggie. Sometimes both Ron and Reggie would show up and get me out of bed to go out dancing. After a long while, I started dancing and meeting people. They finally got me out of the funk that I was in. It got to be fun. We did this for a couple of years. Ron got me to sign up for country dance lessons at the College of the Mainland in Texas City with two of the ladies that we were friends with from Clear Lake. During the eight weeks of lessons, Ron got transferred to Louisiana to clean up a site and Reggie took his place in the dance lessons. We were suppose to learn six or seven dances. Like the Cotton Eye Joe, Texas Two Step, Texas Walze, Shottish, and others. I cannot do any of these dances today.

After Ron moved, Reggie would come by the house and get me. We would work the NASA Road One clubs and have a good time. Reggie began dating on of Ron's close friends that we took dance lessons with and stopped coming by my house to get me. I went out a number of times on Friday and Saturday by myself, but it just wasn't the same. So I stopped running down NASA Road One and moved to League City not long afterwards. I tried the League City night clubs, - two, I believe. But soon I withdrawn back into my shell and stayed home.

The dates I had, was with ladies that I knew by business association or from work. I dated off and on for several more years until 1993 when I started dating Sarah.

I want to acknowledge Ron and Reggie for getting my life going again. I was really in the dumps and do not know what would have become of me if not for these guys. There were several times before these guys pushed their way into my life, I sat on the edge of my bed with my daddy's pistol in my hand.

Ron Gedye and Reggie Hurr

It was always loaded. I had this pistol to my head a number of times. Of course I never pulled the trigger. I would not be here if I did. I can understand the despair that people who commit suicide feel. I am against suicide one hundred percent but I understand what they feel. I think that the ones who do it are cowards. I thought about it enough times and had the opportunity and frame of mind to do it but I always thought about my sons. What would become of them? What will they think? How will they turn out? If I am not around to see them grow up - will they grow up? I wanted to be here in case they needed me and to see what they make of themselves. I am very happy to say that they turned out O K, and so did I.

I will state this again. Getting out and meeting people with Ron and Reggie but life back into me again. I have never had any more thoughts of suicide since that time. I not only want to see how my sons turn out, I want to live a long life with Sarah. I am very interested in seeing how my step sons make out. And I am hopeful that one of these two guys will make me a grandpa one day. It doesn't look like any of my sons will make me a grandpa anytime soon. They don't seam to want any offspring's to springs off of them.

DECEMBER DIVORCE 1989

My wife filed for divorce late in 1989. This was after my two oldest sons graduated from high school. The youngest, Todd, was now in high school and the only son to be considered in the divorce settlement.

At the time of the actual divorce in December of 1989, my oldest son was in the University of Texas at Austin. My middle son lived on campus and was attending the University of Houston in Houston. I was paying for both and most if not all the expenses. After living with me for more than two years, my youngest son decided to live with his momma in a complex on Clear Lake and NASA Road One. I paid her six hundred ninety- five dollars per month for child support for the boy. They/she must have blew the money because a year or so later, after she lost her job and decided to move back to Louisiana with her parents, my son came to live with me. He did not have any money saved from the amount she garnished from my wages. I offered the pay her each month but her lawyer went to the courts instead to make me pay to set up a garnishment plan and to get the amount we decided upon by garnishment. I also paid the state each month to take my money and send it to my ex-wife. The boy not only had no money but had got into the bank account that I started for him when he was born and had spent over half of it. He spent over fifteen hundred dollars of the amount that I scrapped up each year to add into this account for him for college. His momma did not put a penny in it. I regret giving her the account booklet to manage. How could she be so stupid as to let a fourteen year old kid spend all this money besides the amount I gave to her each month. I also paid the insurance coverage for him each month. Maybe she was living to high on the hog. She was making over thirty-five thousand dollars per year. This was very good money in 1989. I also paid her over eighty-three hundred dollars a year in child support. She had only her. She did have expensive taste and liked gold jewelry. I just don't know about her anymore.

I had been trying to sell our house for some time. I had repainted the complete inside. I had painted the outside several years before the divorce so it still looked very good. I had repairs done to the house and garage. I had the house completely re-carpeted. Both of our dogs had passed on a couple years before, so I did not fear that the house would be messed up while we were trying to sell it. The beautiful oak wood floors in the family and breakfast rooms were damaged by dog pee pee. They had to be covered by throw rugs.

I should have tried to keep this house. I think I could have pulled it off. But just me, and Lane, who attended the University of Houston, lived there. Lane was only here on weekends. I would pick him up Friday nights after I left work and bring him back to the campus on Sunday nights. He did not drive - yet.

SOLD BIG HOUSE IN 1990

We finally sold the house in early 1990. I divided the money with my ex-wife. We had gotten together some months before and put a price on everything we jointly owned. I paid her for the furniture and dishes and pots and pans and appliances etc., etc., etc., that she did not want.

When I started working at Foster Grant in the late 1960s, I purchased U S government saving bonds by payroll deduction every month until a year before our divorce. I planned to give her a bond than me a bond and so on until we divided them all up. Well she went into our joint bank account and took one half of the current value of the bonds in cash out of our account. She worked in the trust department of a nearby bank, so she really knew what she was doing. I trusted her and did not think that she would do something like this. She told me that I could have all the bonds. The only trouble was that her name and mine was on all these bonds and I could not transfer them into my name even if she signed papers to let me do it. The bank said it could not be done. To get her name off, and after what she did, I wanted her name off, I had to cash them in and add the amount to my income tax. I had to add about seventeen thousand dollars to my income tax and it put me into a much higher tax bracket. She had already taken over eight thousand dollars in cash out of "our savings account". We had been filing separate income tax returns for two years. She stuck it to me good. This cost me about six thousand dollars in taxes. What a bitch, huh. Since she got the cash, she did not have to pay any extra taxes.

Back in 1979, we purchased the house for one hundred one thousand dollars. I spent over thirty-one thousand in repairs on it in the eleven years we lived there. We sold it for one hundred eight thousand dollars. With seven thousand dollars going to the real estate agents, I figured that we lost thirty thousand dollars. After it being on the market for over six months, this was the best offer we had. It was the only offer we had. My ex-wife was advised that we could get more. If I tried to buy it, they wanted the price to be higher, so I would not do such a fool thing. She finally approved the sale amount. I was not going to pay her more than her half of this amount.

Did I mentioned that the two years plus that we were separated, I continued paying the house note and taxes plus any and all other bills associated with owning/buying a house. Anyway, I took my half of the sale of the house and put it all down on a smaller house in League City. This got my house note down to about six hundred dollars a month with taxes and insurance included.

So we sold this big four bedroom, large den, living room, dining room, breakfast room, utility room, roof covered patio and two car detached garage with walkover cover, with two and a half bathrooms house. This was a twenty-five hundred square foot living space house. I did not need a big house like this for just me to live in so I purchased a fifteen hundred fifty square foot, three bedroom house with garage attached, in League City. This was in early April of 1990. It was just going to be me and Lane (from the University of Houston) on weekends.

Within two months after I moved into my small house, I had all three sons living with me.

In 1991, my ex-wife loss her job and was moving back to Louisiana and my youngest son did not want to go so he moved back with me. I continued to pay child support to his momma for three months after he moved until she notified the lawyer to change the paperwork. Actually I paid her lawyer to change the paperwork to stop taking child support from my paycheck.

Well before my ex-wife loss her job, my oldest son decided to drop out of the University of Texas and moved in with me. Within two months of my buying the house in League City. My middle son who lived on campus for two years decided to live at home and drive to college each day. The University of Houston main campus was only twenty miles from my house. The order of these events was like this. My middle son lived at home all week now, so he got his choice of bedrooms. My oldest son came home, he got the third bedroom. Then my youngest son moved in. These boys were not used to sharing a room and did not want to do so now. My youngest son slept on the sofa in the living room for the next two years.

TODD MISBEHAVING

Although we now lived in Clear Creek High School district, my youngest son insisted on going to Clear Lake High school and I let him. I got an apartment within walking distance of the school. I paid for it for nine months just to be legal and keep Todd in that school that year. It was his ninth grade year and all his friends from The Seabrook school were attending there.

The next school year I purchased a 1987 Ford Ranger pickup truck for Todd to use to continue to go to Clear Lake High school. He was adamant about not going to Clear Creek High school for his sophomore year and I cave in to threats and tantrums to try and appease him. He was really having emotional hard times. I knew that we were not suppose to live in the Clear Creek High district and attend Clear Lake High but I wanted Todd to be near his childhood friends. Todd did not give the school his change of address. I did not realize this and never thought of checking up on it. During the year things were happening but I was not getting any notice from the school because they mailed information to the wrong place and called the wrong telephone number. It took me many months to catch on to Todd's skipping classes. When I caught him, we/he decided it was best for him to move to Louisiana to be with his mom. I moved him to the Denham Springs area the next weekend. He and his mom lived with her parents out in the country on twelve acres of land. It had a one acre pond with nice size bass in it. Todd lived there for about two years or so then came back to Texas to attend college which I paid for.

LAS VEGAS TRIP IN 1990

My brother and I made three trips to Las Vegas. Our first visit was in 1990. The second visit was in 1994. Our third visit there was with our wife's in 1997. This writing is about the 1990 trip.

Some time in late 1987 or early 1988, I purchased a package deal for two to a Las Vegas casino. I did it so my wife and I could go on this trip together. It was for sort of a get-a-way surprise for her. Neither one of us had ever been there so I thought it would be fun and maybe we could rekindle the old flames and start communicating better again. This package was to a casino named Vegas World. It had a two year expiration date. I paid three hundred ninety-eight dollars up front. If we did not use it within two years, we would lose the payment and the trip.

As it happen, conditions worsened around the house and she refused to go to Las Vegas - with me. I sort of forgot about it because of everything else happening at the time. As it were, during the year of 1988, conditions had not improved between us and my wife moved out of the house and into an apartment nearby. This was her way of sending a message to me. She did not want any of our sons to accompany her so they stayed with me. She would still come by and we visited often for the next two plus years.

During this time, my package deal to Vegas World expired. I only realized it when the casino sent notice of that fact. I telephoned them and asked who I could contact about my situation and why I did not make the trip. I wanted to get my time extended if at all possible. I was informed that I could write a letter to the Comptroller of the company. I did write to the guy and explained the situation of my wife leaving me and just forgot about the package deal. I mentioned that I knew that they were good business folks and would understand and should show some empathy for my situation. They actually extended my time for another year but were sure to mention that they would not do so again.

After getting this good news, I went into action to try and get someone to come along with me. I called my brother in Louisiana to ask if he would be interested in making the trip with me. He could not give me an answer right then. He needed to talk it over with his wife. Another problem for his consideration was that we would fly to Vegas. He had never flown before. Still another consideration was that if we flew from Houston, he would have to drive from his house to mine. He had never made this trip to Texas by himself. It is a four and a half hour trip normally but when my brother drives, it is a six hour trip. I mentioned to him that perhaps I could drive to his house and we could fly out of Baton Rouge which was about 30 miles from his home. Another consideration he had to make was, I would buy the airfare tickets (airfare was not included in the package) and expect him to pay half. My brother is very frugal. I also mentioned to him that the package included one thousand dollars in Vegas World casino money to use in their casino. I would give him one half of the Vegas World money to gamble with. As I am very frugal also (it ran in our family - we caught it from our dad), I knew that after we gambled the Vegas World money, we would probably stop gambling. Neither of us would be willing to use our own money to gamble. We were to damn tight for that. Of course the Vegas World folks did not know this fact about the Raffray boys or they never would have sold this package to me so cheap. Both of us have been accused of squeezing a dollar until it hollow. And that is still the word on these two Raffray boys. I am thankful that I have one of my three sons that feel the same way as I do about the way to use money. My brother have one of his four kids that feel this way also.

It took a couple of weeks, but my brother decided that he would come with me after some encouragement from his wife. She thought that he should expand his horizons a bit. He also stated that he would drive to Texas and we could depart from Houston. We picked the date, I got the approval of the dates from Vegas World then made the airline arrangement to depart from Hobby Airport in Houston. This airport was less than twenty miles from where I lived. One month before the extended time was to run out, we made the trip to Las Vegas.

We went to Hobby Airport in my car. We parked in a four dollar a day parking lot and went to our gate to await the flight call. Everything went well. The plane was on time, we boarded, took our assigned seats and took off. My brother had never been on an airplane before. He was a little apprehensive and afraid but was handling it well. We had a smooth flight to Phoenix. When we were descending on our approach to the runway, he got a terrible headache. His face neck and head got really red and I could see the blood vessels in his forehead. I thought that he would have a stroke. It was the air pressure that we were going though as the airplane was approaching the landing strip that was causing his problem. His headache left soon after we were on the ground. A flight attendant gave a couple of aspirins to him.

But they did not do any good at all. Getting on the ground is what stopped his head from hurting.

We changed airplane in Phoenix and before long took off again for Las Vegas. This section of the flight was also smooth. When we started the decent into the Vegas airport, my brother's head started hurting again. The same thing happened as it did at the Phoenix landing. A short time after landing he was alright again. At this time we wondered if this would happen every time he flew in an airplane. He did not want to go through this again. We started thinking about the two stops on the way back to Houston. We were both very thankful that it did not happen on the return trip. If it would have, we would have both missed out on some fun times we had in the future because he would have never boarded an airplane again.

When we got off the airplane at the Vegas airport, there were slot machines everywhere. I made a step and stuck a quarter in the slot. I made another step and did the same thing and again and again. So did my brother. We finally had to stop or we would not get out of the airport. The other problem was, we were spending our own money. This is a NO-NO. We did find out one thing though and that is the slots in the airport does not pay well. We were better off playing slots in the Vegas casinos than at the Vegas airport.

WELCOME TO VEGAS WORLD

We took a cab from the airport to Vegas World. The cabbie, a woman, made some remark about the casino that we were going to that was really funny but I do not remember what it was. I knew what she was talking about after our arrival there. The hotel was located well off "The Strip", although we did not know what "The Strip" was at that time. The route the cabbie took did not enhance our belief that there were many other casinos in Las Vegas. In other words, we did not see any other casinos until we arrived at the one we were going to.

We checked in at the check in desk and got our room assignment and the papers with our package deal outlined in them. There were foreigners everywhere. We really enjoyed hearing the way they talked. Of course we could not understand any of them.

Our room was very small but had two beds and a bathroom and it was comfortable, quite, and clean. And that is all that we could ask for. We did not plan to spend a lot of time in this room anyway. This is all that we needed. We each placed our luggage on a bed and headed down the elevator to the casino. I found the spot where I was to turn in my paperwork for my package deal and get my one thousand dollars in one time play casino money. But first, I got to pull the handle one time on the million dollar jackpot slot machine. I did not win. I also had my picture taken with a million dollars in cash which was on display in the casino. They could not prove to me that it was a million dollars or that it was really real United States currency for that matter. They would not let me count or even touch it. I would like to have climbed up into it and roll all over in it but that was out of the question. They did act like it was real money. I then proceeded to the area where I received my free pair of dice and my free deck of cards. Then I headed to the cashier's window. The requirement was that I had to take four hundred in one time play slot tokens and three hundred in one time play table tokens. I told the cashier to give me seven hundred dollars in slot tokens and three hundred dollars in table tokens. She leaned over to be closer to me and told me that I should take the minimum in slot and the rest in table because I have a much better chance to win at the table. I thanked her and took her advice.

The slot tokens were equal to five dollars. We had to play certain machines that were marked just for the tokens. This sucked. There were not a lot of these type machines. The "package deal" folks there outnumbered the marked slots about five to one. At least this kept the slot tokens in our pockets a little longer. I gave my brother half of the tokens. We waited in line for several folks to finish losing the one time play tokens. I got nine, one dollar pieces for my thirty - five dollar tokens. I believe my bother hit twenty, one dollar pieces for his thirty - five dollar tokens. What a rip off. The cashier lady was correct when the said that these special slots will not pay off. We just messed around in the casino for almost two hours to win a grand total of twenty-nine dollars from the three hundred dollars in slot machine one time play tokens.

I soon lost my nine one dollar coins. My brother lasted over twice as long before he lost his twenty one dollar coins. I finally decided to try to find a five dollar black jack table. I found one and had to again wait in line about a half hour to get a seat. I did not mind this waiting so much. It kept the tokens in my pocket longer and kept me from reaching for my own money. I did not plan to spend any of my own money but guess what. Their plan worked. Just getting me there was the trick. After you are in a casino, any casino, I don't care how tight you are, you will give up your money. You just have to. You may not want to, but you will. Their plan was for the folks to lose the one time play casino money than start spending their own hard earned money. It is a great plan. It will work every time. Well, maybe not every time. Not in my or my brother's case anyway.

This casino stayed in operation because of the package deals it offered. I found out several years later that this was one of the low end casinos. There were many high end and pretty designed and beautiful casinos in Las Vegas that offered top notch entertainment. Vegas World was not one of them. But what Vegas World did worked for them and it kept Bob Strupek, the owner, in business. In the final analysis, they did not know my brother and me very well though.

I sat at the black jack table. I used the one time play token. When I won, they gave me a real casino ship and took my token. Of course when I lost they took my one time play token also. By putting my winnings in my pocket each time I won and using the one time play token until I ran out, I had accumulated some real tokens. I left the table after I was out of one time play tokens. I went and counted up my winnings. I turned my three hundred dollars in one time play tokens into real money. I went to the cashier and cashed in my real chips for real American dollars. I collected about two hundred and fifty dollars American. I got the money in good old green twenty dollar bills. It did occur to me that if I were playing with real money and not one time play tokens, I would have over five hundred dollars. I felt lucky but still would not play black jack with my real money.

All the time that I was playing black jack, my brother was playing the quarter slots near the table game area where I won my money. Earlier we had looked all over the casino for the nickel slots, but just could not find any. We did not want to asked anyone where they were because we did not want them to think that we were cheap- which we were. But we did not want the casino folks or any of the other guess to know that we were. We Raffrays have our pride- you know.

My brother must have converted his twenty one dollar coins into quarters because I don't think that he would have played the dollar slot machines like I did. He would only get twenty pulls on a dollar slot where as if he made change into quarters, he would get eighty pulls. I believe he converted the dollars into quarters. I think that a person have more chance to win on a quarter slot than a dollar slot anyway. I should have converted my nine dollar coins to quarters too. Well, it is to late now.

I went to my brother and told him about my good fortune at the black jack table and tried to get him to go play it. He gave the three hundred dollars in one time table play token to me and told me to play it. I turned these three hundred dollars tokens into about two hundred thirty dollars American. We were in high hog heaven now. I put it all in my pocket and told my brother that we will play the slots on the casino's real money. We had bout four hundred eighty dollars of real American money.

I went back to the cashier and turned forty dollars cash into four rolls of quarters. I gave two rolls to my brother to play with. We used this method the rest of the time that we were in Vegas World. We played the quarter slots for the next two days. When we ran out of quarters, I went to the cashier and got four more rolls and would continue to give two roll to my brother to play with. We did O K most of the time. We would win just enough to not have to continue to cash in for quarters.

The rest of the time we were in Vegas, we played with and ate with Vegas World money. When we came back home, I brought over two hundred fifty dollars of Vegas World real money back with me.

The first night at Vegas World we missed the free stage show that came with the package. We were having so much fun looking around the casino I guess we just forgot about it. We were all over that casino. You know - country come to town. The second night we did watch an old type comedy vaudeville show. It was O K, I guess. It was live and something to pass the time while not spending quarters.

Another of the free gifts in the package was a bottle of champagne that we picked up at the main bar in the casino. Since both of us had quick drinking alcohol for some time before this trip, I gave the bottle to the bartender who was working behind the bar that night. Here we were in the sin capital of our country and neither of us even had a beer. And it would have been free- at that. This is right down our ally. A waitress was always asking us if we wanted something to drink when we were playing the slots. We would ask for water or sometimes a soda. Much of the time we said "no, thanks". The times we did get a soda or a bottle of water, we tipped fifty cents or so. We wanted this money for the slots. A person just cannot drink that much water or soda anyway.

I believe that there were twenty-two or twenty-three floors in the Vegas World Hotel. We saw a sign that said that there was a swimming pool on the roof top. Well we just had to see that. We took the elevator up to the top and sure as shit, there was a swimming pool. We went out there and walked all around it. We wondered how they kept it from leaking. And better yet, how could something that heavy not cave in on the floors below it. I don't remember what floor we slept on. Maybe it was on floor seven, eight, or nine. But I wished that I never saw that damn swimming pool on the roof sign. I did not sleep to good that second night. It is hard to sleep with one eye open. I was trying to keep an eye on the ceiling in our room. I don't know why I wasted good sleep over that. If that pool would have caved in, there wasn't a damn thing any of us could do. We would all be gone pecans. I wondered how they kept it from running over when a big six inch rain came. I remembered later that Las Vegas is in the desert and it doesn't usually get the kind of rain storms that we get in Louisiana and Texas. Thank God.

The two nights we were there, we went to bed early and came back down to pay the slots about one a.m. It was not nearly as crowded and I had been told by friends that have been here that this was the best time to win. They told me the people play the slots all day and load them up for the folks that play them in the early morning hours. Well, after just two days of the early morning playing the slots, I am here to tell you that all of my friends that told me that are full of shit. Yes, that means you Tom, and you Roy, and you too, Ruben, and some others as well.

We did find out while playing the slots in the early morning that that was when the casino folks came to get the coins out of them. Between four and six a. m., these guys would rope off an area and open up and get all the coins in the collection boxes from the slots. They had just sacks and sacks of money. They also wore guns and were not very friendly when I tried talking to them. They did not want us to be to close to them while they did their duties. I guess I can understand that. We just watched them for several minutes and wished we could have a couple sacks of those quarters. They had to hold quite a few hundred dollars each. We had to move a couple times for them to empty the machines we were playing. We were trying to empty them before they got to them. I did not want to play a machine that they just emptied for fear that they reset it to start and I would have to put five hundred dollars back in it before it paid off anything. I don't know how this gig works. Most of the casinos in Vegas claim that they pay ninety-eight or ninety-nine per cent back. Yea, like I believe that. All the money that I saw them collecting made it very hard for me to believe their advertising ratios. I put this advertisement into the same category as with my friends telling me to play the slots from two to seven a. m. They are FULL OF SHIT.

The day we were leaving, we came out of the elevators with our bags and noticed those damn nickel slot machines right near the elevators. We must have passed by them twenty times in the last two and a half days. We were piss off. That just shows to go you. We hailed a cab and headed for the airport having only seen the part of Las Vegas that Vegas World was in. I don/t think we left the casino other than to get a bite to eat across the street the whole time we were there. It was our loss.

As we got into the cab for the trip to the airport, we asked the driver to pass through the part of Vegas that have the big casinos. He did and we were blown away by what we saw. Vegas World was about one mile off "The Strip". We did not see anything while we were there. We had no idea of what we missed by just staying at Vegas World. This was just unbelievable. It was like the videos we all seen on TV but real and in person. I was beginning to think that the whole Las Vegas gambling thing was all made up. But now I saw it in person and the TV really did not do it justice. We have to come back and spend some time in the main sections of Vegas. I will start making plans to come back after we get home.

Barry Raffray pictured with $1 million in cash. No he did not win it.

BIG MAMOU MARDI GRAS

In early 1991, I believe, Don Azwell, of PetroUnited Terminals, made arrangements for me and Mike McKinney, also of PetroUnited Terminals, to ride horses with two brothers from Baton Rouge, Louisiana in the Big Mamou Mardi Gras in Mamou, Louisiana. It may have been a different year but I think that it was in 1991.

The Big Mamou Mardi Gras ride is held on Mardi Gras day (Fat Tuesday) in and around the City of Mamou, Louisiana each year. Big Mamou is known as Big Mamou because there is an even smaller town known as Little Mamou in the nearby area. Just what is the Big Mamou Mardi Gras Ride? It is a horse back ride in the countryside of Mamou, Louisiana whereby the horse riders ask/beg for donations to cook the night of Mardi Gras for a big food festival. The horse ride starts in Mamou and ends in Mamou.

This event has been held for over one hundred fifty years in South Louisiana. The horse or mule (in some cases), riders ware costumes and masks and dance and sing for the donations such as live chickens, ducks, gennie hens, geese, and other food products at each farm house that they stop at in the countryside.

This is an all day event. The ride starts out about seven a.m. Mardi Gras day and come in from the countryside about three in the afternoon. The food stuff items are then, killed, plucked, gutted, cleaned, cut up into pieces and place into a large or several large black cooking pots and cooked for the evening supper and celebration. They may cook gumbo or jambalaya or both and other foods as well. Everyone who participated in the event get to share in the food and any leftovers are served to the general public.

In the modern days, the farm houses where the riders stop has all been contacted before hand and it is known before hand that something will be donated. This was not the case sixty or so years ago. In those days, folks may not have had anything to donate or even have a reason to have a party. All arrangements for donations were made in advance of our ride. We, as riders, were told that we had to perform well before the farmer/ homeowner will give us anything. This meant hooting and hollowing, jumping from the horses and dancing and carrying on- all in costume of course. A bandwagon would be there in front of the riders playing dancing music. There is a lot of carrying on going on. After a good show the farmer/homeowner would throw a chicken or some other foul from his porch. The poor animal would hit the ground running from all the co-motion. The riders chase the foul into the field, yard or pasture or wherever. The person who catches the foul and delivers it to the head captain is revered and held in good standing by all the captains and the riders. The foul is tied by the legs and placed into a pen for safe keeping until time for the butchering in the evening. Then on the riders go to the next house and the same thing happens all over again.

Sometime the farmer would have one of his kids on the roof of his house and after the riders did their dance and put on a good show, he would signal his son to throw the foul in the air in the direction of the fields. This gave the bird a better head start than being flung from a porch. The riders had to run further to catch a bird that was flung free in this manner.

This was to give you some idea of what the Big Mamou Mardi Gras is all about. Now I will tell you of the events of my ride.

We all met and slept at a motel in Opelousas, Louisiana the night before Mardi Gras day. Opelousas is about ten miles from Mamou. Don, Mike and I met the two brothers from Baton Rouge who brought four horses with them. I regret to admit that I do not remember their names. They own a working ranch just South of Baton Rouge. One brother is a lawyer and the other - well I don't know what the other one did for a living. He may be a lawyer also, but he loves to work on the ranch. It seams that is what he mostly did. These two guys were in their early thirties. Don, Mike and I were in our forties. I was forty-seven or forty-eight and the oldest. I had not been on a horse since Davis and Chick Callegan and I rode horses when we were about seventeen years old on the Callegan farm at Lone Star, Louisiana. Lone Star was the location where Davis and his cousin, Chick, lived near the White Castle Canal which was about four miles Southwest from the town of White Castle. So this meant that I had not ridden a horse in over thirty years.

After arriving at the motel, during conversation with the guys, I found out that Don Azwell was not going to ride in the procession the next day. Why, I asked? Don said he had already did that once and that was enough for him. This gave me a little concern because I knew Don usually was ready for anything. But I quickly forgot about his statement as we were having fun and I did not want to put a damper on it.

After supper we went to the house of friends of the guys from Baton Rouge where they were spending the night and where the horses were. It was dark when we arrived there so I did not see the horses then. After several hours of visiting, we headed back to our motel in Opelousas for bed time.

MARDI GRAS MORNING

We all got wake up calls at the same designated time. Met for breakfast and headed for Mamou. Don had set everything up before hand. All we had to do was follow along. We parked and met up with the brothers as they were unloading the horses. Don told us that we had to go sign in for the ride. We went to a building where the signing in and meeting before the ride was taking place. We each signed waivers stating that we would not sue if injured in any way and paid the ten dollars per rider fee.

The guy in charge got everybody's attention and started laying down the rules and regulations. Things like, everyone must be in costume, no riding two to a horse or mule, no guns or knives on the ride, everyone must follow the captain's and his assistants order and instructions or will be ejected from the ride, etc., etc., etc. There were ten or twelve rules. They actually frisked us for guns/knives as we left the building to go to the horses.

There were about fifty riders. We mounted our horses and as we waited for daylight, the captain's assistants line us up the way they wanted to head out of town. We were to ride two riders side by side in a procession throughout the day. Most of the riders were in costume. The Baton Rouge boys were dressed in normal cowboy clothes which was the clothes that they wore on their ranch each day. Mike had on cowboy clothes also and this long riders coat and a mask. I had on Arab dress. It consisted on a long stripped nightgown looking outfit, and a cloth over my head tied on with a strip of black ribbon and a facemask. With my black beard and dark complexion, I really looked like an Arab. I had to pull my nightgown up each time I got upon the horse.

Mike got a horse with one blind eye. Since I was the customer, I got the horse with two good eyes. The brothers had their own horses which was a much better breed of horse than the ones Mike and I rode. Their horses were beautiful and I am sure expensive also.

The Captain headed us out of town. It was just daylight and we could actually see now. Mike and I rode side by side most of the way. The brothers started out just behind us but soon were in the crowd of horses and riders. Mike and I made sure that we stuck together. He rode to my right because his horse was blind in the left eye. We decided it was best to keep the horse that he knew on the side of him that he could not see because we knew that he could tell that his horse friend was near him. We were able to ride like this until the band truck and trailer and the large beer/cola truck drove by us as we approached each house on our ride. Because of the narrow dirt and shell roads, we had to ride single file when the trucks were passing by us.

There was a head captain leading the pack. He had about six or seven assistant captains who strung out among the riders to keep us moving and in line and look for any problems or folks that were not riding a horse. You had to be on a horse/mule to be with this group. Behind us was the large flat bed truck with the Cajun band, the drink truck, a farm tractor pulling a flat lowboy with hay on it for any rider who could not stay on the horse for the complete ride. Behind the tractor was about a mile of cars and trucks that followed the procession into the country side sometimes blowing their horns and otherwise carrying on. No one was allowed to ride the lowboy. It was just for drunks who could not ride any more or tired riders. Nobody came back to town riding in the hay wagon. All riders made the complete ride.

After about one half mile into the countryside we could see the first farm house. The assistant captains stopped all riders about one hundred yards from the farm house. The head captain rode ahead and talked with the owner of the house. The band truck zoomed on by us to get into position on the road in front of the farm house. This scared the shit out of Mike and me. We did not expect something like that to happen. I now wished that I had not signed the release form. There was never much space on the roads in the countryside and fields. The band truck driver was a very good driver. The truck came very close to the horses and the riders each time we approached a house. The driver just tooted his horn and took off whether the riders were ready or not. The truck came very close to hitting me on several occasions. My buddy, Mike, really had a problem with his horse. His one eye horse jumped every time the truck sped by. Because Mike's horse was blind in his left eye and the truck always passed us on the left, the horse could not see what was making all the noise and wanted to turn to the left so he could see with his right eye. Mike had to fight him every time the driver tooted his horn and gunned the engine to come by us. When I heard that toot, I had to hurry and lead my horse to the right to make room for the band truck. Since I was riding on the left side of Mike, I had to rush in front of him or hold up on the reins and duck in behind him. This was the most dangerous time during the whole ride. At the end of the day, Mike and I felt good that we did not get run over by that damn big truck carrying the band.

After the band truck was in place, the head captain blew his whistle, which was the signal for all of us riders to gallop up to the farmhouse, dismount and start dancing. We could either dance with each other or by our selves. The band was playing music. A good time was being had by all. Well, maybe not all, but most. After about a minute or two, the head captain would give a signal to the farmer and the foul would fly. About seventy percent of the riders took off after the birds for this first one. I started to but did not want to leave my house. By the time I decided to hand my reins to Mike to hold my horse and go join the group, they had this chicken caught. It was hard to see much from the ground with all the horses around, so I did not see what was going on. After the bird was given to the head captain, everyone came back to their horses. We all re-mounted our horses and headed for the next house. This is when I notice that all the guys that chased those chickens were all full of mud. They were wet and muddy. Some were worse than others. There had been a lot of rain in this area several days before. The sugar cane fields still had some water in them in some areas. The ditches and canals along the roads we were riding on had water in them as well. It was nasty out there. I kind of liked it high and dry up in the saddle where I was.

We went on about a quarter of a mile and stopped again short of the next house. We knew to be watching out for that damn band truck now. When we were riding the band truck would stay behind all riders and play music. When we left the first farm house, we all got moving and the band truck got behind us. It was that way the whole day. The truck would speed past us to get to the house to play music while we rode up and during the dancing and carrying on while the fowl was being caught. Then get behind us and play softer music when we were walking on the trail to the next farmhouse.

At the second house, I dismounted for the dance but got back on my horse when they let the chickens fly. Boy there were some crazy Coonasses. Some of them were diving into the mud to try and catch the chickens. What a mess. I decided right then and there that I will NOT do this. This getting down and up on a horse was a pain in the ass as it was and was wearing me out.

At the third house, I did not get down from the horse to dance. At the second house, I noticed that a number of guys did not even get off their horses. So I decided to do the same. Well, an assistant captain rode up to me and said, "get off your horse and dance". I did it again. As soon as the birds were flung in the air, I got on my horse to watch the fun. Watching these crazy Coonasses (by the way, Cajun and Coonass, is the same), go after the birds was the best part of this ordeal. I only dismounted one more time the rest of the day and that was for the lunch break.

Meeting interesting people during the ride, I met a number of the riders. Some were young and some not so young. One of the older guys was dressed as a cowboy. It was normal western clothes and a felt cowboy hat. He did not were a mask. I discarded my mast after racing to the first house. So did Mike. What we found out was that we could not see a damn thing with it on. The mask blocked some of our vision and we needed all of our vision on this ride. When galloping and bouncing up and down in the saddle, I could not see anything. Different assistant captains told us several time to put our mask on. We told each one- NO- we could not see a damn thing with it on. They eventually left us alone.

This old rider had told us that this was his twenty-fifth ride. That meant that he has done this for twenty-five years. He was a businessman. He must have a very boring business to want to do this each year. He didn't wear a mask and he doesn't dance either. He never even got off his horse one time during the whole ride. Mike and I got courage from this guy. The captain had mentioned before we started the ride that if we did not do what he or his assistants told us, we would be kicked out of the ride. Well after talking with some of the riders and seeing what was going on, we said to hell with it. We did not wear the mast the rest of the day or get off our horses and dance. We did not gallop up with the group when we did not feel like it either. We just watched the actions as we walked our horses up to the activity with the other more experience riders who did the same. We were learning how to do this thing and it became a little more fun.

We met two younger guys who each rode a small mule. Some folks call them jackasses. That term referred to the mules and the riders. We had a lot of fun talking, riding side by side and watching the antics of these fellows. They wore costumes made out of croker sacks. This is a coarse material that was uses to sack one hundred pounds of corn and other products. Irish potatoes came in this sack also. It is a heavy and strong material. They had hats made of this material also.

One or the other would ride his mule up along the side of you and say "you wanta race"? Which meant- do you want to race. Then he would say that he bet some money that he could beat you to a certain spot. It was always a short distance. He was right. In a short distance race, a jackass is faster than a horse. We never saw anybody take them up on their offer.

I also met this kid from up North- New York state, I believe. He did not have a horse. He was hitching rides with different guys who would ride him. This was certainly against the rules. Every rider is suppose to have one rider to a horse. He walked a lot. I let him ride with me for a while. He/we kept a lookout for the assistant captains. I guess he was never caught because we had a large contingent of riders. As far as I know, he made the complete ride. I saw him again at the end of our ride. This was something very hard to accomplish. Maybe he wrote a book about it.

Lunch on the trail At twelve noon, the beer/cola truck broke out our lunch. It was a length of boudin about eight inches long and a boiled egg. I also had a cola to wash it down.

The beverage truck had been serving since seven in the morning. In between farmhouses, it would drive past us on the route and go really slow so riders could come along side and get their favorite drink, then stop and pull in behind the riders. Some guys starting drinking beer in the early morning. I never saw anyone drunk or even showing the slightest evidence of intoxication.

The truck stopped to serve lunch. We were in the middle of a field on a dirt road. There was not much room on the road. After getting our food, most of the riders were jumping their horsed over ditches on both sides of the road to get to a space where they had some room. These ditches had plenty of water in them. I did not want to try and get my horse to jump the ditch. I had never jumped anything on a horse. I did not know how. I was afraid that I would fall into the ditch.

Mike was trying to maneuver ole one eye into a position to jump the ditch. He finally did it after an assistant captain told us to move to the other side of the ditch. I lined up my horse for a attempt. We made it also. I did not like it. I hurt my balls and butt. I dismounted and ate my boudin and boiled egg and just stood there stretching my legs and rubbing my balls and butt.

After about forty-five minutes or so, we were ready to head out again. The vehicles move out of our way so the riders could jump the ditch again and get to the narrow road and line up for the ride to start again. Ha, Ha. We made it. No problems.

City followers from the time we rode out of Mamou, there was a long line of autos following us. When we went into the fields to get to the first farm house, the autos did not follow. During the complete ride we could see them in a distance. Sometime they were a few hundred yards away and other time they were a mile or two away. They stayed on the black top country roads. When we were fairly close to them, they blew their horns like they were in a parade or something. They hung in there with us the whole day and followed us back into the town and parked before we made it into downtown.

Down the home stretch The afternoon was much the same as the morning. We followed the same routine. I was not going to get off this horse again until this ride was over. We must have made three or fours more house stops. The guys chasing the birds were down to about eight or ten guys. The rest were burnt out or too tipsy for the chase. We had a couple of miles to get back to downtown Mamou. On the way in, the riders got really spread out. We were well over a quarter of a mile long. We came into town through the minority section of town. Black folks were sitting on their porches or standing in their yards watching us ride by. We looked like a worn out bunch of misfits in half costume. Most of these black folks would not even return my waves. I gave this some thought later and came up with my own answer as to why the blacks could care less about us riders. By the way, there were no blacks on this ride.

Mike and I were in the first third of the group to get into town. We were stopped by the captain and waited about thirty minutes until all of the stragglers got to this spot which was a large parking lot of a Stop and Go grocery. With the deposits our horses left on the cement in front of this store, the captain must have made arrangements before hand for us to marshal there. After all the stragglers arrived, the assistant captains lined us up in twos again. The head captain went to the front of the line and got us moving forward. At this time we had no idea of what we were heading into.

VERY LARGE CROWDS

The band truck was to our left and playing good Cajun music as it did all day. By the way, this was live music with violins, squeeze boxes, triangles, drums, cymbals, horns, guitars, etc. There were eight to ten band members. We could not hear or see any thing of significance up ahead. The riders in front of us were now turning to the right. We did not even know where our Baton Rouge buddies were in the line. As we got closer to the street that went right, we could hear noise. Crowd noise. The partying type of noise. When we got to the corner and saw all those people lining both sides of the main street, we could not believe it. This odd feeling came over me. I swelled up inside. It is a feeling that I never had before or since. It seamed that this crowd, that I estimated to be about ten thousand people, were all cheering for me. It is hard to explain how great I felt. It was really strange. There were people everywhere. Clapping, waving, yelling, and touching. No, I did not see any tits. This was not New Orleans. I was really afraid of our houses trampling people. This is how close to the people we were. I was slapping hands. Folks were touching me and my horse. I was afraid that my horse might get spooked and hurt someone. But we made it to the dismounting place o.k. At the finish line we just sort of disbursed. It was every man and horse for himself. Maybe ten thousand people in a town with less than two thousand population. It was great.

This girl came up to me and wanted a ride on the horse. Her male friend was with her. I was afraid of this horse all day. But now, all of a sudden, I was a horseman. I told her sure. I took my foot out of the stirrup. I reached out my arm. She put her foot in the stirrup, grabbed my arm and I lifted her aboard with me. We took off down this side street. She was holding on around my waist. We went about fifty yards and turned around and came back. I was really happy. As I lifted her down another wanted to ride. I looked for Mike and he motioned me to join him. I told this girl and the others standing around that I was sorry but I had to put the horse up. Don was waiting for us when we got there.

I finally saw the brothers again. They were riding girls up and down the street. By the time I arrived where they were, we all headed to the area where the horse trailers were. We unsaddled the horses and put them into the trailers and locked up everything. We walked back to where we signed up early in the morning. This is the spot where the birds that were gathered today would be cooked. The big black pots were already on the fires. Seasoning was cut up and going into the pots. Most of the birds were already plucked, gutted, cleaned and in the cooking pots. These folks don't waist time. While we were still on the horses in the parade, these folks had the fires going, season ready and went to work on the fowl as soon as delivered. I believe someone went ahead and delivered the birds while we were still on horseback.

We were told that the gumbo and jambalaya would be served in about thirty minutes. This sounded great to me. I deserve to eat what I helped go after- sort of. I was looking forward to it, but Mike said lets go. We walked across the street which was not an easy task because the whole town was curb high in beer cans and head high with people. This was one of the things that I noticed when we made that turn to the right on our horses. They let the beer cans fall where they may. I guess they planned to clean the town up on Wednesday. I would like to have had the rights to all those cans. The town must have made so money selling the aluminum.

We walked into a cafe and ordered food. I could not believe it but I went along with the group. If we would have waited just a little while we could have eaten with all the riders. Mike left over half of his gumbo. I don't think he liked it. He must not have been hungry. He is a big guy. That boudin and egg we had for lunch must still be with him. I ate all my gumbo and could have had more. I could not help but think that the food we left across the street was better than what we had in this cafe and we would not have to pay for it either.

After supper, we walked about town a bit looking at the sites and trying not to trip on the beer cans. It was now dark and the town was rocking. It was a big outside party. After we were partied out, which did not take long, we said our good buys to the brother and thanked them again for a great time and headed back to the motel in Opelousas.

Don, Mike and I met for breakfast and talked about the experience. Don had experience the ride years ago and did not care to do it again. I felt the same way. One time was enough for me. It was a great experience but once is enough. I did not get any broken bones and wanted to keep it that way so this would always remain a good memory.

We departed Opelousas for home on that Wednesday morning. I was surprise that I was not hurting all over, especially my butt. I arrived home in good shape. I went to work on Thursday. My butt was still not hurting at all. But I was walking funny. The folks at work who knew where I had been had a good laugh at my expense. My butt did not hurt but my inner thighs were killing me. The inside of my upper legs were hurting badly. I realized that this was from squeezing the horse to try and stay on when we had to gallop up to the farmer's house. I used mussels that I did not know I had. My legs hurt for over a week. This was not the fun part of my great "Big Mamou Mardi Gras Ride". In time the pain went away and I forgot about it but I still have and will always have the memory of the great time I had with my pals who worked for PetroUnited Terminals.

TIME JUST MOVING ALONG

By 1991 I had several relationships, but none that lasted over five or six months. I was floundering about not having much of a personal life. I was still spending twelve hours a day at work and going out to the plant one day each weekend to try and catch up. I always spent more time at work than I should have. I really deprived myself and my family from doing more things together when my boys were kids. Although I put many hours in at work, I did coached, managed, and assisted other guys who coached and managed and I was facility Manager for two years when my middle son played little league football. I did help during baseball, basketball, soccer and football seasons. They all played in at lease two sports from the age of six through seventeen years old. My youngest son played all four sports. We also went to Galveston beach a lot and on many picnics when they were little. I took them crabbing and to some Astros baseball games and the Rockets basketball games as well. But I still feel that I could have done more with them. We played many games at home also. We played card and board games. Still, I think that I could have spent more time with them. I suppose I could have gone to school to see and eat with them more often. We had them all in sports at one time a lot of the time. This meant that I would go with one and my wife would go with one and one would have to play their game without us. During their early years, they were all on separate teams. The baseball teams were combined by the time my older two were fourteen and fifteen years old. They then played on the same team but until this time they were on different teams.

My sons played tee ball, slow pitch baseball, machine pitch baseball, pitcher pitch baseball, football, soccer, and basketball. Kent played soccer and baseball. Lane played baseball and football, Todd played baseball, soccer, basketball and football. They all did good in school at that time also.

Kent and Todd were very bright. They took after their momma. They did not need to study much to pass from one grade to another. Consequently they did not develop good study habits. This was to come into play in a big way when they went off to college. Lane on the other hand had to study for every C or B that he made. He studied hard, starting in kindergarten. He took after me in this area of having to study to get it.

Lane was born two or so months premature. In pre school, kindergarten, and the first grade, the teachers thought that he was immature and should be held back a year. He was also clumsy and used to fall down a lot. He needed eye glasses at an early age. We did not know if Lane had learning problems or not. With all this happening, we decided to have his mental abilities check out by doctors at Louisiana State University. We would drop him off for several hours of testing on several occasions. He tested average on some things, above average on other things and below average when compared to classmates. When put into perspective, Lane, who was born near the end of December in 1971, was in the first grade with kids up to a year older then he was. He was five and a half in the first grade. In Louisiana, a kid did not have to be six years old to be put in the first grade. If you were going to be six in the calendar year, you could start the first grade. We realized that Lane was always the youngest child in his grade by many months. I refused to hold him back. I remembered how I felt when I pulled that stupid stunt in the third grade. If Lane could not make the grade, then the school system would have to hold him back, not me.

I am proud to say that Lane never did fail a grade or a subject for that matter. He did not set the world on fire with his grades during grammar or high school but he never flunked out either. When we moved to Texas in 1978, Lane went into the third grade. All during his school time in Texas, he was one to one and a half years younger than all of his classmates except the ones that may have moved from Louisiana or other states that had similar school requirements as Louisiana did.

In Texas, a kid had to already be six years old before the school year began to enter into the first grade. Lane was seventeen and a half years old when he graduated from Clear Lake High School. His older brother, Kent, graduated the same time, but he did not walk at his graduation to get his diploma as Lane did at Holfins Provillion on the University of Houston campus.

Lane was just twenty-one years old when he got his bachelors degree in Political Science from the University of Houston. He took a year off from school and went to Louisiana to help him Mom (who had moved back with her parents) and grandparents get some things done around the house. While there, he checked into the possibility of becoming a Justice of the Peace in the Parish that his grandparents lived. A year later, I helped him move to Florida to attend graduate school at Florida State University. A year later, I again helped him move again. This time it was to San Marcos, Texas to attend Southwest Texas University to continue work on a Masters degree. He attended night school here. About two years later he received his master's degree in Public Administration. Because of the year he lost in Louisiana and the other year lost in Florida, he was twenty-five years old when he received his master's degree. Not to shabby for a boy who made C's during high school.

Lane made the Dean's list several times when attending the University of Houston. He had a better than 3.5 average grade during his master degree program.

Lane's first job after getting his Master's Degree was working for the state of Tennessee in Chattnooga doing planning for small town/cities in that area. So we packed the things he wanted to move and moved him to Chattnooga. He worked there for a year or so and when the state started cutting benefits, he decided to quit and we moved him back to the San Marcos/Austin, Texas area. He later moved into a duplex with his youngest brother and Brian Bassett, a childhood friend of the Raffray boys. He took his older brother's room. Kent moved into his girlfriend's apartment. Lane then got a job working in a department that supplied information for the state of Texas. They only had three or four people. He finally got a permanent job with the state of Texas in Austin. He worked just a couple of blocks from the state capital building. He helps put information together for the state legislators to use in making decisions concerning the penal system of Texas. He seams to like it alright for now. I believe he will try for other jobs with the state when he see one that he really wants. He is talking about going back to college to add to his degrees.

Kent went on to the University of Texas in Austin. I paid for an apartment for him to live. He registered too late to live on campus. He attended classes here off and on for two years. He decided not to go back. His money supply had dried up or another way to say it is that I stop paying for all the classes that he was not attending. He moved back with me in League City and took part time jobs while he attended Alvin Community College working toward a Communication Associate degree. For several semesters, he and his buddy, Noonie Oats, had their own radio program at the college. This was part of their degree plan. Upon completion, Noonie went to work for one of the largest listened to radio stations in Houston. After a couple or so years, Kent moved back to Austin to share a apartment with friends. He got a job in a warehouse store that sold everything before getting on with a computer game company where he worked for about seven years. He purchased a house in Cedar Park, Texas, near Austin, with his girlfriend. He got laid off by Origin after almost seven years. He had a very good severance package and weathered more time off from work than he wanted but got another job doing almost the same thing he was doing at really good pay. He has changed jobs again as of this writing.

Todd did move to Louisiana with his mom to his grandparents home in his junior year of high school. He attended Denham Springs High school for a short time then quit school again. He took correspondent courses and passed them. He came back and lived with me the next summer and attended summer school here and passed those courses also. We had his credits transferred back to Louisiana. After the summer was over, he went back to Louisiana and continued correspondent courses. He challenged the coursed that he did not take, passed them and took the Louisiana high school equivalency test and passed it and got his GED.

When Todd informed me that he was ready for college I had second thoughts, many second thoughts. But I wanted him to get the chance to go to college and on my dime was the only way he would be able to do it. Maybe he has grown up a little is what I was praying for. I moved him back to Texas. We applied at the University of Houston. They did accept him but as an out of state student which would have cost me much more than being an in state student. He also applied at Southwest Texas University in San Marcos. He was accepted there as well. The better news was that he was accepted as an in state student. Well it doesn't take a genius to figure out where he attended college.

We got him settled in a dormitory on campus. Todd attended SWT for about two years on and off. Until this day, I still do not know how much credit hours he have there. After he quit college, he delivered pizza in a car that I had leased in 1993. It was a little Mercury Tracer. Todd had a heavy foot. He went through two motors on this car and a wreck before I gave it to him to trade in on a Honda Civic after he got a real job with the same computer game company that his older brother worked for.

Todd worked at several jobs in the San Marcos/Austin area over the next couple of years. He lived with his brother Lane when Lane attended SWT working on his Masters degree. Then he lived with Kent when he had a regular job. Eventually he got the job at Origin. Both Kent and Todd started out as temps and worked their way into a company job.

Kent, Todd and their friend, Brian Bassett, rented a three bedroom duplex in a nice part of Austin. Brian was working for the City of Austin at the time. His job was keeping the computers going for the city workers. He later left for a big paying job of maintaining computers for some company in Austin. I remember them having a big party because Brian made the really big time. He was making big money. At the time of this writing, they are still living in that duplex, except Lane took Kent's place when he moved in with his girlfriend. I think Kent got tired of all the smoke. Todd and Brian are big cigarette smokers. Kent is not and neither is Lane for that matter. Thus far, Lane is coping with the smoking situation. For a year or so, Lane did not spent much time at the duplex. He stayed with his girlfriend, but never changed his address. As of this date, December 2001, he is back living full time at the duplex with Todd and Brian but I have a feeling that his will change again before to long.

Time was moving on and 1992 and 1993 just went by. I worked for Huntsman Chemical Corporation. I still put in more hours a day then I should have but I now enjoyed working for Huntsman. I had a high profile job with them. Mr. Huntsman would come by and say hello when he visited the Plant. Of course I enjoyed this. This made me feel good- you know, like I was somebody.

Huntsman Corporation was growing and buying other plastic business and I would have more plants to supply products to. Everybody who was somebody in our styrene or polystyrene plants knew who I was. I was the guy that kept their plants running. I was in charge of all public liquid terminals. These are facilities that we shipped product to which in turned reshipped to our customers and own plants after getting orders from me. The terminals that I was responsible for was: PetroUnited at Bayport, Texas, Deltech Corp. at Baton Rouge, Louisiana, Excello Corp. at New Haven Connecticut, and Itapco in Parkesburg, West Virginia. I was in charge of all tank trucks contracts, tank car rail contracts, leasing tank car contracts, barge and any tanker (ship) contracts for moving product as well as inspection services contract and inventory control. I was also responsible for the negotiation of all contracts. I also did the swapping and trading of product for plant shut downs and to meet our customer's needs. If I could borrow one hundred million pounds of product a year, we would not have to go on the open market to purchase it. Our industry did a lot of swapping and trading during these years. It saved our companies hundreds of thousands of dollars each year by doing so. Anything that it took to move a pound of styrene monomer from one place to another was my responsibility.

I was responsible to keep product available at all the terminals and our Peru, Willow Springs, and Joliet, Illinois plants as well as our Belpre, Ohio, Rome, Georgia, Mansonville, Canada and Chesapeake, Virginia plants. It was fun and I really enjoyed doing what I was doing. It was a lot of responsibility. Life was great - except a little lonely at times when I did not have a lady friend to keep me company.

Barry, Lane, Kent and Todd Raffray at Kent's house in Cedar Park, Texas

LAJITAS ON THE RIO GRANDE IN 1992

During the time that I was single, I had several relationships with lady friends. All of the ladies that I dated I met because of business relationships. We thought that we had something in common and dated for short periods of time and then we each went our separate ways for one reason or another. I was not ready for marriage during these times and told each and every lady that before any relationship ever started. I did not think that I would ever marry again. Who would have me - long term? I was set in my ways and had this thing about being tight with money.

For one of my birthdays, it may have been the forty-eight or forty-ninth - I do not remember which, this lady friend had set up a trip for us to get away for a while. This was for us to spend several days at Lajitas on the Rio Grande in Big Bend National Park which is in west Texas. This was over two hundred fifty miles west of Del Rio, Texas.

We made the trip in my 1982 Cadillac Betruitz. We left League City early in the morning when it was still dark and got on Interstate 10 in Houston and headed west. After we passed through San Antonio, we found Texas to be very dry and desert like. We took Highway 90 out of San Antonio. Than went through Hondo, Uvalde, Brackettville and Del Rio. We had not seen a body of water since we saw Clear Lake as we were leaving League City. We stopped in Langtry, Texas and toured the Judge Roy Bean Salon/Courthouse and Gardens. The gardens were all some sort of cactus plants. In his day, Judge Roy Bean was the only law west of the Pecos River. Langtry was not much to look at, but it is part of American/Texas history. Judge Roy Bean never did sentence anyone to hang. He mainly fined them, if they had money, or put them in jail if they did not have any money. The trials were in his bar/salon. After the trials were over, the salon was opened for business as usual.

We continued on through Dryden, Sanderson, and Marathon into Alpine. We stopped to get something to eat somewhere along the way. I do not remember where we ate but it must have been at Langtry. At Alpine, we took a left on Highway 118 and went straight south for about one hundred miles to the Mexico border. We drove through several mountain ranges. Each mountain had a different name. The tallest was sixty-nine hundred feet above sea level. We arrived at Lajitas after dark and checked into the motel. The folks there were waiting for us. Even in the dark it was not hard to find. It was the only place there that looked like a place where folks could spend the night. I only saw about four buildings in the whole town - if you can call it a town. Early the next morning we had breakfast in the motel and walked around the small settlement. We visited the world famous Billy goat that drank beer and then ate the beer can. He looked like just a plane old regular goat to me. He would not talk back to me when I asked him questions.

At nine a.m. we went to the stable for a horse back trek into the mountains for the day. I was not too crazy about this outing. There were two gals that took us on this back packing trip by horseback. One of the girls was young, in her early twenties and working there for the summer. She was a country girl, but not as country as the other gal. The other girl was about thirty something and looked really rugged. She also looked like she was well into her forties. During our time together, we found out that she was a local gal and lived about ten miles away in the mountains. She loved the outdoors. Her and her husband had two kids and they lived in a shack. They did not have a telephone, electricity, or running water in the house. They had and used an outhouse. She insisted on raising her kids this way. She said that they were a very happy family and had everything they needed. Her husband worked in the area. There was not a lot of work in this area. I guessed that they grossed less than twenty thousand dollars a year in income.

We took off into the desert and mountains to look at the sites. I saw the smallest cactus in the world and some large ones also. We went through some dry riverbeds and saw some drawing on a wall that the gals said were made by Indians many years ago. I don't know if this is true or not.

It was really hot, over one hundred degrees during midday and it was just mid May. We stopped for lunch in a area where a small pool of clear green looking water was. It also had a cave like area that sheltered us and the horses from the heat. The gals made some sandwiches for us for lunch and we also had cold drinks that they had packed. They started out being cold drinks but by the time we stopped to have lunch, they were cool drinks.

We sat their and rested for about an hour and a half than took off again. It would have been alright with me if we headed back to the base now but NOOOOOOOO, we climbed higher on the mountain. At one point we could see down to the small settlement where we came from. It looked many miles away. We followed a trail on the edge of this mountain. We were on a damn cliff. I did not like it at all. The drop looked like a mile down. I let my distaste for this trail be known to all. The country gals said to not worry because the horses did not want to fall off either. My thoughts was - just suppose I had a horse that had a falling out with his or her horsemate back at the stable and the bastard wanted to commit suicide. Huh? What about that?

At one point we had to jump the horse over a gorge to get to the other side to proceed down the mountain. Why in the hell did they take us on this path? What in the hell am I going to do now. This is horseshit. I did not want to sit on the horse while he did the jumping. I thought about getting off the horse and jumping over it myself. But that was not a good idea. I did not think that I could make it. I was scared shitless. It seamed about five or six feet wide and I was second guessing rather I or the horse could jump that far. One girl said to kick my heals into the horse's side and he will jump over the gorge. Suppose I piss the horse off- what then? I would not want to be kicked in the sides and told to jump over something. That would make me NOT want to jump. Now all three gals were on the other side already and shouting encouragement to me. I felt like a pussy. I was the only "guy" on this trip and I was sure in the hell NOT a manly one. Well shit.

Here I am. I went over thirty years between riding horses when I did that ride in Louisiana less than two years ago. And here I am again on the back of a damn house. But this time I am two damn miles up on top of some damn mountain. At least in Louisiana I was on flat muddy ground. The fall may not have killed me. But here- there is no way that I will survive a fall from up here. Why in the hell do I get myself into this kind of situation? Yea, lets go for a horse ride, it will be fun. Way up here without a parachute or any protection against a fall. What I gonna do? Whoo is me-whoo is me.

I loosen the reins that I was holding tight because my horse wanted to follow the others and I was not ready yet. I pointed the horse toward the narrowest gap between these mountains and nudged the sides of my horse with my heels. He jumped over the gorge much to my happiness. I maintained my balance on the horse and did not fall off when we landed on the other side. Although my nuts and ass was hurting, I was happy. I did/could not talk for a while. I was trying to catch my breath and not letting the gals know that my nuts were up near my navel and my ass and both legs were hurting.

Every so often, one of the girls wanted me to get off the horse to look at something small on the ground. I told her "NO". Just like in the Big Mamou Mardi Gras ride in Louisiana, I was tired of getting off and on the horse and did not do it again until I got off of it once and for all. This is horseshit. Enough is enough. No more of this up and down shit.

It was after five p.m. when we got off that damn mountain. I could see Lajitas in the distance. We made it to a green pasture where one of the girls opened the gate and closed it after we rode through. We rode to the banks of the Rio Grande where we would make camp for the night.

As we were resting, the two gals set up two tents after they took the saddles and gear off of all the horses and turned them loose in the green pasture. The horses quietly went to visit with several other horses at the other end of the pasture. I could just imagine my horse telling the others what a pussy I was on the ride in the mountains. You know how word gets around by horse mouth. I could hear them all laughing and having a good time. The bastard should keep his mouth shut. Anyway, I don't think that I will ever be coming back this way again. And if I do- I sure am NOT going to ever go riding a horse in the mountains. I am taking that OFF my bucket list. Come to think of it, that was never on my bucket list to begin with. Why in the hell am I here in the first place? Oh, I remember, my lady friend is very HOT and good looking and she thought it would be fun. My friend and I put on our swim suits and went to a safe area and played in the Rio Grande while our guides built a fire and started cooking supper. Now this is having a good time. Back on flat, well almost flat ground, and having someone else cooking for you while you just play in the water. This is the good life. What more could a pussy errrr I mean manly man want.

We were called when the food was ready. These gals did a great job. The supper was good and they even baked/cooked a cake over the outside fire for my birthday. We had the happy birthday song with a guitar that one of the girls played and ate cake. We did not have ice cream, just cake. This was a fun time. We were all going to sleep under the stars. The rugged gal did not sleep in a tent. She really slept under the stars with just a blanked and saddle for a pillar. It was cool and pleasant during the night. The stars were just a wonderful site to behold. No pollution out here, just beautiful stars and planets. My lady friend wanted to roll in the hay with me for my birthday. I was reluctant at first with the other gals so close but succumbed to her wishes. Today was May 18th.

We got up the next morning to a great outside cooked breakfast at eight a.m.

It was very good and we enjoyed it very much. We then got dressed and waited for a person to pick us up by raft.

A male guide in a raft showed up at our camp site. He was there to pick us up for a twenty mile trip by raft down the Rio Grande. We said our thanks and good byes to our horse back tour guides. I told them how happy I was to be at the river alive and well even though the inside of my thighs were really hurting now. These were the same muscles that I found out I had when I went on the Big Mamou Mardi Gras ride a couple years earlier. My nuts got back in place last night and were doing just find. Everything was a O K.

We got into the raft. There was a mother and adult daughter couple and two others already in the raft. This was a large raft and we had plenty room. There were several other rafts on the River. The guide was a young Mexican American. He told us about the Rio Grande and the different sites as we approached them. I ask him a question a couple of times. He did not like being asked questions. After answering each time, he started his spiel about the river and gorge from the beginning. I guessed that he had it all memorized and he had to start at the beginning or he could not remember anything. A question interrupted his presentation of our passage way as he memorized it.

He had the two large paddles that he paddled and controlled the raft with. He paddled us along until noon. He then pulls into a designated spot for lunch. The other rafts were in this area also. He made sandwiches and we ate well and had a soda to wash it down with. After an hour or so, we got under way again.

About five p.m. we arrived at the landing which marked the end of the river trip. We all got into an SUV and were transported back to Lajitas. The rafts were placed into a huge trailer and also transported back to Lajitas.

We spent that night in the motel again. The next morning we drove around Big Bend National Park and visited several other locations within the park. This is a very large park and would take several weeks to see everything, if that was possible.

In this area of Texas, I believe that the park rangers and employees of the park are the best paid folks there. Everyone else works for minimum wage or not much more than that. I do not know how well the resort does in a years' time. I cannot believe that they or setting the world on fire with profit.

On the fourth day, we started the long trip back to League City. We said good bye to the mountains, valleys, Rio Grande, cactus, cliffs, horses and heat. Thank God that this was mid May. August would have been pure hell. This I am sure of.

Top: Barry Raffray in Judge Roy Bean's Bar and Courthouse in Langtry, Texas west of Pecos, Tx.
Bottom: Barry's friend Victoria on right and the two gal guides

Top: Barry Raffray looking at a watering hole
Bottom: The cowgirls singing happy birthday to Barry. He is trying to cool off.

Riding down the Rio Grande

1993 SUMMER TRIP TO BELPRE, OHIO PLANT

I had a meeting set up with the plant manager at our Belpre, Ohio polystyrene plant and one of our barge company representatives. I had decided before this business trip to tie it in with a mini vacation that I needed desperately. I pre-arranged to take several days of vacation while on this trip. I thought that I wanted to do some white water rafting in West Virginia while I was in the area. It seamed like a fun thing to do at the time that I planned my trip.

Belpre, Ohio was not an easy location to fly into. You either had to fly into Columbus, Ohio or other larger cities and drive. Since I planned to do some white water rafting in Beckley, West Virginia, I set up my flights into Charleston, West Virginia and I would drive to Belpre for my meeting and also meet with my friends and business associates at General Electric who are based in Parkersburg, West Virginia. Parkersburg is across the Ohio River from our Belpre plant. I planned to get a lot accomplished on this one trip. After the couple days of

AFTER RAISING SUGAR CANE | 259

meetings I would drive back to Beckley which was below Charleston and spend a couple of days there white water rafting. Then head back up too Charleston for my flight back to Houston. What a plan. And I did it all by myself- almost.

I flew from Houston to Cincinnati in a large jetliner. I changed planes in Cincinnati. I knew that I would have to change planes but I did not know that it would be a tree top airplane. It was a thirty or so passenger airplane with two propeller engines, one propeller on each wing. I was not too happy with this. The one flight attendant placed the ten people or so on this flight in certain seats. This was to balance off the airplane. They did not want one side heavier than the other. We took off. I wondered what I had gotten into. Everything seamed to be going o k. I started a conversation with the guy across the narrow isle from me. I guess he started the conversation after he noticed that I was a white knuckle flyer. I admitted that I did not care to fly and when I did, I preferred the larger airplanes. After this conversation, several other passengers stated talking with me. It seamed that I became very popular in a very short time. I thought that it must be my accent. I was asked it I ever flew into the Charleston airport before. I told them that I had not. They all clamed up and looked the other way. I became unpopular in a hurry. Maybe it was my bad breath or something. As the airplane continued, we hit a few bumps in the air. I do not know how pilots manage to hit bumps this high in the sky that bounce the airplane around like that. But they always do this when I am on the plane. I think that somehow they know that I do not like hitting bumps in the sky when I fly. They do this on purpose just to piss me off and make me afraid, and this one did it to. I guess I mumbled something each time we shuddered, because the nearby passengers would giggle. I do not recall what I was saying or mumbling. After about thirty minutes the pilot announced that we were making our approach into the Charleston Airport. All he had to do for the announcement was to turn around and push the drapes aside and make his statement. I looked out of my window and said "mountains". The guy across from me said "yes, there are mountains all around here". He then informed me that the Charleston Airport was on top of a mountain. To which I murmured - "SHIT". I guess it was more like a shout than a murmur. The passengers all laughed or giggled. It was not a funny matter to me. I grabbed the seat arms and held on tight.

The airplane started to descend. I could not see a runway. What is the pilot doing, I thought. I was still holding on to the armrests very tightly. We kept getting closer to the ground and I still could not see any ground from my window. Looking out of the window on the right side of the airplane, I could see ground. But there was no ground on my side of the damn plane. What is this? I almost shit when I saw over the cliff. The airplane was almost on the ground and all I could see was the wing over a cliff which went straight down for a mile. I think I yelled SHIT again followed by DAMN. I do not remember me saying anything, but everyone on the airplane started laughing out loud and looking at me. Even after I knew we were on the ground, all I could see was over this cliff. The left wing of the airplane, my wing, was extended over the cliff. If the pilot had hit a pot hole on the runway, over the cliff we all would have gone. I am sure that I lost all my color. I did not understand what I was told when they said the airport was on a mountain. Boy, I sure in hell understand it now. This is an experience that I do not care to do again. And I never did do this again. I went back to going through Atlanta.

Heading to Belpre for the meetings my knees were still shaky when I got off the airplane. I got my rent car and instructions how to get down off this mountain and in the direction to Ohio. After getting my luggage, I headed down the mountain. It was very curvy. I did not have to step on the gas at all. In fact I had both feet on the brakes and was hoping that the brake held up on this little car until I got to the bottom.

I had some beautiful scenery on the turnpike heading to Ohio. I tried to hug the mountain side of the highway the whole way. There are cliffs all the way to Ohio. I could not go as fast as everyone else. I was too afraid. These local drivers were doing eighty or more miles an hour and left me in their dust. This was fine with me. I could not drive that fast. I was too afraid of this winding, mountainous highway. I was also trying to see some of the scenery while driving. It was just awesome, but I would not want to live there.

I eventually made it to Belpre. The next day we had our meeting. That night I had dinner with the General Electric folks at a nice restaurant overlooking the Ohio River. I passed a good time visiting with my long time friends Sandy Haynes and Mary Jo Buffington. We talked about the styrene monomer business and our families and many other things. The next morning, I headed back south through Charleston to the small town of Beckley, West Virginia.

WHITE WATER RAFTING

I was to meet a friend who lived in Roanoke, Virginia at the motel in Beckley, West Virginia. My friend was already there and waiting when I arrived. We went to lunch and afterwards drove around the area site seeing and pickup brochures on white water rafting.

The next morning after breakfast we headed to the Little White River. There were people everywhere. We was about to buy two tickets when I noticed this lady that was upset. We ask her what the problem was. She started talking about white water rafting. She saw the movie shown to first timers and decided not to go with her husband and older kids. What movie, I asked. The one that this facility shows to promote rafting, she responded. Well, I had not seen this movie. I told my friend to hold up on purchasing the tickets until after I watched the movie.

The guy behind the counter put the movie into their VCR. I watched very attentively. I did not like what I saw. I decided that I did not want any part of white water rafting. I told my friend that I would wait there until their rafting group gets back and hoped they all got back alive. The folks running the place told me that they had different levels of rafting trips. Some were on calmer waters than others. I liked this idea. Why didn't you say this before? Most of the folks there were college age kids and wanted the more exciting/dangerous white water rafting trip. This was not what I wanted or the lady that was so upset.

As it turned out, the river was lower than normal and the water was not flowing at the dangerous level. We purchased our tickets and got a raft with five young Ohio State football players. Until we got under way, I was concern about what these young fellows would do. They were a good group of guys. The smallest one was huge. Well over six feet tall and about two hundred forty pounds. They made me laugh and feel more at ease. When we had to walk the raft over low area, they took charge and carried it without my assistance.

There were about ten rafts on the river at the same time. Each raft had a guide who instructed us as what to do and when to do it. The guide was the boss. He let us know what to expect and when to expect it and what was coming around the bend. We each had paddles and he told us when to paddle, how hard to paddle and in what direction to paddle. Most of the time we were just drifting along very slow. This was in between the rapids. This was an all day trip, so they just took their time. We stopped in several areas along the River to get into the water and just play. I did it one time. When it was time to get back into the raft, I did not have the arm strength to pull myself up and into it. These rafts were large and had large round sides. I was the last one to get in as we got under way again. The football players were diving off the raft and climbing back in so easy that it pissed me off. To get me into the raft, one of the kids grabbed my arm and lifted me into the raft like I weighed thirty pounds. I thanked him for his help. Without it I would have continued to go floating in the rapids that we were now approaching.

The kid that helped me was about six feet eight inches tall and weighed about two hundred ninety pounds and very strong. I was happy that he was sitting just in front of me. I felt really secure. We stopped several more times in deep water but I did not get out of the raft because I knew that I could not get back in without help. I did not want the kid to think that he had to look after me or impose on him the whole trip. I just stayed put.

We traveled some rough rapids and really had to work to paddle and anchor our feet in the raft to stay on board. I was having fun at last. With all the excitement during this time, I did not find the time to be afraid. During the rough rapids, we had to paddle like a son of a gun while trying to hold on and not fall out of the raft. It was very exciting. On some of these rapids, even if one of the young strong kids had fallen out of the raft they would have been hard pressed to survive the ordeal their bodies would have gone through.

All the rafts pushed to the bank at a designated spot to have lunch and take a break. We got under way about an hour later. We went through several more rapids and some of the folks floated in the river along side the rafts in the calmer water. The floaters would get back into the rafts to go through the rapids. I failed to mention before but we all had to ware safety equipment on the rafting trip. We had plastic helmets on our heads and floatation device vest were a requirement. The latter made it really easy to float with the current. I had fun the first and only time I floated.

At the end of the run, we all boarded old yellow school buses for the trip back to the starting area. This trip was as exciting as going through the rapids. We had to ride on dirt roads in the mountains. These old buses took up the whole road. Us passengers were either rubbing upon the side of a mountain or looking over a cliff. Sometimes it felt like we were riding on air and the rear wheels were not on the road because of the hairpin curves of the roadway. Several times we met a vehicle and had to come to a complete stop and maneuver to get the vehicles by each other. I thought that I would die several times on the way back. After arriving back, I promised never to do this again in this part of the country. They could not GIVE me a ticket for another ride on the river or on the bus for that matter.

I enjoyed the scenery and the country side, but I would not want to live there. I get to damn cold in the winter time and I would not like to drive on those roads and highways all year long. No way, Jose.

After saying good-bye to my friend, I headed back north to Charleston for the mountain top take off. I was not looking forward to this but I had to do it. I found, much to my delight, that taking off from the Charleston, West Virginia airport was much better than landing on it. I could see the cliff on the take off but we were a little distance from it. Maybe twenty or thirty yards or so. Anyway, it was nothing like the landing experience I had there. I've said it before and I'll say it again. I do not ever want to land at the Charleston airport again. Once in a lifetime is enough for me.

Barry and Victoria are on the raft. See if YOU can find them. This is on the White River near Beckley, West Virginia

1994 HOUSTON FLOOD

I had purchased another package trip to Las Vegas some time before we made the trip. My brother drove over from Louisiana again. He had a much more exciting trip than the one in 1990. This package deal was also for Vegas World Casino. But before I get to the trip, I will tell you about the terrible flood that was happening when my brother was driving from his home in Louisiana to meet me and my house in League City, Texas. The 1994 trip to Las Vegas almost did not happen.

1994 was the year that the Houston Ship Channel caught on fire. We had a lot of flooding in this area from rainfall. The flooding burst petroleum pipelines that ran under the Houston Ship Channel. This caused the sparks that started the fire. The fire burned out of control on the flooded channel until the source supplying the pipelines was cut off and blocked in. It was a big mess. Seeing the fire on the water flowing in the ship channel was an awesome sight.

My brother was driving from Louisiana to accompany me for our second trip to Las Vegas. He had left the Baton Rouge area before midday. It is about a five hour drive from his house to mine. At six p.m., I started getting telephone calls from his wife and daughters asking if he made it yet. They had seen on television the terrible rainstorms that we were having all across East Texas and the mess that was happening on the Houston Ship Channel. They wanted word that he had arrived is good shape. The fact was that he had not made it to my house and I had not heard from him. I did not have any idea where he was. I had heard on the news that I-10 between Winnie, Texas and Houston was closed because of sections being under water. Our normal path between our homes was on this section of Interstate 10. After the third call that I received from his daughter saying she thought that he was near Mont Belvieu, Texas, which was about thirty miles from my house, I decided to go and look for him. I started getting worried for two reasons now. Number one, we did not know where he was and number two, it was getting dark and we had to leave before nine the next morning for the airport to make our flight to Vegas.

I told my niece to tell her momma that I will go look for him. I ran to my car and headed north on Texas highway 146 in the rain. This highway would take me to Mont Belvieu. I did not know if I could get there or not. I drove my car which was a 1992 Mercury Grand Marque. I was a big and heavy car. I made to through Seabrook and La Porte without any problems. There was not much traffic out. The weather reports were warning drivers to stray off the roads and highways all day. I am happy to report that a lot of folks listened to the weatherman. It was also an opportune time or good excuse for folks to miss work. I went through the Baytown Tunnel without any traffic around. This was very unusual. I was really worried that it might be full of water. But it was not. In fact, there was hardly any water at all in it. The tunnel authority does a great job of keeping traffic moving but I do not remember seeing another vehicle while I drove through it.

When I arrived near Interstate 10, there was seven feet of water over highway 146 and under the I-10 overpass. Mont Belvieu was just a couple hundred yards on the other side of the overpass. The road was blocked off. There were state of Texas trucks and workers parked there just watching the water and making sure no on moved the barricades they had set up.

I parked in a Taco Bell parking lot on the right hand side of highway 146. Next to the Taco Bell was an Exxon station on the corner of highway 146 and the west bound entrance onto I-10. I could not get to the Exxon station because of the high water and the barricades on 146. Across 146 from where I was parked was a small Mobil gas station. The Taco Bell and Exxon station was at a higher level than the highway. Water was running down their drive entrance to 146. The Mobil station had a ditch all the way in front of it except for a driveway entrance which was covered with about three or four feet of water at this time. You could not see where the entrance started or ended. All the business places did not have any water in them. They are all higher than the street/highway.

There was no traffic at all on the interstate. It was under water to the west toward Houston and to the east toward Winnie. Here at highway 146, it was high and dry. There were several other folks parked near me waiting for the water to go down. We talked off and on giving each other what updates we heard over the radio. We all could hear the fire trucks and ambulances sirens in the distance. We did not know what they were for because we could not see them. After some time, I heard over the radio that there was a chemical spell at Exxon's Baytown refinery and the Baytown Tunnel was shut down. Now I was trapped. I could not go forward because of the water and I could not go back home even if I wanted to. I turned off the radio and just sat there.

After about two hours, one of the state workers came wading through the water to back up his state truck and check the barricades out. He was not available to talk with before this time. He had an emergency portable radio and I had been picking up information from the truck's emergency radio since I arrived by just listening to it. I asked the driver how much have the water went down. He told me that he had been there for eight hours and the water was still coming up and he did not expect it to go down tonight. Oh shit, said I. Although the rain was letting up, he said the water had to come to this spot before it would drain off. I really felt bad now. I had been here for three hours and could not do anything. I could not even get to a telephone to call my niece back to give them an update. I knew that they were really worried now. These business places had been closed for hours.

After hearing what the state worker said, a guy in a Chevy S-10 pickup said that he had to get on the other side of I-10 to check on his house and family. We waded across 146 and felt his way where he thought the Mobil station driveway was. We got in the water to check it closer. He came back and said the he was going to try it. He said that the two most important things were to not go into the ditch and to keep the engine running. We could see that I-10 exit coming from Houston on the other side of the Mobil station. It looked to be high with only a couple of inches of water. This is what we estimated from what we could see from our position. He may make it.

He started up his truck than lined it up where he thought the driveway was and started forward. Water came almost up to his window. The stretch of deep water was about eight yards wide. This was from the side of highway 146 onto the Mobil station property. He made it. I looked very close where he drove through the water. I watched as he drove to the back of the Mobil station property and come out on the east bound exit ramp of I-10. This is going the wrong way of course but there was not any traffic because it was blocked off about two miles toward Houston where Greens Bayou was OVER I-10. He went up the ramp the wrong way. I could see his taillights as he crossed over the four lane I-10 and started down and getting on the west bound ramp going the wrong way. I lost him for a while. Then there he was again. He made it down going the wrong way, made a left turn onto highway 146 on the other side of the deep water and underpass.

Several of us saw that he made it. I jumped into my car. I drove to the Mobil station entrance. I tried to line my car up as he did his little truck. I knew it was over three feet deep over the driveway. I started out slowly. About half way I gunned it. Water came up to my windshield, but I made it. All of this took about fifteen seconds. I did the same thing that the guy before me did. I went the wrong way to get on I-10, crossed it and the wrong way to get off I-10 and back to highway 146. As I looked back toward the Taco Bell, I could see other folks were now doing the same thing at I did.

There are several motels just off the interstate in Mont Belvieu. I knew that my brother may be in one of them. My brother drove over in his son's new small pickup truck. My niece told me the color and make of it before I left my house earlier today. I checked every parking space at the first motel and did not see what looked like the truck. I drove to the next motel. There were cars and trucks parked everywhere. I bet every room available at the motels there was taken by folks stranded one way or another. I kept looking and then notice the Louisiana license tags on this new looking pickup. I could not tell what color it was because of darkness. I went to the desk clerk but she would not tell me what room my brother was in. She rang the room for me and sure nuff, it was him. He was surprise to hear from me. He told me what room he was in. I drove around to the back and parked and walked to his room.

Well, he was all nice and cozy. He had been in bed eating a large bag of potato chips and watching television. The potato chips were his supper. He sure was not going to buy any food in a restaurant. I told him that Liz, (his wife), was worried about him and had the red ass because he did not call and let her know what the hell is going on. And that he should have called her and me and let us know that he was o k. He let me know that it was long distance to make those telephone calls. I knew it. This boy is really tight with money.

I told him that I thought we could get back to my house by going back the way I came. I had heard a report on my car radio sometime before now that the Baytown Tunnel was reopened and the plant emergency was over. He grabbed his stuff and we left.

It had stopped raining for about an hour, but started up again as soon as we got into our vehicles. He followed me back onto highway 146. We took a left and headed to the I-10 overpass. Oh shit. A black Texas Highway Patrol Officer was blocking highway 146 before I could get to the ramp. I got out of my car and told him that I needed to get to the other side by going on I-10. He said that he could not let me do that. It was too dangerous. That was why he was sent to this spot to stop the folks from doing what I had done earlier. He said that suppose another driver get on I-10 by doing this and we get into a wreck. He just could not let us do that. He told me that I might be able to drive on the service road to the Old River bridge and cut across I-10 to the service road on the other side of I-10 to get back. Shit, this is a long way to go when I could see where I needed to go and it was just a couple hundred yards.

The Old River Bridge was about five miles east toward Winnie. I mentioned to my brother to follow me. I headed east on the service road. My brother was on my bumper. It was raining cat and dogs. The road was in good shape as far as water was concern. We went about three miles than I cut across where I thought I could get on I-10. My brother was still on my bumper. I then cut across the medium and got on the I-10 east bound heading west. I was afraid to go all the way pass highway 146 to come back the same way behind the Mobil station because the damn trooper would see us and may have a buddy on the side we were trying to get to and jack us up. Then there would be no trip to Vegas for sure - if we were in jail. We were heading in the right direction but going the wrong way on I-10. I saw an area that looked like cement between I-10 and the service road. I went for it. As soon as I hit it, I know that it was mud. I could not do anything about it now. My brother was on my ass. I gunned it and made it through to the black topped service road. So did my brother. For a guy eight years older than me, he could keep up real good.

We drove another three or so miles and there was highway 146 two hundred yards ahead of us. But there was just too much water on the service road to get to 146. We were very close to the Exxon property now. We had stopped to look it over. Yes we were getting soaking wet. We were in about four or five inches of water now. I cut over the curb for the Exxon station with my brother on my tail. The water had come up some since I was last on this side of I-10. We drove around the back side of the station and crossed unto the Taco Bell back side of their property. We came out of the Taco Bell driveway near where I was parked earlier for a couple of hours.

We made a left onto highway 146 going south. We were about thirty miles from my house. We made it through the tunnel at Baytown, through LaPorte, through Seabrook, and through Kemah and to my house in good old League City. We were both very happy to be there. It was almost midnight now.

My brother called his wife and got his ass chewed out for not doing so about seven hours earlier. He told Liz to let his son, Brian, know that his truck was alright. It saw a lot of water and mud but was alright too. My brother saw a lot more of Texas than he bargained for on this trip. He was forced to divert off I-10 near Winnie, Texas. He was lost a lot of the time and by the grace of God, ended up back near I-10 in Mont Belvieu. He was just following the traffic. He could have ended up anywhere if he followed another vehicle. But he turned left at Dayton to follow the guy in front of him. He did not know where he was but did see the sign that said highway 146 and took it.

We both slept good that night. The next morning after daylight, we checked over our vehicles. We did not find much mud. I guess all that water cleaned it off. More surprising to me was that my car was not wet inside. I guess I did not stay in the deep water long enough for it to seep into my car. Thanks be to God. A couple hours later, we headed to the airport for the flight to Las Vegas.

1994 LAS VEGAS TRIP

We took off from Hobby Airport in Houston and landed in Phoenix, Arizona to change airplane. We had to wait an hour or so for the next scheduled flight. This was my brother's second airplane trip. We all boarded the plane for the next leg of the flight at about four thirty in the afternoon, Phoenix time. It was well over one hundred degrees outside. There were about a dozen airplanes lined up to take off in front of us. The pilot came on the radio and said if we did not take off before the temperature hit one hundred twenty degrees that we would have to wait until it cooled down to take off. What the hell is this all about, I thought. He then announced that it was one hundred nineteen degrees and there were now just two planes ahead of us. I looked at my brother and said "shit, I hope we make it". But I was worried about this temperature thing. I had never heard of it being to hot to take off before. Of course I had never been in a place where the temperature got this hot before either. Before we got to the take off position, the pilot came back on the radio and said that we were going back to the gate. It is one hundred twenty degrees. Double shit. We are stuck here now. What we gonna do?

I was pretty much upset. First of all, to restate, I never heard that an airplane could not take off it the temperature got to one hundred twenty degrees outside before. The pilot said that this applied to the type airplane we were on. My thought was why can the plane take off at one hundred nineteen degrees and not at one hundred twenty degrees. It is just one lousy degree. I cannot tell the difference in one damn degree. It seams to me that this is cutting it close. Suppose the thermometer is lying and it is two degrees off. I don't like this one damn bit. I am now suppose to trust a damn lying thermometer.

They made us all get off the plane back at the gate. It was hot inside the airport even with the air conditioner running. A little later my brother saw an afternoon newspaper with headlines stating that the temperature reached one hundred twenty-one degrees. He purchased a paper to show the folks back home how hot is was in Phoenix. He said that this will show the Louisiana folks back home just how lucky they are to be living there. This is the hottest temperature either of us had ever been in.

Some time after we de-boarded the airplane an ice cream man pushing a cart came into our section. He was selling Hogindos ice cream on a stick. Many folks formed a line to buy some. My brother got in line behind me. When I finally got up and ordered our ice cream on a stick, my brother asked how much it cost. The man said that the price was two dollar and fifty cents each. My brother said, "WHAT - I don't want one". I told him that I was buying but he still said "HELL NO". He just could not bring himself to eat ice cream on a stick that cost that much. Back home he could get a half gallon for that price. I purchased only one. I enjoyed eating it and tried to eat the stick also to get my money's worth. I had to spit the stick out. I was afraid of splinters sticking in my mouth. It was good, but certainly not worth the price that I paid. The truth be told, I am cheap too.

It was nearly six in the evening before the temperature cooled down enough for us to start re-boarding the airplane again. We took off about a half hour later. We arrived at the Las Vegas airport in due time. We did not pay much attention to the slots there on this trip. We knew how they did not pay off. They were there just to rip us off. Been there and done that before and was not going to do it again.

After getting our suitcases, we got a cab and headed to Vegas World. We were much smarter and wiser this time around. This was our second trip and we knew where the nickel slots were, if those bastards did not move them in the past four years.

I checked us in the hotel and although I was not suppose to get any casino money this time, they gave vouchers to me for over three hundred dollars in cash. This was real money. I did not question them on it. I took the money and ran. When we got to our room, I told my brother about the cash that we were going to get. We had both brought more money with us than the last trip figuring that we needed to spend our money this time. But this windfall changed that. We were in high roller heaven now.

After we went down to the cashier and received the cash, I gave my brother some. We played the nickel slots but soon got bored. After all we were not rookies. We were gambling men and wanted to play for high stakes. We went to the quarter slots. Since we already had real money, I stayed away from the blackjack/twenty-one tables. I came to play the slots and see more of Las Vegas.

After playing the slots and refusing drinks from the waitresses many times, we decided to go walk and eat at another location. Upon arrived, at some distance away, we noticed the tall monstrosity of a building that was being built on the Vegas World grounds. It was going to be a new casino called The Stratosphere Casino. It will be over seventeen hundred feet tall and have a roller coaster near the top on the 109th floor. When we left Vegas World and walked by this building we noticed some shoddy cement work and remarked that we hoped that they fixed that better than it was before they opened for business. NOTE: When we went back to Vegas in 1997, they had corrected all the problem areas that we saw this day. How do I know, you ask. Because we went back and checked out the areas that we saw before, before we went into the new building.

We continued to walk for about a half mile. We found a restaurant that advertised a special for about three dollars. We went in and ordered a meal. After we departed the restaurant, we walked a bit further away from Vegas World and there was a line of casinos on both sided of the street. It seamed like we walked a mile from our casino to get here. There were vagrants lying on the sidewalks. Also drunks and folks begging for money and panhandlers as well as just plain poor folks. Several people were shouting out things for no good reason. One woman shouted something about religion at my brother as we walked by. He told her "yea, yea". She seamed to get pissed and followed us for about ten or fifteen feet shouting before she went back to her spot on the sidewalk. I started to get a little nervous. I looked back to be sure that that woman or anyone else wasn't trying to do something to us even though it was still daylight and realized just how huge the Stratosphere really was. It was something else. They boasted that it was the tallest building West of the Mississippi River. I guess it was.

We walked into all the other casinos and played slots in each one. I won some money from every casino that we went into. Not much money, just a couple dollars from each one. If I hit twenty quarters and that put me ahead in this casino, I left and went into another one. There were a lot of them side by side. Some were sidewalk casinos. They had some big name ones from the old days also. I just cannot remember the names.

We were in one casino and I noticed a number of nickel slots in a large circle. There must have been ten machines there. The best part was that nobody was playing these machines. This seamed strange to me at the time. I pulled a nickel from my pocket and placed it into the first machine I got to. It went straight through and made that noise when it hit the trough. I thought this one is out of order. I put my nickel in the machine next to it and it went straight through also. Huh, what is wrong here, I said. I replaced the nickel with a fresh one from my pocket. It went through just as the first nickel did. I tried two more machines. The same thing happened. After the first machine did this, I looked around for one of the casino helpers and continue to look around each time my nickel made the noise hitting the tray. I was half way around the circle of machines. My brother had been doing the same thing that I was doing. After five machines, I got the message. I do not know how many machines my brother tried. We may have passed all ten by this time. The message I got was on each machine and on a huge sign above them as well. These were five dollar machines. We hauled ass from there as fast as we could walk. Some distance away we stopped and looked back. How could we miss all the signs stating five dollars. We had our minds set on nickel machines since we arrived and that is what we saw. We looked around to see if anyone was watching us. No one was. They were all busy losing their money and did not have time to notice a couple of tight coonasses from Louisiana put nickels in five dollar machines that would not work. We laughed at ourselves all the way into the next casino.

After several hours of playing around and looking at the sites in this area, we headed back toward Vegas World. It was getting dark but the street was well lighted and it was much cooler than on the walk over earlier in the day. On the earlier walk it was really warm. You might even say that it was hot. There was a good breeze on that walk but it blew hot air. We had never experience that before. The only reason we did not sweat through our clothes was although it was hot, the humidity was very low. It did not feel as hot as it was.

Just as the last package deal to Vegas World, we received two different stage show tickets. That first night we watched a variety show. It was o k. But when this guy did a bicycle act it was unbelievable. This guy was incredible in what he did on a bicycle. He did an act on a two wheel and one wheel bike that was hard for me to believe. I thoroughly enjoyed that part of the stage performance.

During these shows, they try to sell you drinks and stuff. They make big bucks off the drinks. If you are in the casino gambling, your drinks are free but not so at the stage shows. We still did not drink alcohol and finally told the waitress who kept trying to wait on us. We did order sodas so we would buy something and tip her. Damn they were high. We could as well ordered mix drinks and just left them there for that price. After the stage show, we played more slots and later on went up to bed.

The next day we played different types of machines and I played something called Keno or something like that. I tried several games of bingo for big money pots. I found an area in the casino where you can bet on any kind of sport that is going on in the world. I did not try that. I played this game where you bet on numbers then spend this big wheel and try to land on your number. It didn't work. You cannot win at this game. I tried several other games but cannot remember the names of them either.

I did quite a bit of watching other people play black jack, poker, roulette and other high stakes games. I did not want to lose all my "free" money on the slots or on anything else for that matter. I certainly did not want to lose any of my own money. I got spoiled on our first trip when I took over two hundred fifty dollar back to Texas that I did not have when I got to Vegas.

At some point during this trip, I shook hands with Bob Strupek. He was the owner of Vegas World and was building the huge hotel and casino called Stratosphere. Upon my return back home, I ended up buying six hundred shares of Stratosphere Hotel and Casino stock. I had over seven thousand dollars tied up in that stock. I really thought that Strupek would make a go of it and took a chance. More on this later.

The second evening we went to the stage show again. This time it was an Elvis impersonator show. This was the heavy set Elvis. Just as the last time, my brother and I sat at a table for two. All the tables were close together and either tables for two or four. The guy came out and introduced himself and told us a little about him before he started the show. The first thing he said was, "my name is William King and I am from Tennessee". I did not hear the rest of what he said because after he said his name, my brother said, "I wonder if he is kin to Nigger-Boy King of Plaquemine". This just broke me up. I started laughing and looking around to see if anybody heard what my brother said. There were all kinds of races of folks sitting around us. I could not tell if anyone overheard or not. Nigger-Boy King is my brother's neighbor in Random Oaks just outside of Plaquemine, Louisiana. He is a white guy but he is known far and wide as Nigger Boy. I have been knowing him for over twenty years and I do not know his real name. I guess it was a legitimate question to ask. Nigger Boy liked to slick his hair back and always tried to sing over the mike whenever he got drunk at different functions he attended. I saw him attempt this myself on several occasions. He would piss off the band members by getting on stage and grabbing the microphone. When he was restrained, he would sing along and throw the lead singer and the band off key. They hated to see Nigger Boy coming. Also, I think that he was originally from out of state. He may have come of Tennessee and when he got to Louisiana found out that it was the place for him.

These nick names in Louisiana is not that unusual. I've known Mr. Nigger Ourso all my life. He was a sugar cane farmer until he retired a number of years ago and gave the business to his children. As with Nigger Boy King, I do not know or remember how Mr. Nigger Ourso got his name.

Then there is T-Nig Salvadres who worked for Cora Texas sugar house. T-Nig is French for the nigger. His oldest son is T-Nig Jr. which in French means the nigger junior.

There is another person back home that is name nigger something but I cannot recall enough to tell you who he is. So between White Castle and Plaquemine, Louisiana there is Nigger Boy King, Mr. Nigger Ourso, T-Nig Salvadres Sr. and T-Nig Salvadres Jr. All of these white men answer to the name of nigger and are not embarrassed, ashamed, apologetic, or angry because of it. It is accepted and even the black folks in the area address these men with these names without animosity. Because they know them to be straightforward folks and not an evil bone in their bodies. It is just a name and is accepted by all in that area. These guys names are not meant to degrade or tease or make fun on them or any race of people in any way or form. Still, my brother had me going there in Las Vegas.

I thought Mr. King did a credible job on all the Elvis songs he sung and played. He was dressed and looked like Elvis also. I really enjoyed his performance. He did a good job.

The next morning we got ready to leave for the airport. We caught a cab in front of Vegas World with an older couple who was headed to the airport also. They talked about the MGM Grand, TashMaHall,

The Lexur and other casinos we haven't seen. We said "damn", we've been here two times and there is still more casinos to see. The cabbie told us if we haven't seen "The Strip", we haven't seen Vegas. He also said that we were in the po-dunk part of town. This made me feel really good - NOT. The driver detoured from his normal route to the airport and drive us down "The Strip" so my brother and I could see what we missed. We had not ventured this far from Vegas World. Now these were the nice casinos. We were in awe of the site of them. We decided right then and there that we would make another trip to Las Vegas to see these casinos someday. What a pisser.

Nothing exceptional happened on the way back home. We again stopped in Phoenix to let off and take on passengers heading for Houston. The next day, my brother headed back to Louisiana. The whole Houston area was getting back to normal after the flooding and fire disaster on the Houston Ship Channel. Many plants had been shut down and were now being started back up. Things were looking up.

This in the end of my second book- please be looking for my third book to follow before to long.
Thanks you for reading.
Barry Franklin Anthony (Butch) Raffray